Last Dance at the Hotel Kempinski

ROBIN HIRSCH

Last Dance at the

Hotel Kempinski

Creating a Life in the

Shadow of History

UNIVERSITY PRESS OF NEW ENGLAND

Hanover and London

University Press of New England, Hanover, NH 03755
Printed in the United States of America
5 4 3 2
CIP data appear at the end of the book

for Leona, Sasha, and Benjy

and in memory of my parents

Contents

Part II
The Man Who Danced with Marlene Dietrich
(1964–1973)

Part III
Towards Home
(1972–1982)

Epilogue
(1991)

Acknowledgments

There are many people to thank. In particular, those who appear in this book, most of them by their real names. I have tried to honor their experiences and their memories. Where details, events, or speeches are reported, they are of course in part a fabrication, if only by virtue of the shape that any telling of a story takes. Where any of them offend, I apologize, in most cases profoundly. Where any of them are in error, I can only say that this is a work of memory, not of history, and that the truth at stake here is emotional, not factual. Nevertheless, I was trained as a historian, the emotions recorded here are bound up with matters of great historical importance, and, however lightly I may tiptoe through my own life, the burden of other people's lives weighs heavily upon me. I have tried therefore to be as true to the letter of those lives as to the spirit. And to all whose lives are touched on here, for better or worse, for richer or poorer, I am profoundly grateful.

Some of this material first appeared in print in *Culturefront, Forward,* the *New York Jewish Review,* the *Village Voice,* and *Western Humanities Review,* and to the editors of these journals I am grateful for support at a time when I was fumbling for a form.

To the New York Foundation for the Arts, the Queens Borough Library, Poets and Writers, and the National Foundation for Jewish Culture, I am grateful for support of a blessedly tangible kind. I am equally grateful to the law firm of Stecher, Jaglom, and Prutzman for the use of their magnificent printer, to Linda Caffin and Daniel Engelstein at Vladeck, Waldman, Elias, and Engelhard for bailing me out with their remarkable scanner, and to various householders in Fair Harbor, Fire Island, for the use (knownst and unbeknownst to them) of space in which to escape my children and finish my manuscript.

Some people have been enthusiastic supporters of this material, as it developed, over more years than many of them might care to admit.

Nevertheless, for their encouragement and support over the years I would like to thank Muriel and Peter Bedrick, Vincent Byrne, Janet Coleman, John Kallas, Jess Korman, Mardee Kravit, Lois Meredith, Rosalind Miles, Tamar Rogoff, David Rohn, Nick Ullett, Eric Werthman, and the communities of the New Works Project and the Cornelia Street Cafe, where all this material first saw life. I feel particularly indebted to Rachel Cowan, Molly Fowler, and Rip Keller for their contagious enthusiasm in the early stages; to Marc Kaminsky for a generosity of spirit which kept me going during some dark moments in the middle stages; to Elinor Fuchs for opening her beautiful house so I could perform sections of *Kinderszenen* for the kind of sophisticated theater audience one dreams of and trembles before; to Sonia Gluckman and Richard Edelman for their help in translating some of this material to the stage; to Martha LaBare, Kurt Lamkin, Marilyn Lubin and Joan Schenkar for helping to bring this material to new audiences; to Pam Bernstein, Gail Hochman, and Lucie Prinz, who at various stages have given me generous professional advice; to Robert Youdelman, who has been of unstinting and inestimable counsel to this project since before it began; and to Ava and Robert Siegler, whose friendship continues to sustain both my family and my work.

To Phil Pochoda, my editor and quondam agent, I owe a particular debt for his unflagging commitment in both capacities to arm wrestling this thing into print. That it exists as a book at all is entirely due to him and to his many cohorts at UPNE, who have been uniformly gracious, thoughtful, careful, and enthusiastic.

Finally to my wife, Leona Jaglom, who has borne with me through all of this with extraordinary grace and understanding, and to my children, who continue to teach me more than they can know, I owe more than I can say.

A Note on the German

The German language is almost a character in this book. I have tried on the whole to let it speak for itself. Obviously there are occasions where such speech may not be understood. On such occasions, rather than append a glossary or footnotes, which might prove an even greater stumbling block, I have chosen to include a translation in parentheses.

I have tended to err, however, on the side of *not* translating (though I have on occasion tried to paraphrase as unobtrusively as possible). I have in particular erred in three gray areas: first, where translating an idiom, particularly a Berlin idiom, necessarily diminishes it (a favorite expression of my mother's, for example — *Getü und Geta* — means "much ado about nothing" or "song and dance" or "big fuss," but nothing resonates like the original); second, where (mostly in direct speech) the general drift of what is being said is intelligible from the context or from repetition (my father, for example, had as many German words for *angry* or *be quiet* as the Inuit have for *snow*); and finally, where I am simply stumped.

In this last category the key word is *Jäcke* (pronounced, and sometimes spelled, *yekke*), which informal etymology attributes to the *Jäcke* (jackets) which German Jews in Palestine, the most fastidious of immigrants, insisted on wearing even when working in the fields. The name was of course an insult foisted on them by earlier settlers from Eastern Europe. It has, however, formally entered the language (Yiddish, Ivrit, German) and a *Jäcke*, ungrammatical though that plural may be, is now an almost standard term for German Jew. Even *Jäckes* with a gift for self-deprecation use it. It is, in its mish-mash of etymology and nuance, untranslatable. It is also, in some respects, the subject of what follows. It therefore appears, *aber selbstverständlich* (but, of course), untranslated.

Prologue

(1988)

Preserve This Child

"Martha wants to know what to wear."

"I don't know. Whatever you wear to a conventional bloodletting."

I am not uncivilized. My wife is a clinical psychologist. Our son was barely a week old. And here we were, new and excited parents, about to submit our beautiful, tender, sweethearted boy, whose journey into the world had been hard enough, to the sharp and terrifying instruments of a certified *mohel.*

A *mohel,* in the Jewish religion, is a ritual circumciser. Traditionally, on the eighth day after the birth of a male child, after sunrise and before sundown, in a ceremony that goes back to Abraham, the boy's foreskin is cut off.

"This is the twentieth century," my mother-in-law protested. "They can do it in the hospital. It's barbaric. Why are you doing this?"

Why *were* we doing this? Neither of us is an observant Jew. We fast on Yom Kippur, we attend the occasional seder, even more infrequently we hold one, but we don't keep kosher, we rarely worship, and we belong at the moment to no shul, mostly because two years ago we moved to Brooklyn and we have yet to find one here which answers to our peculiar, secular, vague, uneasy needs. And yet, one of the few things we had decided before the birth was that if we had a boy we would have a *bris*—a ritual circumcision. Now, as the hour approached, a flood of feelings, questions, memories, apprehensions overtook me.

Had I had a *bris?* I didn't know. Certainly I had been circumcised, but had there been a ceremony? My father is dead; my mother is elderly and no longer remembers.

I was born in London during the war. My parents were refugees from Germany. How anxious, I wonder, would they have been for so conspicuously foreign an occasion. The family doctor was German Jewish. Perhaps he had done it. On the other hand, given how conspicuously foreign my parents seemed to me growing up, and given also my father's bullhead-edness, perhaps I had *doch*, as they would have infuriatingly put it, had a *bris*. And did I not have a godfather, that spectral figure on my child-hood's horizon, and is not a godfather in childhood legend the one who holds your penis during the act?

If there had been a *bris* who would have been there? Certainly no immediate family beyond my parents. All my grandparents were dead—both my grandfathers had died in Berlin, mercifully, long before Hitler; both my grandmothers had lived to die in concentration camps. My mother had a sister—but she had escaped with her two children to South America. My father had a brother—but he had fled with his wife to Amsterdam, where of course the Nazis followed; by the time I was born they had been moved into the Jewish quarter. One widowed cousin of my father's had also ended up in London. Perhaps she would have come. The rest of what had been two large, vibrant families were either dead, about to die, or scattered across the earth.

Bris or no *bris*, I think of my parents choosing to have children in a foreign country, in middle age, during the Blitz, and I think of it as a decision of extraordinary, almost palpable, courage. In the face of the destruction of their families it seems such a life-affirming act that if I dwell on it, I weep. But I weep also for another, more complicated, reason. For the inevitable failure. For parents old enough to be grand-parents, for the enormous emotional and psychological gulf that sepa-rated them from us, for the hated foreign language which they were too old to shed, for the rigid nineteenth-century German precepts by which they sought to bring us up in postwar England.

And yet here am I, more than forty years later, and some of the con-tours of my life have a familiar shape. I live in a foreign country. What remains of my family is scattered. My mother, my sister, and my sister's two daughters live in London. My mother's sister, whom I met once in my life—twenty-three years ago at my sister's wedding—is dead. Her two children, my only cousins, survive. One, Ellinor, lives in Beer Sheva—we have seen each other half a dozen times over the years, each time in a different country. The other, Gert, lives in Buenos Aires. We have never met.

My father's brother lives in Amsterdam, childless at the age of eighty-six, having survived hiding, betrayal, Auschwitz, and the death, eighteen years ago, of his beloved wife after a series of strokes, the delayed and deadly aftereffects of her own imprisonment, starvation, and torture.

So, in terms of immediate family, there are eight of us in five different countries. Scattered about the globe, all these years later, we are shards from the explosion and there is very little holding us together.

And here am I in New York, six months older than my father was when I was born, and here, miraculously, is Alexander. And now, suddenly, however briefly, we are nine. And complicated, turmoil-ridden, tenuous though my family history has been, it is still, willy-nilly, a Jewish history, and there is still a tattered fabric to sew him into.

And so I look for a *mohel.* And in the process some of the loftier thoughts evaporate. And certain inescapable realities begin to present themselves.

How, for example, do you audition a *mohel?* We had avoided finding out the sex of our prospective child so that when Alexander emerged, tiny, misshapen, and covered in blood, we weren't exactly ready to roll. On day two, bleary-eyed, exhausted, I called around, soliciting names. By day three, I had four possibilities. But day three was Friday and from sundown Friday to sundown Saturday, these guys go into seclusion. So I had to move fast. I connected with two of them and the wife of a third.

Mohel Number 1 — this was beginning to feel more and more like a TV show — lived in New Jersey, had trained in Israel, and was also a cantor. I had in fact seen him in action: an acquaintance whose son had been circumcised had the entire thing on video. He sang nicely, the baby didn't seem to cry unduly, the whole thing was over quickly, and the cameraperson had had the taste to fade out during the central act. But maybe the *mohel* was just a little young . . .

Mohel Number 2 was an old-timer, the most orthodox, and probably the most experienced. What was my Hebrew name? That was easy — David. And after whom is the child named? Well, his middle name, Max, was my grandfather's name and my father's middle name.

"And your father's Hebrew name was . . . ?"
I didn't know.
"Well, Max would have been either Moshe or Meir."
"O.K."
"And your wife's Hebrew name?"
"Darling, what is your Hebrew name?"
"Darling, I don't have a Hebrew name."
"I'm afraid she doesn't have a Hebrew name."
"She doesn't have a Hebrew *name*—is she Jewish?"
"Of course she's Jewish."
"Well, thank goodness for that."

The wife of Mohel Number 3 was a businesswoman. "*Mazeltov.* The *bris* will be next Wednesday. Between sunrise and sundown. End of the day is no good, he is booked. Telephone—home and hospital." Two hours later the rabbi—he is also a rabbi—calls us at the hospital. I explain that

I am as interested in the social and historical context of the ceremony as I am in the religious, that my son is the offspring of two families which have both suffered losses in the Holocaust, but that as far as orthodox religion goes, there isn't too much of that. I am being tactful—my wife's family is highly acculturated, in most quarters antireligious, and in some quarters hysterically so.

Mohel Number 4 didn't get back to me until Saturday night, by which time I had pretty much made up my mind. And the winner is . . . Mohel Number 3 had done the deed on the son of a friend of a friend. The grandfather, a surgeon, was impressed with his work. He had been recommended by a distinguished liberal rabbi. Also, Mohel Number 3 was the fifth generation of *mohel* in his family, he had written a scholarly book on circumcision, which he promised to send me, and above all, he had a voice that sounded real on the phone.

Reading the *mohel's* book the night before, I learned a number of things. For example, that the ritual of circumcision, according to the Talmud, is one that the Jewish people have always observed with ecstatic joy—this was clearly one for my mother-in-law; that the removed foreskin was customarily buried in the desert—what would he do, bury it in our garden? and that, contrary to my childhood legend, it is not the godfather who holds the boy's penis during the *bris*, or even the boy, it is traditionally one of the grandfathers, and this—the office of *sandak*—is a signal honor. When Leona's father arrives I will ask him to be the *sandak*.

The ceremony was set for 1:30. I had called what little family there is, some friends, bought smoked salmon, champagne, one bottle of kosher wine, thirty three-inch gauze pads, Neosporin ointment, rubbing alcohol, flowers, candles. Behind closed doors, on a quiet city street, in the middle of an ordinary Wednesday, normal-looking men and women and even the occasional child would assemble, and a man with, as the jacket of his book told me, one of the most comprehensive collections of circumcision instruments in the world, would, after a few Hebrew words, cut off my son's foreskin in our living room. Why were we doing this?

"Why are you doing this?"

It's half an hour before the ceremony and the question comes from Ingrid, a writer, a Jew, who lives most of the time on an island off the coast of Maine. There is no challenge, no criticism, it is a simple open question. But I don't have a simple answer.

"I don't know exactly," I say. "It's a mystery. It has something to do with family, something to do with community. Somehow I felt it was important."

"Are you nervous?"

"Of course I'm nervous."

When Alexander was born—at the moment he was born, after six hours of transitional labor and two and a half hours of pushing—I looked round the delivery room, into which Leona had been wheeled two hours earlier. When we had come in, it had been spotless, sterile, gleaming. Now, with Alexander's painful arrival, it was covered in blood, instruments, rags. But mostly blood. Blood was everywhere—on the walls, on trolleys, on equipment, on the gowns of the doctor and nurse, on the bed, ankle-deep, it seemed, on the floor. In a petrie dish, swimming in blood, lay the placenta. It was as though a terrorist had thrown a bomb. And in the midst of the wreckage, his head in a bandage, I held my new-born son and murmured, over and over again, as much for me as for him, "Everything's going to be alright. Everything's going to be alright."

Amazingly, almost everyone I called is here. We are maybe two dozen. I look around—writers, psychoanalysts, filmmakers, rock musicians, lawyers, business people, television producers—not exactly a crowd Abraham might have anticipated, not exactly a family. And yet *doch* a family—a lateral family, a chosen family, the only kind of extended family a decimated family can have. And, *mirabile dictu*, there is even real family. In addition to Leona's relatives, there is one distant cousin of my father's, Herta, whom I discovered living in New York a dozen years ago. From Berlin in 1939, she had escaped to Shanghai. And from Shanghai after the war she had come to America. And here she is with her husband, Lacy, a Hungarian Jew who had spent the same ten-year period in the Jewish quarter of Shanghai but whom she had not met until New York, and here they both are with their American daughter and their son-in-law and their two-year-old granddaughter, Kayla, the youngest of all present.

The *mohel* arrives. We go upstairs. I have set out candles, the wine, the gauze, the alcohol, the ointment, on a table, and a chair for the *sandak*. The *mohel* takes off his jacket and puts on a white coat. He lays out his instruments. We discuss the matter of Alexander's Hebrew name. Alexander, it turns out—the Great, not the Little—was a benefactor and protector of the Jews and his name is thus acceptable as a Jewish name. Max we have decided will be Moshe. And, as a Jewish boy is named also after his father, he will in addition be ben (the son of) David.

Leona holds him, kisses him. I kiss him. She retreats with him to the landing. I stand with his godfather, his grandfather, and the *mohel*, four Jewish males awaiting with varying degrees of anxiety the arrival of a fifth. His godmother brings in Alexander and presents him to his godfather. His godfather presents him to his grandfather, who sits in the chair opposite the *mohel*. And the *mohel* says, "*Boruch haba*. Blessed be he who has come." And Alexander is placed on the table. I read from a poem written by an Irish friend who cannot be here. In the best Irish tradition it begins, "Shalom—Alexander Max," and it continues,

> Journey well, Alexander Max
> And make with us this loose pact—
> You will laugh a lot,
> And always ask—why.

The *mohel* introduces himself, jokes about his instruments, places the ceremony in a brief historical context, recites the traditional blessings, and asks me for permission to carry out the act. I read from a prayer by Rabbi Chaim Yosef Dovid Azulai:

> I am prepared to fulfill the divine commandment of Ritual Circumcision. Presently, my son will be brought into the Covenant of Abraham as it is written in the Torah: "At eight days shall every male be circumcised unto you for your generations. . . . It shall be a token of the covenant between Me and you."
>
> I appoint the Mohel, here present, to act in my behalf and perform this Ritual. I pray to God that our son will be a pride to his mother and myself, that we may raise him to be learned and righteous and that we may share with him in the fulfillment of his life.

And the *mohel* begins. My father-in-law holds his grandson, gazing intently as the *mohel* clips back the foreskin and cuts. And cuts. And Alexander cries. And I stand beside his grandfather and I squint my eyes and reel back so his grandfather's head comes between me and my son. And I hear the sound of cutting. And I hear the sound of crying. And after an age the *mohel* looks up and presents the bloody stump for my inspection. And he says, "A nice Jewish boy." And I smile wanly. And he soaks a piece of gauze in Schapiro's Naturally Sweet Concord Grape Wine from Rivington Street and Alexander bites on it like a sailor in the British navy and he stops crying. And the *mohel* recites the blessing, "*Elohenu velohay avosenu* . . . Our God and God of our fathers, preserve this child for his father and mother, and may his name be called in Israel: Alexander Moshe ben David."

And the *mohel* bandages the tiny wounded penis. And when he is done he produces a miniature red, white, and blue knitted yarmulke with the legend "I ♡ NY" crocheted around the edge, and he places it on Alexander's head and he holds him up and people laugh and there is applause.

And Alexander is returned to his mother.

And the rabbi and I settle up.

And down in the kitchen Leona's mother, who has stoically resisted the temptation to come up, knows that the barbaric ritual has come to an end.

And Lacy, my father's distant cousin's husband, who finds himself here in Brooklyn via Hungary, Romania, Yugoslavia, Shanghai, and the Upper West Side, breaks the challah and says the blessings over the bread and the wine.

And we open the champagne and we dig into the bagels and cream cheese and salmon, and slowly the terror and the mystery recede, and we are once again in a pleasant light-filled house on a pleasant street in the borough of Brooklyn, New York City, and the year is 1988 if you count from the birth of Jesus, or 5748 if you count, as the Jewish calendar counts, from the Creation. And no one cries. And there is only the faintest memory of blood.

Part I

Kinderszenen: Scenes from Childhood

(1935—1964)

Conjecture

It was in the spring of 1935 at a costume ball in Berlin that Herbert met his future wife. He was not expecting to get married. He had a lifetime behind him already. He was two years older than the century, he had fought in the First World War, he had been decorated. In the twenties, his father ailing, he had nursed the family bakelite firm through the ravaging inflation. Now in the thirties, as Hitler rose, he was taking advantage of the export side to travel more frequently abroad: he had secured visas permitting business travel to Holland, to France, to England. He knew one day he would have to get out. He had known it for years. He was preparing the way. Perhaps that was why he had never married.

In Berlin, in the Jewish community, there were still dinner parties, and Herbert, when he was in town, was still a welcome guest. He was highly regarded in the Jewish community: he had been an early Zionist; he was well respected in business and professional circles; and he came from a good family—his father had been dead for almost ten years now, but his mother was robust and he still lived with her and his younger brother Georg and the two remaining servants in the large family apartment on Michaelkirchstrasse.

He was strong in appearance and in manner—he was handsome, with black hair, dark skin, strong features. He was strongly built—he had been a rower. And he had strong opinions, which he had no inhibitions about expressing.

There are some men whose refusal to cultivate certain social niceties in no way diminishes their appeal. Herbert was such a man. He did not make or value small talk. He had little patience for those less well informed about political or economic issues than himself, and little tolerance for those whose information led them to conclusions other than his own. And yet he could be charming and beguiling, particularly to women. And he had certain eccentricities which seemed to belie the tough exterior. He manicured his fingernails. He smoked his imported cigarettes in a holder. And every so often he would produce a comb and a pocket mirror, even at the dinner table, and check his immaculate jet-black hair, with the razor-sharp parting on the left-hand side, which never needed combing.

He was careful with money, parsimonious even. Perhaps he was saving. Perhaps, some members of the Jewish community suspected, on his trips abroad he did not leave the country empty-handed. But on such subjects, while he was willing to dispense advice, he was not willing to be drawn out. His own affairs were private matters, not to be discussed. They bordered on the personal. And there the line was very clearly drawn.

In short, Herbert was a man respected, admired, sought after, if perhaps not loved. His younger brother, Georg, shy, musical, more of a scholar than a businessman, was loved. He had even recently become engaged to be married. Herbert, four years older, had never married. Now, at thirty-seven, the world in which he had grown successfully to manhood, the world of which he had become so securely a part, the world for which he had fought and which he had helped in concrete and tangible ways to create, the world of business, of finance, of enlightened but not assimilated Jewry, this whole subtle and complex world was threatened by a force more vicious, more violent, more volatile than anything he or the newspapers he read so avidly could accurately predict.

Some Jews had left, some were preparing to leave, and yet in many respects life, and the institutions which both reflected and sustained it, continued very little changed. The climate was certainly different, but businesses were not yet appropriated, synagogues were not yet closed down, and even large-scale celebrations for Jewish professional groups were still occasionally held.

And so it was that one spring night at this precarious moment in history Herbert found himself in the Grand Ballroom of the Hotel Kempinski, dressed as a Turk, with a scimitar and a white carnation, at a costume ball given by two of the remaining Jewish fraternal organizations. He was sitting with a group of friends from his old rowing days when a dark-haired, hazel-eyed Egyptian queen touched him lightly on the cheek with a bunch of cat's-paws and said, "*Du gefällst mir*" (You I like).

"What's your name?" Herbert asked her.

"Nefertiti," she replied.

Her real name was Käthe Lewald. She was thirty-three. She had been married once before, to a bohemian, a Jewish vagabond, a *Luftmensch*, as her father had contemptuously called him, whom she had met at a similar ball. But that was fifteen years before, when she and the world were younger and there was hope and experimentation in the air. Her parents had been bitterly opposed to the liaison, so in the spirit of that earlier, carefree time, they had eloped. When a year and a half later the marriage collapsed, her parents had, not unhappily, taken her back. She had an older sister, Herta, also divorced, who had two small children. Mercifully, she thought, given what was happening, she had had none.

Herbert danced with her all night, and when the ball was over he and his brother Georg took her home in their open roadster. Georg was preparing to emigrate to Holland with his fiancée, Bertel, a fashion designer. The only stumbling block was his mother. He wanted to get her out of the country before it was too late, but she was unwilling to leave. Herbert said there was no hurry. Käthe shrugged and said the Nazis were beneath contempt—all that marching, all that *Getü und Geta*, so much ado about nothing, how could one take them seriously. She gave them each a cat's-paw. Herbert gave her his carnation. They said good night.

Over the next three years, in between trips abroad, Herbert pursued her. Käthe's mother called him the last of the *Blumenschmeisser*, the last of the flower throwers. But after the Nuremburg Laws at the end of '35 and the brief respite of the Olympics in '36, the clouds got darker very quickly. Herbert's father was dead, his brother had left, very few of his friends remained. In the summer of 1938 his mother finally relented and moved to Amsterdam, into a room which Georg and Bertel, now married, had prepared in their apartment. And shortly afterwards, on the very day when Jewish males—visa or no visa—were forbidden to leave the country, Herbert himself got on a train and attempted to travel for the last time out of Germany.

At Emmerich, at the Dutch border, where George and Bertel and just months earlier Herbert's mother had crossed freely into Holland, the train was halted and two SS men with guns entered his compartment and took away his passport.

Early that morning, Käthe had heard the new ordinance on the radio. Frantically she had telephoned him at the office. "Quick. Take a train to the remotest border crossing. Emmerich. Perhaps the news will not have reached there yet. *Schnell. Schnell.* No good-byes."

Herbert's suitcase was always packed. He bought a one-way ticket, boarded the train, found an empty compartment, closed the door, pulled down the blinds, examined his passport. It had a red *J* for *Jude* and visas permitting business travel to Holland, France, and England. As of this day they were no longer valid.

Now, alone, at night, at Emmerich, at the very brink of freedom, Herbert sits in a locked compartment and waits. After an hour the SS men return. They unlock the compartment. They look down at Herbert in his overcoat and hat and gray silk scarf. He looks up at them. Then they give him back his passport. "*Weiter*," they shout into the corridor. Then they get off and the train moves slowly into Holland.

Käthe, however, stayed on. She had a fashionable crafts studio just off the Kurfürstendamm, she was well connected with the German aristocracy, she had her own mother to worry about and an older sister who had two young children and was trying desperately to get a visa. Finally, on the night of the 9th of November—Kristallnacht—the last remaining lights were extinguished. Käthe's studio was spared, but it was all over. With the help of an influential countess, she shipped a small quantity of her own wrought-iron work, some family china, some silver, and two or three pieces of furniture, to London.

Things moved with an extraordinary swiftness now. By the New Year her sister, Herta, had somehow managed to persuade a well-placed former admirer to call the appropriate official and was expecting any day now three visas for Uruguay.

"Uruguay?" Käthe said, "I can hardly pronounce it. It's so far away. When . . . ?"

But Herta shook her head, as much as to say, "Not in front of the children."

The sisters made their good-byes. And then Käthe took a final leave of her mother—her stubborn, cynical, infuriating mother, Luise, who so admired Herbert, who even liked London, but who refused to give up the splendid Lewald apartment with the crystal chandelier in the salon and the grand piano on which now no one played.

Herbert had taken furnished rooms in Mayfair. When Käthe arrived she lodged discreetly at a hotel in Berkeley Square until the 16th of February, 1939, when, after a brief ceremony at the Kensington Registry Office, they moved together into Grove End Gardens, a block of flats in St. John's Wood, Käthe Lewald having now become Mrs. Herbert Hirsch.

Sir Hirsch

My father used to tell this joke:

> Two Jews meet in Paris after the war.
>
> The first one says, "Don't I know you from somewhere?"
>
> The second one says, "I don't know. It's possible."
>
> The first Jew says, "So, what's your name?"
>
> The second one says, looking down his nose, "Maurice de la Fontaine."
>
> "Maurice de la Fontaine," says the first Jew, impressed. "But, wait a minute, don't I know you from Berlin, from before the war? Of course, it's Moritz Wasserstrahl. Come to think of it, I knew you back in Poland when you were plain old Moishe Pishe."

This is significant for two reasons. One, my father never told jokes. Except this one, and some obscure Chinese proverb about two men on a journey which even I could tell was more of a moral tale.

However, this joke, the Moishe Pishe joke, was clearly a joke joke. It stayed with me, though, not because it was funny, but because it spoke to something frail and uncertain at the heart of things. In some telling and enigmatic way, it uncovered my own secret longings and pierced me in my most private dreams. It was a joke which made you laugh, but it was also a joke which, if you had a child's dull sense of what your family and thousands like them had survived, on some profounder level made you cry.

And this of course is the second reason.

My parents were refugees from Germany, arriving in England before the war, settling in London, at No. 154 Grove End Gardens in the not unfashionable district of St. John's Wood, and having me, Robin Marc David Hirsch, and shortly thereafter my sister, Barbara Eve Louise Hirsch, in the intervals between the bombings. Growing up after the war, like the children of other German Jews who spoke German or at best the kind of English the Nazis spoke in war films, we knew, without ever having to articulate it, that it didn't exactly facilitate the much-hoped-for assimilation if one arrived at school each day under the burden of a name like Treppengeländer.

"Smith?"

"Present."

"Thompson?"

"Present."

"Treppengeländer?"

One didn't exactly blend in.

Doubtless to mitigate this, my parents cast about for a suitable English name. The woman in the next bed to my mother—they were clearly down to the wire—suggested Robin. My parents wanted a name which could be pronounced by those scattered members of the family and friends who had managed to escape and who were now living out the war in Holland, Australia, America, Shanghai, Sweden, Switzerland, Palestine, Uruguay, Bombay. Robin fit the bill. The news was dispatched throughout the war-torn world, and doubtless in New York the Schoenheimers, who had fled Berlin for Paris and then, when the Nazis caught up with them, Paris for New York; in Amsterdam my father's mother and his brother, Georg, and his brother's wife, Bertel, who were not yet in hiding; in South America, my mother's sister, Herta, who was negotiating her way with her two children into Argentina; doubtless even in Berlin my mother's mother, Luise Lewald, who had yet to be deported to Bergen-Belsen; doubtless all over the world German Jews took note of the event, breathed a collective sigh of relief, and said, in German or the various languages they were painfully acquiring: "*Ach ja*, Robin, *Gott sei Dank*, a name we can pronounce."

That my parents couldn't pronounce it was of concern, of course, only to me. My father, when he could remember the name of his firstborn son, called me "RRRawbeen" with that long low rolling guttural German *r* which to this day gives me the shudders, and my mother would attempt to ingratiate herself with some appalling endearment like "Robienchen." This was as English as it ever got.

My second name, Marc—with a *c*, very unusual in England—came from my father's father, Max, long since dead of a heart attack in Berlin before the Nazis were anything more than a lunatic flicker on the Bavarian horizon. Somewhere in the genealogical mists, the traditional family *Vorname* had been Marcus, which I was spared.

I had a third name, my only "normal" name, David, which I assume was intended as my Jewish name, although given its junior position in the lineup and my parents' almost total lack of interest in, let alone enthusiasm for, anything religious, it may have been more in the nature of a concession to Judaism. Combined with my second name, however, it had one curious advantage. Magazine subscriptions were generally filled out: last name, first name, initials of all other names. As a result Hirsch, Robin M. D. was perhaps the only child in England who was regularly addressed, at least on labels, as Doctor.

The name, however, which loomed largest and which gave me the most trouble and which my father's one joke caused me most painfully to wince about was of course my last name, my family's name, Hirsch. It marked me permanently and indelibly, from the moment I was first aware of such things, as a foreigner.

In an art class at Arnold House when I was perhaps six or seven we had to draw a castle. On my castle I put a flag and on the flag in bold letters I put SIR HIRSCH. Patiently the teacher explained to me SIR HIRSCH was not correct. LORD HIRSCH would be acceptable, but a knight is known by his first name. If I were a knight, I would be SIR ROBIN. There was no way of erasing the mistake so my castle stood for all the class to see, with the egregious name still flying. SIR HIRSCH. Even after the drawing came down and I took it home and my mother praised it—"*Ach, ist doch süss*"— it continued to haunt me.

But I could dream. I would lie awake at night while Barbie slept in the bed opposite and my parents quarreled or my mother wheeled the tea trolley into the living room, and give myself names:

> SIR ROBIN
>
> SIR ROBIN HIRSCH
>
> LORD HIRSCH
>
> LORD DAVID HIRSCH
>
> LORD DAVID
>
> THE MARQUESS OF GROVE END GARDENS
>
> VISCOUNT GROVE

VISCOUNT GROVE OF ST. JOHN'S WOOD

VISCOUNT GROVE OF ST. JOHN'S

Occasionally I'd come down to earth and it would be plain old DAVID GROVE.

And then one night it all fell suddenly, majestically, into place: R. MARC daVID. No major changes, just a slight adjustment. It was perfect. A certain enigmatic foreign suavity, short, pithy, powerful, and yet the whole bathed in an insouciant aristocratic *je ne sais quoi*. I could imagine whole shelves of books by the distinguished author, R. Marc daVid, or a concert series at the Albert Hall by the internationally renowned violinist, R. Marc daVid. And he clearly wasn't German at all.

Or Jewish, for that matter.

Which is why, when my father told his only funny joke, I was not generally disposed to laugh.

But, no matter. From the age of seven or eight I was R. Marc daVid, at least in my private dreams. And there no one could touch me.

Nazis

Arnold House School was of course named after the great nineteenth-century educator Thomas Arnold, headmaster of Rugby. It was around the corner from Grove End Gardens, and the boys of Arnold House were a colorful presence in the neighborhood. They wore red blazers with green trim and school caps and ties to match. Crocodiles of Arnold House boys could be seen snaking their way through the streets of St. John's Wood on constitutionals, with one master at the front looking down and making conversation and another in a parallel configuration bringing up the rear. It was one of the leading preparatory schools of London before the war, and for newly arrived refugees like my parents it was a reassuring sign of a calm and orderly universe.

Then, in September 1939, war was declared. Immediately every refugee was suspect. Tribunals were set up and all enemy aliens, as the Home Office dubbed them, regardless of whether or not they were Jewish and had fled for their lives, were subject to official scrutiny and the suspicion that they were Nazis. In June 1940 the males were interned. "Collar the lot!" said Churchill.

So, one early summer day, less than two years after arriving in England, my father found himself on a train again with other Germans, other Jews, headed for Liverpool and the Isle of Man. My mother with hundreds of other wives waved good-bye at the station. Six weeks later a parcel she had addressed to Herbert Hirsch, c/o Central Camp, Douglas, Isle of Man, was returned with "Sent to Canada" stamped across it.

Thousands were sent to Canada. Hundreds drowned when the Arandora Star was torpedoed in July.

My mother in a panic telephoned the Home Office, scanned the lists, found out nothing. Terrified, she waited for news. Then, very early one morning, at No. 154 Grove End Gardens, the doorbell rang.

"Yes. Hullo?"

There was no reply. She opened the door a crack, with the chain on. There on the doormat was a bunch of cat's-paws. She knew it must be my father, but when she unhooked the chain and looked in the corridor she didn't recognize him. He was wearing a beard and had lost considerable weight. "Sent to Canada," it turned out, had been a mistake.

But such mistakes were not uncommon during those six long years of the war, and many families, bewildered by the bureaucracy and the way they were treated by a country in which they had sought asylum, never quite managed to free themselves of a countervailing suspicion and took refuge in the company of their own kind, where speaking their native language would not automatically be regarded as treason.

For the balance of the war my father, together with the other older men in the building, did anti-aircraft duty on the roof. This was mostly a nighttime occupation, with a tin hat, looking—and listening—for German planes and rockets and alerting the building when a bombing seemed imminent. The entire population of Grove End Gardens—babies, children, mothers, fathers, relatives, visitors, air raid wardens—would then wait out the alert in the basement.

Down in that basement, at the bottom of one of his Berlin trunks, beneath the bakelite samples and the records of his rowing club and his letters home from the Western Front, carefully wrapped in a gray silk scarf, my father kept his Luger with two bullets and the Iron Cross (Second Class) he had been awarded as a young artillery officer in the German army.

Now, a quarter of a century later, a naturalized British citizen in a tin hat, he stood on the roof of Grove End Gardens, carefully shielding his half cigarette against the dark, draped London night and scanning the sky for his erstwhile countrymen.

Did he ever permit himself to wonder, I wonder, whether any of the men who flew the planes or dropped the bombs or launched the rockets were old enough to have fought in that earlier war to end all wars and whether, by some ghostly chance, one of them might have stood shoulder to shoulder with him in those desperate, muddy, blood-soaked trenches at Verdun?

One night Grove End Gardens was hit and the top three floors of one wing were destroyed. But the alert had been given and everyone was in the basement so there were no casualties. After the war I used to go up on

the roof and, terrified, edge over to the gaping hole. I don't remember
that I ever had the courage to look down it.

The building next door was totally demolished in another attack, and
after the war this bombed site became our favorite playground. It was far
more enticing than the spacious garden that was available to all the
tenants of Grove End Gardens, with its sandpit and little flowerbeds.
Here there was rubble and undergrowth and mystery and a place to hide.
And if one picked one's way through the jungle, dirty and scratched and
bleeding, one could come out at the wall beyond which the boys of
Arnold House were playing soccer in their gray flannel shorts and their
gray sweaters with the green and red borders, kicking the ball across the
macadam and shouting to each other in their authoritative high-pitched
voices.

I was going to go over that wall. I had of course been over the wall
before, several times, in the evening or on the weekends when the school
was deserted. But now, suddenly, at the age of five and a half, I was
withdrawn from the Alexandra Road Nursery School which Barbie and I
both attended, taken down to Bond Street, to Mallard and Frobisher,
School Outfitters, and fitted out with an assortment of the familiar red
and green togs. How my parents afforded it I don't know, although I do
remember one remark of my father's to the effect that Mr. Smart, the
headmaster, had been very good to them in the early days, and I always
assumed that meant he had had some understanding of what they had
been through and had let their son into Arnold House at a fraction of the
normal tuition.

"But I paid him back later, every penny."

So now, properly attired, I was going to go in the main gate around the
corner on Loudoun Road with the other boys, and *I* was going to kick the
ball across the macadam, and I was going to become part of the great
English school tradition.

My first memories are all of smells: the tar on the playgrounds, the wax on
the linoleum in the hallways, the wood on the desks on which generations before me had carved their initials, the perfume of Miss Rigby, the
school secretary, as she wafted by in her butterfly glasses, the unexcavated
dirt in the cracks of the parquet floor which for some arcane reason we
lay down on during Miss Tyrer's class in my first term. The floor was an
almost too perfect vantage point from which to look up Miss Tyrer's
dress. To this day I am astonished at the energy, time, and ingenuity
devoted by five-year-old boys to attempting to look up the dresses of

female teachers no matter how prim or ancient or haggardly. It wasn't that we expected to find anything in particular there, indeed it was the air of mystery, of otherness, attaching to it that was the inducement—in that respect it was like the rubble in the bombed site. And the last thing we really wanted was for the veil of mystery to be torn away. After all, as Robert Louis Stevenson, the adventure writer, so wistfully put it, to travel hopefully was better than to arrive.

Every morning before school, then briefly at the eleven o'clock break, and then again at lunchtime, and at 4:30 after school ended, there would be pickup games of soccer in the playground—and in the summer term, cricket. And twice a week, on Tuesday and Thursday afternoons, the entire school in its red and green blazers would file its way through the streets of St. John's Wood to the Underground station and take the train almost to the end of the Bakerloo line, where, perhaps two hundred strong, we would troop into the ample locker rooms, change into the appropriate apparel, and disport ourselves on the fields of Canon's Park— soccer in winter, cricket in summer.

I was never one of the great sportsmen—or sportsboys, I guess you would call them—of Arnold House, but I loved soccer, and as a cricketer I developed a real talent as a wicket keeper. I eventually made it into the Second Eleven for soccer—which meant we played the Second Elevens of other schools on some outer field while everybody watched the two First Elevens battle it out on the main field, and we trooped in and used the showers second, and sat down to have tea and cream cakes, after the match was over and we were clean and exhausted, at the tables farthest away from the center of the clubhouse dining room.

But for five glorious matches in my final summer I made it into the First Eleven for cricket. However, while I was a good wicket keeper, I wasn't a very good batsman, and on the Friday after the fifth match, when Mr. Smith went down to the gym to put up the names of the teams, I was back in the Second Eleven for cricket too. No more teas in the center of the room, no more cheering, no more applause.

Mr. Smith was both the maths teacher and the sports coach. He was also the school disciplinarian. Whenever you had transgressed one of the more serious School Rules—perhaps by looking up the dress of one of the female teachers—you would be sent to see Mr. Smith. This was a fearsome prospect since it meant interrupting his maths class and ex- plaining what you had done wrong. In mathematical terms, being sent to see Mr. Smith equaled corporal punishment. A decision was somehow arrived at as to the number of strokes you would receive, and an appoint- ment was made for after school in that same gym where the names of the teams were put up. Mr. Smith would greet you holding a gym shoe. You would hold out your hand with the palm up. Mr. Smith would bring the shoe up above his shoulder and then down with a rush of air on your outstretched palm. If your hand flinched that particular stroke didn't count. It was always a number between three and six. And then the same number on the other hand.

The gym wasn't really a gym. It was a low one-story structure where we would leave our belongings during school. Attached to it was a room with benches along the wall and mats on the floor where Mike Guttredge, the scion of a famous boxing family, taught boxing. Boxing was voluntary, but my father was adamant from the moment I first stepped into Arnold House that I take it. So every week for seven years I went down to the little white room to box. I hated it. I had a certain amount of style but no stomach, so that I was really good at exhibition matches and terrible when it came to the real thing. Bobby Lorenz, the younger and smaller of two vivacious Jewish brothers, would come at me every week with incredible energy, aiming a fusillade of punches at me from below and driving me into a corner, whereas once a year at Seymour Hall in public, at an exhibition match, I would go three rounds with David Macaulay, a quiet studious Scottish boy, and leave him with a bloody nose.

Perhaps in the long run all this orchestrated pummeling did some good because I remember very few fights breaking out in school. And I remember only two which I started. One was with a boy named Hunt, a tall blond furry crypto-Nazi with glasses who made what I took to be an anti-Semitic remark and whom I did a Bobby Lorenz on, pummeling the shit out of him in a corner. The other was more complicated.

I had a friend called Kleeman—David Kleeman—my first best friend at school. He lived in a house—already for me a sign of distinction—on Ellsworthy Road. His father was a tall remote man with a pinched mouth and a hearing aid. His mother was a rather portly lady who would occasionally serve food but who for the most part kept to herself in one portion of the house or occupied herself with her daughter or the maid or some older female relative. Mr. Kleeman was in business of some kind and I assume, to judge from the house, very successful at it. The Kleemans were Jewish but that seemed somehow incidental, ancillary to their Englishness. They never had anything to do with my family socially. They were simply the family to whom Kleeman would return every night and at whose house I would occasionally be permitted to play. In his life, I imagine, my family played a similar role.

One day at school, in the washroom, where we lined up at lunchtime at a row of sinks, Kleeman, directly behind me, turned to a boy in an adjacent line:

"Hirsch," he said, "is a Nazi."

The room smelled of carbolic soap. I felt that rush of fear and blood that beset me every week in the boxing room.

"What did you say?" I said, turning round.

"I wasn't talking to you," said Kleeman and turned to the boy in the adjacent line. "Hirsch's parents are German. I heard them. They speak with an accent. They're Nazis. Hirsch is a Nazi."

I don't know what happened. I do know I let fly, but with what success I don't remember. I think the fight was broken up. It didn't matter. I was crying anyhow. "I am not a Nazi," I cried into the sink, "I am not, not, not a Nazi."

That was the end of my friendship with David Kleeman and the beginning of a vague realization that, while there was something different about being Jewish in England, there was something even more different about being German Jewish. It was ironic, of course, because all of us had been kicked out of England in the thirteenth century and none of us had been allowed back until the seventeenth when Cromwell let us in, so we were all, so far as the English were concerned, parvenus. Only some of us were more parvenus than others.

Bar Mitzvah Boy

When I was eleven we moved to a larger flat in Marlborough Mansions on Cannon Hill—stately, peaceful, almost but not quite in Hampstead. It was farther away from the center of London, it had not been bombed during the war, and there was no bombed site next door to play in. It was also farther away from Arnold House, and I would come in every day by bike or on the bus.

The boy who sat next to me for my last three years and who, if for no other reason than prolonged proximity, replaced David Kleeman was Robert Atkin. Robert Atkin was also Jewish, his parents lived in a house no less splendid than the Kleemans' house, and they were a hell of a lot less remote. Mrs. Atkin, I think, was Czech, and even Mr. Atkin, I learned years later, was born abroad. But compared to my parents he spoke a flawless English. He had a rubber company in Tottenham with the impeccably English name of Cannon Rubber, so I was inclined to overlook his wife's accent as a charming affectation and assumed they were at least as English as the Duke of Edinburgh.

Robert was eight or nine months older than I, an extraordinarily nervous boy who would finger everything that came to hand and ask unending questions. He was the only person I ever knew, even at the age of ten, who could give my father a run for his money. He had the unspeakable chutzpah, in my father's study, to leaf through the papers on my father's desk, an act of such inconceivable lèse-majesté that my father was actually taken aback. All the while Robert would keep up such a barrage of questions, pronouncements, opinions on this and that—the weather, the stock market, the state of the nation—that my father was, I think, in a tiny corner of his heart, disposed to smile.

One day an engraved invitation addressed to Mr. and Mrs. Hirsch and Master Hirsch arrived at Marlborough Mansions. It was from Mr. and Mrs. Atkin and it requested the pleasure of our company at the Bar Mitzvah of their son Robert and a dinner following. The Bar Mitzvah was to be at the Abbey Road Synagogue which was round the corner from

Grove End Gardens, and the dinner following was to be at Selby's, a catering establishment in the heart of the West End. "Following" of course was not to be taken literally, since the Sabbath would not end till evening and the festivities would not begin till after sundown.

I had never been to a Bar Mitzvah. I had only rarely been inside a synagogue, and never an Orthodox synagogue like the one on Abbey Road. I didn't quite know what to expect, although I assumed it would be solemn and dark and forbidding, and there would be chanting and a great deal more Hebrew than in the services my parents attended on the High Holy Days and to which we were dragged along. I didn't know whether to look forward to this occasion, on which Robert would become a man, with joy or with foreboding.

In the end it was no contest. My father called me into his study and I knew it would be foreboding.

"Rrrawbeen," he said, making me stand as usual by his desk. "You are a friend of Robert's and I think it would be a good idea if you would make a speech."

"Oh, no, but . . . ," I began—and I thought, I'm not really a friend, certainly not his best friend, and I don't want to get up in front of all those people, and anyhow they probably don't want some little twelve-year-old barging in on their Bar Mitzvah. But I didn't get any of that out.

"It will be ten minutes long. You should say he's your best friend, how well you know him, how a great occasion this is, *und so weiter.*"

"But . . ."

"So . . . you will go to your room and write. And in an hour you will show me."

So I went to my room, and tore my hair out. After an hour, I had written, "Ladies and Gentlemen, I am Robert's best friend," crossed that out and put, "Ladies and Gentlemen, Robert is my best friend, and this is a great occasion." Clearly, I was in trouble. Indeed by the morning of the Bar Mitzvah I did not have two sentences strung together and the outlook was very bleak. The afternoon I knew would be spent in my room, sweating blood.

We entered the synagogue late, my father having berated me at length about my nonexistent speech. My mother and sister were directed upstairs, and my father and I entered the main chamber. It was indeed dark and solemn and forbidding. Up on a dark burnished dais the cantor chanting and behind him the golden pipes of the organ and somewhere behind them invisible, the choir, and in the pews men in dark suits and black hats adjusting their shawls and swaying in prayer. And up in the balcony, separated from us, the women. I tried to find my sister who I thought must be even more lonely in all this than I, but I couldn't, and I felt the vague apprehension that looking up at the women might well be forbidden and I stopped doing it.

The appearance was solemn, but underneath the solemnity there was evidently a great deal of business going on. Men davening and throwing in the occasional *omein* seemed, on closer inspection, to be carrying on all manner of conversations—the weather (which was glorious), the stock market, the children, Israel, the Chief Rabbi (who was in attendance), and all sorts of other matters to which twelve-year-olds, who are not yet men, are not privy. Perhaps, I thought, after today Robert will be having these covert discussions every Saturday morning.

My father, not being a member of this synagogue and having few acquaintances amongst the cream of English Jewry, was perhaps little more at home than I. But he had a wonderful tallis in a blue velvet bag, he scorned the rituals which seemed second nature to the other men, and he had no compunction about asking questions of any neighbor. In a way I think I was proud of him for not at any moment surrendering to a sense of otherness.

Eventually ten men were called up to the Law, the tenth being Robert who acquitted himself with his usual energy and then launched into his Haftorah portion. The rabbi complimented him, addressing him, his parents, his family, and the congregation at large on the importance of this occasion, and after what seemed to be an age relinquished the dais to the cantor for the concluding prayers, and then a glass of wine was lifted and kiddush was said, and a final blessing proclaimed, and we filed out into the sunlight.

I spent the afternoon writing out in capital letters on four tiny sheets of paper some extremely hard-won words on the subject of my friend Robert and the greatness of the occasion and praying to the great Jewish God that He would show some sign of His powers by interceding on my behalf and making it impossible for me to deliver my speech.

We drove into the West End—my mother, my father, and I (my sister was not on the invitation and was left to her own devices). At the elaborate entrance to Selby's the doorman enquired whether we were here for the Atkin Bar Mitzvah and we were motioned inside and up an enormous staircase. Here we checked our coats and were motioned into an ornate antechamber. Beyond the antechamber I could see Robert and his family arrayed in a reception line and beyond them what seemed like thousands of people digging into the hors d'oeuvres and swilling champagne. But between them and us, at the entrance to the reception room, stood an enormous, elegant, imposing figure in a red frock coat and a clipped mustache—the toastmaster. I began to tremble as we approached him. He bent down toward us.

"May I see your invitation?"

"My son Robin would like to say a few words."

"I beg your pardon?"

"My son Robin is the best friend of Robert Atkin and he would like to say a few words."

A look of incredulity passed over the toastmaster's face.

"I'm afraid that's quite impossible."

I hardly dared to hope—did God really exist?

"He has a speech prepared, he is the best friend of the Bar Mitzvah boy."

"I'm afraid the speech list is already printed. Now may I see your invitation?"

And then, holding up the invitation, in tones which have resounded in every colony of the British Empire, he announced: "Mr. and Mrs. Hirsch and Master Hirsch." Did I detect a slight sneer in the emphasis on "Master"? It didn't matter; we were through and I was free.

We went down the receiving line until we reached Mr. Atkin, whom my father had not met.

"My son Robin wanted to say a few words but the man in the red coat said no."

Oh my God, I thought, how can You do this to me?

"What a wonderful idea," said Mr. Atkin.

"How charming," said Mrs. Atkin.

"So, you will arrange it," said my father.

Mr. Atkin motioned the toastmaster over to the receiving line and explained that Master Robin Hirsch, at some point in the proceedings, would like to say a few words and please arrange it. The toastmaster scowled and looked at me, as much as to say, "You little wog, weaseling your way in here and disturbing the order of events; I'll arrange it alright." And with much shaking of hands and smiling and clapping of backs we passed on to the hors d'oeuvres, the reception line reconstituted itself, and the toastmaster went back to his appointed position.

I couldn't eat. I could hardly talk. I kept thinking of the printed speech list and me penciled in somewhere between Her Majesty the Queen and the State of Israel. I clutched my four tiny pieces of paper and saw that the ink was beginning to run.

Dinner was a seven-course meal for two hundred people at tables scattered throughout a vast ballroom. The average age of a table seemed to decrease in direct proportion to its distance from the top table. There was what seemed to be a young people's table adjacent to ours, but ours was the children's table and we were at the other end of the earth from where Robert was sitting. At least I assumed it was Robert, because there was only one diminutive form in a long line of distinguished heads at the top table. Robert was the only person I knew at this enormous gathering, apart from my parents—and they mercifully were also a million miles away. I didn't know a soul at my own table although we all introduced ourselves and everyone seemed very friendly. There was indeed a speech list with a printed menu on the facing page. Every Jew in England with a title seemed about to propose a toast.

"My Lords, Ladies, and Gentlemen, Reverend Sirs,"—the entire room fell silent as the toastmaster's voice cut through the hubbub like an icebreaker—"Pray silence for Sir Louis Gluckstein, who will propose the toast to Her Majesty the Queen." Up at the top table, Sir Louis got to his feet, adjusted his microphone, called on us all to rise, and gave us the Queen.

Course after course arrived, and course after course I looked at in a kind of catatonic terror.

"What's the matter, why aren't you eating?" asked my neighbor, a beautiful and solicitous cousin of the Bar Mitzvah boy.

"Um, um, I can't eat," I mumbled.

"My Lords, Ladies, and Gentlemen, Reverend Sirs, pray silence for the Right Honorable Maurice Edelman, M.P., who will propose a toast to the State of Israel." Two hundred chairs pushed back, two hundred glasses raised—"The State of Israel."

More courses. The father of the Bar Mitzvah boy spoke, the uncle of the Bar Mitzvah boy spoke, the Bar Mitzvah boy himself at some significant moment spoke. More food. More food sent back. And then again the icy voice of the toastmaster.

"My Lords, Ladies, and Gentlemen, Reverend Sirs, pray silence for . . ." —and then the longest pause in history, and finally with all the contempt he could muster, "*Master* Robin Hirsch, who will address you." Two hundred pairs of eyes consulted their speech lists, two hundred frowns appeared on two hundred faces, and two hundred heads turned expectantly to the top table.

Meanwhile, down at the other end of the room, I pushed my chair back, unglued my clammy thighs from the seat covering, and, in a rash moment, decided to clamber aboard the chair. I vaguely remember the look of apprehension on my neighbor's face as she saw me standing up on one of Selby's delicate gold-painted party chairs, my knees shaking, my trembling hands holding on to four tiny pieces of paper. "What are you doing?" she whispered.

"My Lords, Ladies, and Gentlemen, Reverend Sirs," I began in a tiny voice, "Robert Atkin is a friend of mine and this is a great occasion." Two hundred chairs started to shuffle round in my direction. "I just wanted to say a few words from this end of the room."

And somehow I guess I did. I finished, there was what seemed to be riotous applause, my neighbor looked at me with a mixture of admiration and concern and said, "Oh, now I see why you couldn't eat," and asked the waiter to bring back all the courses I had returned. The sweat poured down me, the weight of generations seemed to depart from my shoulders, and I ate like a pig.

After the meal was over, the tables were cleared away and the room made ready for dancing and a cabaret. People came over to me and patted me on the head, and my erstwhile table companions protected me with a certain proprietary interest. Finally the toastmaster sought me out. "Master Hirsch," he said, and the sneer seemed to have melted away, "Mr. Atkin wants your speech to be on the record."

"What do you mean?" I said.

"The proceedings at the top table were being recorded," said the toastmaster, "and you were supposed to come up and speak into one of the microphones."

"Oh," I said, "nobody told me."

"Well, Master Hirsch," he said, "I wonder whether you would accompany me to the studio at the other end of the room and we can record your speech in there."

"Why, certainly," I said, and we went, the two of us, he in his red frock coat, me in my gray flannel shorts, into the studio and cut a record.

When we came out the band had struck up and there was dancing. I had managed to give my parents the slip and had begun to make friends with some of the cousins, Charles from Bradford in the north of England, and Valerie, the beautiful one, and all sorts of others far too proud and too sophisticated to go out on the floor and do a fox-trot.

"Ladies and Gentlemen," the bandleader said, after the dancing had been under way for some time, "we crave your attention for the cabaret." So we all gathered round. The children were pushed to the very front and sat on the floor, and behind us, on chairs out of breath, a sea of grown-ups. "Ladies and Gentlemen," said the bandleader, "Selby's is proud to present for your delectation, a very special artist and a very special event. Ladies and Gentlemen, Serena and her Dance of the Seven Veils."

I don't think any of us children knew what the Dance of the Seven Veils was, I suspect Selby's had a standard cabaret for evening events and perhaps was not used to catering Bar Mitzvahs, and I'm absolutely positive that Robert's parents hadn't the faintest idea what was in store for their firstborn son. If Bar Mitzvahs were about coming of age, some of us indeed came of age that night.

With a trombone and a roll of the drums and a couple of spotlights Serena was suddenly in our midst. Cousin Charles and I exchanged glances. Could this really be true? Maybe God did exist after all. Bump, bump. She removed a long filmy pink veil and looked for an appropriate blue-jowled businessman to caress with it, but the only ones within touching distance were Charles and me and the other children. The veil sailed past our noses and floated down in front of our uncovered knees. Was this really happening? Another veil and another. Bump, bump. The music picked up and her thighs were so close we could touch them—were you supposed to? Finally her whole body was revealed to us, with sequins strategically placed to obscure and at the same time to highlight the critical areas. A final flourish, a final roll on the drums, a touch with the brush on the high-hat cymbal, and then, as suddenly as she had appeared, she was gone.

The following January, in my first pair of long trousers, I had my own Bar Mitzvah, in the German Jewish congregation to which my parents belonged. No Chief Rabbi, no grand reception, no long-playing record, and no Dance of the Seven Veils. I had been accepted at St. Paul's School, founded by John Colet, Dean of St. Paul's, in 1509. I was Bar Mitzvahed in my new school uniform, a black blazer with a white badge, a black cap with a white ring, and a black tie. And in my hand a velvet bag and round my neck a tallis.

Getting and Spending

I knocked on my father's door.

"Who is it?"

"Robin."

"*Who?*"

"Robin."

"*Ach, ja,* RRRawbeen, *komm' ma' rein.*"

His study was filled with papers and cigarette smoke. "*Was willst du?*"

"It's Saturday. Can I have my pocket money, please?"

"And what have you done to deserve pocket money?"

This was a weekly ritual. I hadn't done anything to deserve pocket money. On the other hand, I hadn't usually transgressed sufficiently for it to be denied. But I had to stand patiently by his desk, waiting, begging, for my father to relent.

We were on rationing, not for everything, but for certain things, into the early fifties. When rationing came off sugar, sweetshops, which had been barren, began to sprout all kinds of wonderful and arcane flora—Mars Bars, Smarties, Cadbury's Milk Flakes, Rowntree's Fruit Pastilles, Bassett's Licorice Allsorts. I could, if I had money, go down to the local newsagent, where, in terms of sweets, a healthy assortment of packaged goods was available amongst the magazines and the index cards advertising "Chest for Sale—40 inches," "Used Car—marvelous body," "Rubberwear—please ring," and other messages the deeper meaning of which was lost on me. But my overwhelming passion was to get on my bike and pedal down to the sweetshop on Boundary Road, where the real exotica were exhibited in glass jars. I'd lean my bike against the window, open the door with its tinkling bell, and inhale the heady aroma of boiled sweets and loose chocolates and roasted coffee beans and nuts and dates and raisins and glacéed fruit. I could spend hours just looking and making my mind up, and when I was ready I'd ask for a quarter of a pound of this and a quarter of a pound of that and the shopkeeper would spoon each precious purchase into a neat white paper bag which he would twirl nonchalantly over and over until he let go and two ears appeared at the corners and the bag was miraculously sealed. And then he would line up my bags and total them, and if I had any money left I'd add a Tiffin Bar or a packet of Maltesers or a small Cadbury's Bournville with Roasted Almonds, please. And then the agonizing choice of how much to eat right away and how much to hoard for later.

On this particular Saturday, after wheedling my two shillings out of my father, I ran downstairs, unlocked the cellar, and pedaled my bike furiously down Cannon Hill, down West End Lane, down Abbey Road, until I came to Mecca. There I loaded up with every treasure two shillings would get me. When I returned home I had eaten myself silly.

"Where were you?"

"I went out on my bike."

"*Wo?*"

"Oh, down West End Lane."

"*Warum* West End Lane, how often have I told you."

"Oh, it's alright, I know what I'm doing."

"How far did you go?"

"Not far."

"Not far. You have been gone two hours and a half."

"Well, I rode around."

"You went to the sweetshop."

"Er, yes."

"*Herr Gott noch Mal.*"

"It's alright, I went the back way."

"And how much did you spend?"

"Not much."

"*Wie viel?*"

"A shilling."

"*Was?* A shilling? On sweets?"

"Well, yes."

"Let me see."

"What?"

"Your purchases."

"I can't."

"Why not?"

"I've eaten them."

"*Bitte?*"

"I've eaten them."

"You've eaten them? How much do you get for a shilling?"

"Oh, not much."

"A shilling. *Es ist nicht zu glauben.* Let me see the other shilling."

There was no other shilling. I fished in my pocket. It wasn't in my right pocket. It wasn't in my left pocket. "Um. I. Um. I. It's. I can't find it."

My father sits and glowers. I invent.

"I had it. It was here. Maybe it's. When I put my bike away. I must have. Dropped it."

My father cuts a cigarette in half, lays one half aside, stuffs the other in his holder, clenches his teeth, doesn't light it. "Alright, we do down." He puts on his tattered house jacket. "Take the torch."

I take the torch. We get in the lift, say nothing, go down two floors, get out, walk down to the basement.

"Switch on."

I switch on. I walk up and down the cold dark cement hallway. I look everywhere. My father stands and lights his cigarette. I unlock the cellar door, wheel out my bike, light the candles, move the suitcases, paraffin heaters, accumulated bric-a-brac, search the floor. Hopeless.

"*Also.* Keep looking. When you find it, you can come up."

He leaves.

Two hours later, with a hole in my stomach, I come upstairs. "Dinner's ready," says my mother.

"I'm not hungry."

"Tell Daddy to come in."

"Why can't Barbie tell him?"

"Ach, Robienchen, *mach nicht immer so ein* fuss."

I knock on the door.

"*Ja*, who is it?"

"Robin."

"Who?"

"Robin."

"*Who?*"

Trembling, I open the door.

The Queen's English

My mother's sense of humor was riper than my father's; this was not hard since my father's was barely discernible. My mother's usual entreaty to us after we had been beaten, which happened not irregularly, was "Ach, Robienchen (or Barbarina), go in, apologize, make him laugh." Even under the best of circumstances this would have been impossible.

My mother, on the other hand, laughed readily. She laughed at her own mistakes, she laughed at the pretensions of others, she even at a distance laughed at my father. But that was a special laughter filled with mysteries we would never fathom.

In everyday life, she had all kinds of jokes and stories and allusions which she would translate—Berlin jokes, lunatic jokes, refugee jokes. And while translation is not the best medium for such things, and the atmosphere at home was far from radiant, a sense of my mother's underlying good nature always came through.

But the occasions on which she really shone were unpremeditated. One day a friend of mine came over for tea. We didn't have friends over often, partly because my father would come in and scowl after a few minutes as much as to say, "You still here?" and partly because my mother would make an embarrassing fuss—tea and cakes in the living room—when all we wanted was to laugh among ourselves in the kitchen. But there were children of other refugee parents who understood the arcane German rituals, and with them my sister and I could at least groan sympathetically and roll our eyes. But even these occasions were rare.

So how it came that Herbert Levy, who was one of the leaders of the youth group at the Belsize Square New Liberal Jewish Congregation, a congregation of refugees to which my parents belonged and in whose youth group, the Phoenix, my sister and I found a totally unexpected and blessed sanctuary, how it came that not only Herbert Levy but a young American cousin of his were over for tea one day I cannot imagine. But there they were in the living room with my mother pouring tea and making conversation in her Berlin accent, and my father coming in from time to time to see what took so long, and my sister and I grimacing and sweating on the sofa.

"So, vot brings you to zis country?" my mother enquired. "It is here a very different country England from America, *nicht wahr?*" "You are *immer noch* in school in Chicago, *nein?*"

To each of these Herbert Levy's fifteen-year-old American cousin replied with the same uncomprehending stare and the same ever-so-polite midwestern, "I beg your pardon, ma'am?"

Finally, my mother, irritated, unable to bear it any longer, said, "Vot? You don't understand ze vay how vee English speak?"

From Ashes

There opened up before me in the wake of my Bar Mitzvah two very different lives.

One was at St. Paul's, where, after much terror and examination, I became a scholar, and where, as a scholar, together with the one hundred and fifty-two other scholars, I wore a little silver fish to remind me of the miracle on Lake Galilee where Our Lord gathered in His nets one hundred and fifty-three little fishes after his awestruck disciples had failed to land any.

The other was at the Belsize Square New Liberal Jewish Congregation, the congregation founded just before the war by German Jewish refugees to which my parents belonged and to which one dreary Sunday morning Barbie and I were dragged as a kind of punishment for having reached double figures.

Sunday mornings were now spent trying desperately to decipher Hebrew with a German Accent—not to make sense of it, but to get through it, not even one sentence at a time, but rather one word, one letter. This was no yeshiva—*Gott behüte!*—this was a touching, awkward attempt by German Jews who were beginning to establish themselves in England, who for the most part had never possessed great religious conviction, and who, having fled Hitler and lost much, had little reason to discover it now, to provide for their children some vestige of a Jewish education which would not interfere with their English schooling and which would get them out of the house on Sunday mornings.

Sunday school in which haphazardly I was prepared for my Bar Mitzvah passed in a fog. But on reaching my thirteenth birthday, as my Bar Mitzvah approached, I was invited to join the congregation's youth group, the Phoenix—or the Furnix, as my parents religiously called it. My parents let me join, I suspect, not for any great benefit that might ensue, but because this would get me out of the house on Saturday nights, which was even better than Sunday mornings.

The Phoenix turned out to be balm. I never expected it. I thought at best it would be Sunday school in fancy dress. But it wasn't. It wasn't at all.

I never knew it was possible to laugh so much. Of course we had common grounds from which to laugh, we children of German Jews. We laughed at the language of our parents, of the teachers in Sunday school, of the dignified old rabbi, who barely spoke English at all and who conducted his services in a mixture of German and Hebrew—too much Hebrew, some of the grown-ups felt. And we laughed at the language of the fat new rabbi, who conducted his services in a mixture of Hebrew—less Hebrew—and an accented and high-flown English, which impressed many of the grown-ups but few of us children, who knew he was full of hot air and faulty syntax and who giggled away at services on Friday night or Saturday morning and hoarded the latest flower of Impossible English to share on Saturday night at the Phoenix.

Laughter lifted the soul. It leavened every activity at the Phoenix, from committee meetings to drama rehearsals, from swimming matches to brainstorming sessions, from editorial palavers to dancing parties. Membership in the Phoenix was the best Bar Mitzvah present I got. I felt as though I'd been let out of prison, that suddenly I was in a free country, peopled exclusively by ex-cons like myself, all thirteen to seventeen years old, all of whom spoke the same language, understood the same jokes, and shared the same appetite for the sudden free blissful and ravishing air. I felt as though by some miracle I had found my long-lost comrades and they had found me. I felt as though I had come home.

Within weeks, Sunday school fell by the wayside. After all, I had been Bar Mitzvahed. Any given Saturday night was fuller and richer than the Haftorah portion I had struggled with for over a year, and besides Sunday mornings were now devoted to an extension of Saturday nights at the Finchley Road Swimming Baths. Here at ten we would meet, a dozen or more of the movers and shakers, and we would plunge and dive and cavort and chase, Gerald and Peter and Daniel and Paul and David and now, to my astonishment, me, and the girls, Susan and Ruth and Jeanette and Miriam and Sheila and then, sixteen months later, Barbie. And in the chasing and the screaming and the laughing and the splashing the serious history of the Belsize Square New Liberal Jewish Congregation and the solemn purposes of its youth group would be washed away and the past and the future would be blotted out and there would be only the exhilarating and unselfconscious present, and the bewildering curve of a leg or a glistening shoulder or the faint swelling of a breast, and a sudden, inchoate, and heavenly longing.

And after swimming, heady with chlorine, tingling, refreshed, jumping and clowning and taking over the entire pavement, we would repair to a coffee bar called the Dorice just down the Finchley Road, where we would order cappuccino and pastries and make miserable for an hour the life of the middle-aged Austrian waiter, not to mention the dignified refugee patrons. "Ach, so, I hef a Hot *Schokolade mit Schlagsahne* and fifteen straws for *meine Freunde.*" And the entire table would dissolve in laughter.

Why we were never kicked out was a mystery. And why the management allowed us to come back week after week was another mystery. Perhaps it had something to do with the fact that the owner too was a member of the Belsize Square New Liberal Jewish Congregation. And that the swimming party, as often as not, contained one of the daughters of the fat new rabbi, who—it was a pleasure to note—did not in any way that I could discern resemble her father. And perhaps also that the exuberance and high spirits of youth, irritating though they might be, offered a certain complicated consolation, a promise of hope and continuance, to a clientele mired in loss and displacement.

The Phoenix had three leaders. They were all of an age that sat at some eternally fixed spot between the oldest of the members and the youngest of the parents. Still, questions hovered in the air above their head, just as they hovered over the heads of our parents, of the rabbi and cantor, of the teachers at Sunday school, of every disconsolate customer at the Dorice. Everyone older than us had stories, but they were shrouded in mystery and silence, hinted at only in rumor, amplified only by conjecture. Every story begat questions, but questions never begat answers, only further questions.

The leader of all leaders, the founder of the Phoenix and for years its presiding genius, was Charles Gutmann, or KarlHeinz as he was known to the parents. He lived round the corner with his elderly widowed mother, who, it was rumored, held him in thrall. Was there a father? Was he dead or were they divorced? Or had he indeed, as rumor had it, abandoned Frau Gutmann? And if so, when? And if early, how early? And had she thereupon bestowed upon the infant KarlHeinz all her grief-ridden passion and jealousy? And ten years later, when the time came to flee with him to England, had she secreted a number of large gems inside the dress that little KarlHeinz had been made to wear for the journey? And how could they not have been searched at the border? And what, exactly, had been discovered?

In everyday life Charles was a junior English teacher at a minor public school, with aspirations towards acceptance there which did not quite jibe with his work at the Phoenix or his impassioned Sunday school remonstrances on the subject of assimilation. Nevertheless, in the course of my four-year passage through the Phoenix, Charles Gutmann, its indomitable leader, became in the outside world a Justice of the Peace and head of the English department. His mother, growing more tyrannical with every year, gloated at these accomplishments and continued to intercept his phone calls.

No doubt Charles's dedication to the Phoenix sprang in part from the excuse it gave him now, after so many years, to escape from the old dragon, at least on Saturday nights. Still, it was from Charles, more than from any of our teachers at school, that we acquired an appreciation, however meager, for a fundamental kind of humane learning. It was through endless committee meetings at the synagogue with Charles presiding, through endless sessions at Charles's flat with Frau Gutmann leering and wheeling in *Streuselkuchen und Kaffee*, that the complex network of life at the Phoenix was sustained, that club quizzes were concocted and Saturday night revues were born and the club magazine was produced and a young people's lecture series was developed, in short, that the entire cultural and social fabric of a community was stitched together. And it was in the course of all this activity, so freely undertaken, so consuming, so filled with laughter, so different from school, that we first began to discover, however unintentionally, the history into which we had been born and the language into which circumstance had thrust us.

Charles had as a sidekick a small dour man named Richard, who worked as a salesman in the furniture department of John Lewis. Richard had spent the war years underground in Europe and the years after the war in D.P. camps, so that he came to England late, alone, and disadvantaged, and while he had mastered the new language, he was never able to shed the old accent. Through the aid of refugee organizations he had found a room and eventually a job. Perhaps on the one hand his work at the Phoenix was a way of paying off a debt, perhaps on the other it offered him the only kind of home a man who has lost everything can find. Every week he would put aside a few shillings from his salary at John Lewis against the day he would be able to afford a flat of his own, and every week, also, he would scour the *AJR Information*, the refugee newsletter, in the hope of finding some news, however final, of the family he had last seen on a train crossing the border into Poland. Had he jumped at the border, I used to wonder, this small, wizened, inconsiderable man? Had he slipped away by himself or had he been left behind? And the SS, with their boots and greatcoats and dogs and machine guns, how had he eluded them?

One day, in the *AJR Information*, a sister turned up, alive and married, in Israel. Richard kept a small clipping from that issue in his wallet and every so often he could be seen in a corner studying it and shaking his head. And then one Saturday night Richard was gone. He had packed his belongings into one small suitcase, had gathered his shillings together from under the mattress, had taken the bus down to Regent Street to the offices of El Al, had bought a ticket to Tel Aviv, and that night had flown to Israel to join his sister and her husband and the two small children and to live out his life in the hot days and cool nights of the Galil.

Every so often Charles would receive a letter or the Phoenix a post-card: Richard was working in the kitchen, making yogurt; Richard was working on the fish farm; Richard was working with his brother-in-law in the banana groves; Richard was becoming a citizen; Richard was, at the age of thirty-nine, doing his military service. Gradually, inevitably, the members who had known Richard grew older and left, and the postcards became fewer. Eventually, by the time of the Six-Day War, even the letters to Charles stopped coming.

The third member of the triumvirate was W. H. Levy, an actor manqué, whose family included theater people from the German, Austrian, and Yiddish stages. Nobody knew what the W. stood for—it was doubtless some German name of which he was ashamed. The H. stood for Herbert, which is how he was known. It was of course my father's name, but two more different spirits it would be hard to imagine.

Herbert was responsible for introducing drama into the Phoenix. He was fluent in both German and English, so that on the grand occasions when the Belsize Square New Liberal Jewish Congregation paused from its collective business of worship, worry, and building and let down its collective hair at the annual dinner dance, Herbert would perform some-thing from Schiller, something from Shakespeare, and serve in the pro-cess as a bridge between the generations. Somewhere between arriving in England as a nine-year-old boy with his parents before the war and join-ing the Phoenix in his late twenties as a leader, his dream of a life in the professional theater had foundered. As a teenager after the war he was tested for an important role in a film opposite Jean Simmons, but his father suffered a heart attack and the struggling family handbag business which his parents had started and which enabled him to go to school needed more hands and his were the only ones available.

The dream of becoming an actor on the English stage, of carrying on the family tradition in another country, in another culture, in another language, had died, but if there was some profound disappointment I couldn't detect it. Indeed, as far as I was concerned, the laughter which rippled through the Phoenix, the joy which bubbled up through the floorboards and which infected every life there, had Herbert as its source. On certain Sunday mornings on the pavement outside the Finchley Road

Swimming Baths Herbert could be found making aeroplanes with his arms, laughing his infectious high-pitched unstoppable laugh, and leading two or three or half a dozen of the bravest and least ruly of the Sunday swimmers in an aeroplane race to the Dorice. And at the Dorice as often as not it was Herbert who started the chaotic ordering and Daniel or Michael or Paul or occasionally, timidly, me who followed suit. And the laughter which sooner or later engulfed the whole table and overwhelmed the restaurant started as a ripple, a nudge, a whisper from Herbert—a remark of Herbert's into the ear of a neighbor, a wink of Herbert's across the table at one of the girls, an order of Herbert's delivered in languid and supercilious English to the Austrian waiter and then punctured with an abrupt eye-popping outraged Wagnerian, "Vot? No vipped cream?!" As far as I was concerned, Herbert was the bringer of light.

When I joined the Phoenix, Herbert was rehearsing the first act of *The Importance of Being Earnest* for the upcoming dinner dance. Herbert himself took the role of Ernest, and Charles, who revealed an unsuspected talent for farce, played Algy. Richard, who took his job very seriously, was stage manager. "No," he would say in his ineradicable accent, "ze correct line is 'To lose vun parent, Mr. Verzing . . . ,'" and out of his improbable mouth would drop like a stone yet another of Wilde's immortal soufflés.

"Richard," Charles would bellow, "You are murdering Wilde, and, what is worse, you are murdering me! Herbert, how do you expect me to act, to be 'free', to quote the Herr Regisseur, if I am chained to a text which this dwarf, this nitwit, cannot even pronounce."

Charles could not, for the life of him, remember his lines, but he was a gifted improviser and before an audience of refugees Wilde's immaculately honed words and Charles's desperate interpolations were not readily distinguishable. Indeed, the scene proved so successful that the synagogue charged Herbert with working up a full evening for which the Belsize Square New Liberal Jewish Congregation would rent a real theater in Westbourne Grove, real costumes from Bermans', and produce a night to which tickets would be sold to benefit the building fund.

"*Gott im Himmel,*" said Charles, "now I have to learn my lines." But it was a lost cause. He wrote them out on Bermans' starched white cuffs, on pieces of paper scattered strategically about the stage, and on the inside of the cigarette box which Herbert had, as a result, more trouble wresting from him than perhaps any Ernest before or since. "And, Richard, don't you dare, don't you DARE, clean up the stage before the show. If those pieces of paper are not EXACTLY where I want them when I come on, I will come straight off and I will kill you. Do you understand me?"

"What kind of job is stage manager, if not to keep everything clean and in order?"

"RICHARD!"

"Alright. Alright."

Lady Bracknell was played by a girl, old before her time, who had lost her parents during the war after fleeing to Belgium and who had been adopted as a six-year-old when the war ended by relatives who had escaped to England. She was treasurer of the Phoenix. Whenever she rang Charles at home, Frau Gutmann would pick up the phone and tell her he was unavailable. Her name was Lilian.

Lilian was almost four years older than me. She was seventeen, an age so immeasurably far away that I could scarcely conceive of it. Certainly she was too old for the Sunday morning frolics at the Finchley Road Baths. But she had always been too old for that, I imagined. There was a gravity to her that was missing from the others. There must have been that gravity to her even when she was my age, although I couldn't imagine her ever having been my age. One day, I thought, she would marry Charles.

Sometimes, after a committee meeting or a rehearsal or cleaning up on a Saturday night, I would find myself walking with Lilian to Swiss Cottage, where she lived and where I caught the bus. Miraculousy I discovered that I could talk to her, that for some unfathomable reason, I was not hopelessly tongue-tied in her presence, and, more astonishing still, that she would listen. When I got on the bus I would be barely able to contain myself. It was not that she was beautiful, she was far from beautiful. It was not that I lusted after her, although sometimes at night in my bed in the dark, after my parents had finally retired, I would hold my pillow and imagine her naked. It was rather some quality about her that made things safe. Somehow I knew I could talk to her about things I hadn't even realized I needed to say.

"What is it, Robin?"

"I don't know. I don't know. Things are terrible at home."

For the grand event at the Twentieth Century Theatre in Westbourne Grove, Herbert decided to add the trial scene from *The Merchant of Venice*. I found myself cast as the Duke of Venice, a small and thankless role which I thought anyone could pull off, but the words I had to say were formal and weighty and I couldn't quite get my mouth around them fast enough, and I watched enviously as Shylock and Antonio and Portia battled it out in speeches I seemed somehow to have known since before I was born.

The trial scene was performed one Saturday night for the members of the Phoenix. The members tolerated it because a dance was promised afterwards and perhaps also because the anticipation of the grand event had in one way or another fired the imagination even of those who were not directly involved. Gary, a new boy, delivered his lines menacingly and with conviction as Shylock, Daniel nobly offered his breast as Antonio, ably assisted by Paul as Bassanio. Even my difficult first speech as the Duke went better than I had expected. Indeed, everything was going well until the entrance of Portia with her maidservant, Nerissa, who was being played by my sister. When I, swathed in a turban as the Duke, asked for their credentials and Nerissa was about to reply, nothing came out. Numb, I looked at Barbie and waited. Nothing. Dimly, through the darkness of my own frozen and desperate gaze, I realized that she was helplessly, uncontrollably, laughing. At least I thought she was laughing. She had her back to the audience and tears were streaming down her face.

Royal Command Performance

Jews and atheists and the occasional Buddhist—I knew only one, the Crown Prince of Thailand, who always beat me at table tennis—were excused from Morning Assembly at St. Paul's. We still had to be in the main door before the bell rang, but we congregated in the upstairs theater while the vast majority of the school drank blood in the chapel or whatever muscular Christians do first thing in the morning.

Actually, there were quite a few Jews at St. Paul's, 10 percent or so, which was extraordinarily high for an English public school. Some of the more observant would gather in a neighboring classroom to hold a morning service. This was even more frightening and alien than the glimpses I'd had of Chapel. Boys I knew from class, shy, retiring, scholarly types, would suddenly in this clandestine context transform themselves beyond recognition. Yarmulkes, tallisim, tefillin would mysteriously appear and for a brief and eerie moment Mr. Rainbow's room, unbeknownst to the goyim, would be transmogrified into a nineteenth-century shtetl shul. And then just as suddenly, in the midst of davening, the bell would ring and all the arcane Jewish paraphernalia would be spirited away and the Christians would saunter in and we would all be jaunty schoolboys again.

One morning in 1959 the prefect in charge of Jews tells us that there won't be time for morning services because the High Master has an Important Announcement. We are herded down. We shuffle in and take our places on the stairs and in the aisles and when we have settled Trickle begins. "Why Trickle?" every entering thirteen-year-old would ask. "Because he's such a drip." The name had acquired a kind of magical incantatory quality which was now more frightening than if we had called him by his real name, Mr. Gilkes. He was a tall, imposing man, with none of the warmth that Mr. Cook, the Surmaster, radiated without effort. His was a totally public persona. He would have made an admirable Prime Minister.

"As you know," Trickle began, "this year marks the 450th anniversary of the founding of the school by Dean Colet, and in honor of the occasion Buckingham Palace has announced that Her Majesty the Queen and His Royal Highness the Duke of Edinburgh will visit us in the late spring. We have had instructions from the Palace that this will be a strictly informal visit. There will be two rehearsals.

"Now, Mr. Davies, if you would be so kind," and Mr. Davies at the organ was of course so kind, and struck up "Onward Christian Soldiers," and five hundred Christian soldiers sang out lustily and we Jews held onto our satchels and tried not to hum.

For the next several months the school swung into relentless action. The Combined Cadet Force prepared an honor guard for the Royal Visit which marched incessantly up and down the paths of the front quadrangle, stamping, shouting, and presenting arms. A special toilet was built for Her Majesty at a cost, it was rumored, of three thousand pounds— no one was allowed to use it, instructions having been somehow conveyed from the Palace that the Royal Behind was not to sit uncovered on any surface that had previously been sat on. And a production of Milton's *Comus*—Milton was an Old Boy of the school—was being readied in which I, amongst other aspiring thespians, would make my Royal debut. We even rehearsed our normal classroom business, some of which to an outsider might have appeared far from normal.

In Mr. Parker's French class, for example, in an attic at the top of the school, we were required to present, neatly arrayed on our desks, nose drops, cough drops and tissues, on pain of being banished to the Lepers' Table around a corner under the beams. Mr. Parker would appear from an inner room in an immaculate gray suit and gray silk tie, limping from a war wound, and swing himself painfully behind his desk.

"Alright," he would snarl, "Eyes on me. This is a double period. I am going to read to you from André Gide. I want you to lean back, close your eyes, and drain in the sound."

Under such circumstances I was an easy mark. I had the misfortune of being assigned to the front row inches from Mr. Parker, close enough to receive his spittle on my face, with Jacobs at the next desk prodding at me until I gave way. If I was lucky I could disguise my outbursts as coughing and be removed to the Lepers' Table. On less fortunate occasions I had been banished from the room.

"Bon. On commence. 'La porte étroite' par André Gide." Mr. Parker begins. Jacobs starts stroking my leg. I bite my lip. Stedman-Jones behind me inches forward and starts snoring just loud enough for me to hear. Other people start snoring. I bite down harder on my lip.

Suddenly to my rescue comes Walsh, who has already won a music scholarship to Cambridge and is coasting blissfully through the remainder of the academic year with absolutely nothing to fear. "Please, sir, excuse me, sir."

Mr. Parker continues reading.

"Please, sir, excuse me, sir, I have a nosebleed, sir."

"Lie on the floor," Mr. Parker does not even look up.

"Sir, I think I need to see Nurse, sir."

"*Parterre.*"

"Yes, sir."

Walsh lies on the only available floorspace, in the aisle by the door. Mr. Parker continues. After twenty minutes or so with our eyes closed, those of us who are not twitching with suppressed laughter are genuinely asleep.

Suddenly the door opens and the unctuous voice of the High Master can be heard in the hall saying, "And here, Your Majesty, is the Middle History Eighth under our senior modern languages master, Mr. Parker, studying French."

Mrs. Bryan, the matron of the boarding house, who is impersonating Her Majesty, enters and falls straight over Walsh. She is prevented from getting up not just by Walsh, who is holding onto her, but by the press of the entourage which follows her into the cramped room and tumbles on top of her—Nurse and Cook, who are impersonating ladies-in-waiting, and the Head Boy.

"Nosebleed," Mr. Parker informs them, and then to us, snarling, "Eyes closed, lean back, drain in the sound."

The Head Boy, Cook, Nurse, and Mrs. Bryan pick themselves up, Mr. MacIntosh, the hapless master impersonating the Prince, looks on glumly, and Trickle, imperturbable, says, "Well, I'm glad to see, Mr. Parker, that you have not in any way modified your style for this occasion. Walsh, I think you better see Nurse."

"That's what I thought, sir."

"*En français!*" Mr. Parker bellows.

"Sorry, Mr. Parker."

And our last stolen glimpse is of the Royal Party bumbling out of the door with Walsh, head back, the last to leave, repeating for our benefit, "*Le nez, le sang, il course. Oh, oh, oh.*"

The actual visit of course couldn't live up to this. The honor guard stamped its feet and presented arms, Her Majesty didn't use the toilet, but she did come through the theater just as Mr. Harbord happened to be rehearsing *Comus*. I had desperately wanted to be in this production and timorously had auditioned for one of the smaller speaking parts, that of the younger brother. This, Mr. Harbord regretfully informed me, he had promised to someone else. However, there was the part of a lion still open, one of Comus's bacchanalian followers, and while there were no words and I would have to wear a full body suit and mask and have to dance, which he was sure I did admirably, it was one of the more important of the animals and carried a great deal of responsibility.

So, dressed in a forty-pound lion suit, I danced with fifteen other animals in a hazy half-light while Scalchi as Comus and Mr. Thorne as the Attendant Spirit recited Milton's luscious words and Her Majesty the Queen, His Royal Highness the Duke of Edinburgh, the Head Boy, Trickle, and several equerries and ladies-in-waiting passed quietly through the auditorium.

Keats

Caius Marius Constantine Hendtlass was a thin wisp of a man, with a high noodling tenor and glasses. He was named after two noble Romans: the general, Gaius Marius, who in the year 101 B.C. was elected consul for a fifth time, hailed as "the savior of his country," and honored with a triumph; and the Emperor Constantine the Great who, more than four hundred years later, moved the seat of the empire from Rome to Byzantium, changed its name to Constantinople, and made Christianity the official religion of the empire.

C. M. C. Hendtlass taught classics at St. Paul's. He also taught fencing, which in the pantheon of sports at St. Paul's where rugby stood at the acme, occupied the same dismal latitude as chess. He lived with his widowed mother and his sister, Elizabeth Victoria Boadicea Hendtlass.

When I arrived at St. Paul's, a raw and nervous thirteen-year-old, in my black-and-white cap, my black tie, my black blazer with white badge, my first pair of long gray flannel trousers, and my first awkward collar-detached shirt, Mr. Hendtlass was made my tutor, which meant that he would advise me (and my parents) on my future academic career. In my second year, when I moved from V alpha to VI alpha, he also became my form master. It was here, in VI alpha, before I turned fourteen, before I faced the Great Barrier Reef called the General Certificate of Education, that the critical question of my academic future had to be addressed.

St. Paul's, like most of the great schools of England, measured its prestige in the number of boys it managed to get into Oxford and Cambridge, and in particular the number of boys who managed to win scholarships. Since there were many nineteenth-century endowments at the universities which offered scholarships in classics and far fewer which offered scholarships in anything else, pressure began to be exerted early on those boys who, four or five years hence, might bring glory on the school, to specialize in classics.

So when, one Monday afternoon in tutorial, Mr. Hendtlass called me up to his desk and enquired as to what I might be specializing in once I had crossed the Great Barrier Reef and I said English, it was the wrong answer. First of all, it was not possible to specialize in English—one could take it only as a subsidiary to history. And second, the school strongly advised that I study classics.

In the course of that year, when I demurred, and when my parents were consulted on the matter, it was made clear that I could of course specialize in whatever I wanted, provided that my parents agreed, but that equally my scholarship to the school could of course be taken away.

As far as my father was concerned my desire to study English was the desire of a dilettante. I spoke it already, didn't I? And, so far as he could tell, without an accent. "*Latein und Griechisch sind wenigstens* important, since you refuse to study anything *praktisch.*"

So, the following year, I found myself in the Lower Classics Eighth with all the whiz kids from the Remove, watching in awe as they tossed off a dozen elegant Greek hexameters for breakfast and then sat around cracking jokes in Latin. By the end of the first term I had demonstrated, I thought conclusively, my utter inadequacy as a classicist.

I was in despair. None of my friends from VI alpha had moved with me into the Lower Classics Eighth. Mr. Hendtlass and my parents had conspired to send me to Siberia. I knew no one. I was a dullard. No one wanted to know me. I felt utterly alone.

One day, on an impulse, I made a completely unsolicited, and for me quite terrifying, foray into the science department. I had developed the notion that in one dramatic move I could not only free myself but also forestall my father's ire. Rather than waste another two terms stumbling around the foothills while my brethren scaled the peaks, I would grit my teeth, heed my father, and bend my efforts towards something "*praktisch.*"

I had in my youth at Arnold House—from the age of perhaps nine to the age of perhaps eleven—been something of a mathematician, although the facility had then begun to wear off. But, as a result of the peculiarities of the English school system, I hadn't even the most passing acquaintance with physics and chemistry. So the laboratories, with their rows of bunsen burners and their acrid smell and the alien technicians who guarded them, were indeed a foreign country.

I am amazed, in retrospect, at my temerity. Somehow, out of some mysterious alchemical combination—part desperation, part chutzpah—I managed to convince the science masters that I had missed my calling, that if at this late date they were to let me into the Lower Maths and Science Eighth, they would see, I would prove another Einstein—he was a German Jew, too, you know, like my parents—and I would bring glory and reknown to St. Paul's by winning a scholarship to Oxbridge in physics or chemistry—or both, if necessary.

When I announced my acceptance at home, my father said: "How can you give up Latin and Greek? *Ich versteh' das bloss nicht.*" And his voice began to rise.

By the end of that year I had demonstrated my inadequacy both as a classicist and as a scientist, and so it was that when I finally sat for my scholarship three years later, it was in history. And I didn't even take English as a subsidiary.

My academic confusion was nothing compared to the confusion that was developing on the domestic front. As I crawled blindly over the lip into adolescence, things began to go haywire at home. My father would storm down the long corridor at Marlborough Mansions with me stumbling backwards ahead of him and my mother going, "Ach, Herbert," as we passed the kitchen. More often than not I would make it to my room, tumble in, and lock the door in time. Outside my father would pound and rage: "*Mach die Tür auf* or I break your neck." My mother would follow him down the corridor— "Ach, Herbert"—and he would turn on her: "*Halt die Klappe zu, verdammt nochmal, ich warne dich.*" And he would bellow and pound till the big thick door seemed about to crack, and I would sit on the bed in the farthest corner of the room and cover my ears and try to keep it all out.

And eventually the storm would subside and my father, bellowing and sputtering, would march back the entire length of the flat, the heels of his shoes thudding into the carpet, his voice retreating, yelling as he passed the kitchen, "*Und du, lass mich bloss in Ruhe,*" and he would charge back into his study, the door thundering shut behind him.

And an eerie silence would return to the flat. And then, when it was safe, my mother would emerge from the kitchen, tiptoe down the corridor, and knock diffidently at my door.

"Go away. Leave me alone."

"Ach, Robin, don't take it always so serious. He doesn't mean it."

"Leave me alone."

"Can't you just maybe go into Daddy and tell him you're sorry?"

It got worse. I developed fits. At the unlikeliest provocation—whenever my mother or father smoked, for example, which was almost all the time—I would shudder and tremble and rush to my room. I would sit on the bed and cover my ears and try to block it all out.

Things got so bad that when I was fifteen I suggested that maybe I should see a psychiatrist. I barely knew what a psychiatrist was, but at least I could pronounce it, which was one up on them.

And for them, of course, there was something suspect, improper, shameful even, about the whole notion. For them the discoveries of Dr. Freud, their fellow Jew and fellow exile, who like them had fled Hitler and found sanctuary in London, who had lived out the last year of his life, as war erupted, on Maresfield Gardens, half way between Grove End Gardens where my parents started out and Marlborough Mansions where we now lived, whose son Martin, Fellow of the Royal Society, had been interned like my father on the Isle of Man, whose relatives were members of the same German Jewish congregation on Belsize Square to which we belonged, whose granddaughter or grandniece or great-grand-something-or-other at a tender age had even gone to the pictures with me at the Odeon Swiss Cottage, for them the great uncharted territories which Dr. Freud had begun to uncover were as alien and forbidden as the bedchamber of Her Majesty at Buckingham Palace.

"*Komm her,*" my father called me into his study. "I want you to write with this pen."

"Why?"

"Don't ask. Write. Here, it has four different nibs. Write carefully. Which do you like best?"

Some weeks later an appointment had been made for me to see a psychiatrist. If I had known anything about psychiatry, and if I had been less terrified, I would have burst out laughing. Dr. Mannheim was a caricature of a Viennese psychiatrist. In his late seventies, almost bald, smoking, nervous as a sparrow, his suit crumpled and stained, his study piled to the ceiling with books and papers, he alternately darted around the room and slumped in a dilapidated fauteuil.

"Here, Robin, I want to give you a test. This is an inkblot. You know what an inkblot is? I want you to look at this inkblot and tell me what you see." He thrust an inkblot under my nose. "Hm? What is it? Hm?"

"It's an inkblot."

"No, no, no. What is it to *you,* what does it look like, what do you see?"

It looked vaguely like a rib cage, but I felt silly saying it looks like a rib cage to this jittery dickybird and I thought I would be giving too much away, so I said, "It looks like a cow."

"Aha!" said Dr. Mannheim, "from this I deduce that your relationships with human beings are not what they should be. Let me tell you about my father." And for the remainder of the hour he proceeded to tell me how he hated his father, how he had always hated him, how he hated him even now, though he had been dead for forty years.

When the time was up and he said I could leave, I saw on his desk four careful samples of my handwriting.

As a result of my test with Dr. Mannheim—which I suppose I must have passed—it was arranged that I should see a specialist in the treatment of adolescent disorders at the Tavistock Clinic. For the next three years on Monday and Wednesday afternoons, while my schoolmates at St. Paul's were marching and countermarching in the Combined Cadet Force (which they did on Mondays) or churning up the rugby field (which they did on Wednesdays), I would disappear from school, climb to the top deck of a No. 73 bus for Baker Street, and furiously dream up things to say to fill the stony hour which lay ahead. For three years, twice a week, autumn, winter and spring, I would arrive at the clinic, sweating, and wait to be called. For three years, twice a week, Dr. Dugmore Hunter, a tall, courteous, white-haired English gentleman, would rise as I entered the room and motion me to lie down. For three years he would take his place in the chair behind my head, cough discreetly and indicate for me to start talking. And for three years, I would stammer and strain and try to keep my soul from flying away. For three years Dr. Hunter said barely a word and when the hour was over rose from his seat and silently watched me leave. And for three years at school I participated in sports only informally at lunchtime or after school, and in the cadet force only on special occasions like Field Day or Annual Inspection or for a week in the summer at RAF camp. My schoolmates thought I was lucky and that I suffered from some exotic disease, like Keats.

Leading-Cadet Hirsch

"The Annual Inspection of the Combined Cadet Force this year will be conducted by a distinguished Old Boy of the school, Field Marshal Viscount Bernard Montgomery of El Alamein."

We all knew about Monty. He was a nebbish, he'd had a totally undistinguished school career, he'd had a totally undistinguished career at Sandhurst, but by dint of hard work he'd risen in the ranks, gone to Africa, defeated Rommel, and saved the country from the Germans. Then he came back and saved the rest of the world with some American named Eisenhower who was now president of the United States—indeed they'd planned and executed the entire Normandy invasion from their joint headquarters in Trickle's study.

Annual Inspection was at best a dreary business—five hundred of us ranked in platoons, schoolboys pretending to be soldiers, standing on the tarmac behind the school at the height of summer, dressed in thick itchy woolen uniforms with boots, buckles, belts, and webbing mercilessly polished, rifles with fixed bayonets at our sides, waiting for the Inspecting Officer with his aides-de-camp to walk up and down every single line looking at our nose hair. After this there would be demonstrations by the different arms of the cadet force. I was in the air force, but I was hardly the stuff of which the legendary RAF was made. Indeed it was largely because I was so inconspicuous a presence that I found myself this year in the central role of the air force demonstration. I had been volunteered.

We were going to demonstrate a parachute jump. The force of landing in a parachute is equivalent to jumping off a thirteen-foot wall. I was going to be strapped in a parachute harness with a rope attached. At the end of this rope would be six other air force cadets who would collectively represent the Wind. I would climb a plank suspended between two ladders thirteen feet above a mattress. At a given signal I would jump. After I landed the six cadets representing Wind would pull me across the playing field until I released myself.

The day arrives. It is of course the hottest day of the year. Teachers in gowns, parents in lightweight suits and summer dresses are arrayed on the playing field stands. We are arrayed five hundred strong on the tarmac, which is melting. We wait. We wait interminably. We mutter. I wonder about my parents out there on the grass with their German accents—please God, may they not speak to anyone.

Eventually, instructions filter down to our platoon commander and we are told to stand easy. We wait some more. Trickle, the Head Boy, and the Senior Under Officer appear from a balcony on the second floor looking for Montgomery. They confer. The Senior Under Officer descends. Trickle and the Head Boy withdraw. On the tarmac now boys faint. Members of the Physical Training squad in white shorts and short-sleeved shirts rush in and remove them on stretchers.

Finally, after two and a half hours, a black bullet-proof Alvis roars round the school and onto the tarmac and a little man in a beret jumps out. He is followed by several larger men in military hats. Platoon commanders now spring into action, bringing their exhausted troops to attention. Trickle and the Head Boy reappear on the balcony. The little man strides up to the Senior Under Officer and begins the inspection. He looks at boots, he looks at trouser creases, he looks at pimples. It takes forever. After inspecting a given platoon he instructs the platoon commander to turn his men in a different direction. After he has finished with the last platoon he disappears inside the school and reappears on the balcony with Trickle and the Head Boy.

Platoon commanders are busy bringing their troops to attention and turning them round again. "Platoon, atten . . . SHUN," is heard all over the tarmac.

"Platoon, left . . . TURN."

"Platoon, right . . . TURN."

"Platoon, about . . . TURN."

When we are all back facing in the original direction, the Contingent Commander shouts, "Contingent, shoulder . . . ARMS." This we had carefully rehearsed. Up, two, three; over, two, three; down.

"Contingent, present . . . ARMS." Arm, two, three; rifle, two, three; stamp—five hundred feet come crashing down.

"Contingent, forward . . . MARCH." This too we had carefully rehearsed. We march forward, closing ranks until all five hundred of us are marching in place with our nose in the nape of the neck ahead of us.

"Contingent, . . . HALT!" We halt.

"Contingent, stand at . . . EASE! We stand at ease.

"STAND . . . easy."

This is the moment for Montgomery to address us.

"Men," he begins in his clipped voice. Then he explains how hot it is and how if you're in the desert fighting the Germans as he had been it can be beastly uncomfortable, which is why he had had our platoon commanders turn us around. Then he asks us to sit on the ground. This we have not rehearsed and is in fact impossible. We are so close that there is not enough room. Nevertheless we try. We slide down our rifles and manage to get the seats of our trousers onto the melting macadam. Then he tells us how important we are to the defense of the country and how important the country is to the defense of the rest of the world and how considerate he has been in having us sit down now and how when we have two million men under our command as he had had we will remember this day.

He concludes and we climb back up our rifle butts, black tar stuck to our behinds.

"Contingent, atten . . . SHUN!"

"Contingent, remove . . . HEADGEAR!" Head, two, three; up, two, three; down.

"Contingent, three cheers for the Inspecting Officer . . . HIP, HIP . . ." And from five hundred throats "HURRAYYYY . . ." and five hundred arms with five hundred berets go up in the air.

Twice more. And then, "Contingent, replace . . . HEADGEAR!" Up, two, three; head, two, three; down.

This of course is where it all breaks down—five hundred berets are now balanced incongruously on five hundred heads. However, the army is never at a loss.

"Contingent, stand at . . . EASE!" Stamp. "STAND . . . easy." We stand easy.

"Contingent, adjust . . . HEADGEAR!" Shuffle, shuffle, five hundred rifles slither between a thousand legs, we adjust our berets.

Then we march past the reviewing stand and salute Montgomery who salutes us back and then the entire cadet force breaks up into demonstration units.

My parents are there and dimly as I climb the ladder I can make them out on the fringes of the crowd, my mother in a summer dress and a hat with a veil, my father in one of his German suits, smoking. We go through our routine half a dozen times and suddenly Montgomery and his party are upon us. We line up. The Air Force Commander explains that this is a parachute demonstration, that Under Officer Williams, Sergeant Groves, Corporal Walsh, Corporal Stedman-Jones, Leading-Cadet Jacobs, and Leading-Cadet Sorkin will be representing Wind and that Leading-Cadet Hirsch crouching in the parachute harness will now climb the ladder and jump off the equivalent of a thirteen-foot wall.

I climb. I walk out on the plank. At the signal I jump. Wind, however, keyed up by the importance of the occasion, starts running before I hit the ground, with the result that I miss the mattress altogether and land with the rope wrapped between my legs and Wind already tearing across the playing fields in the direction of the tarmac. I am screaming because not only can I not reach the harness release but the rope is in danger of ending my sex life before it's even begun. We are mere specks in the distance, long past the playing fields, three-quarters of the way across the parade ground, before I finally get free and Wind rushes headlong into the school wall.

My father says later that he heard Montgomery tell the Commanding Officer, "Damned effective show."

Or as my father says that night at dinner, *"Nicht schlecht"* (Not bad).

Or as my mother says, "Ach, all this marching, all this uniforms, they always have to make *so ein Getü und Geta.*"

The Purpose of Life

After a year in the silent company of Dr. Hunter it was decided, in order to relieve the pressure at home, that I should become a boarder. So for my last two years, as I prepared for my scholarship, I boarded at school during the week and took the No. 28 bus home through London on the weekends.

Like everything else at St. Paul's, the boarding house had its own hierarchy and my seniority in the school at large counted for nothing. I went to bed with the thirteen-year-olds, and every night at ten I would wait for the dormitory prefect, some enormous rugby player, to fall asleep, so I could slip out with my books and sit on the toilet in the winter cold committing the details of Queen Elizabeth's Parliaments to memory.

"But why you have to study history is beyond me. You couldn't have stayed with science?"

In the December following my eighteenth birthday I went up to Queens' College, Cambridge, wrote feverishly for a week, was interviewed by an eccentric young history don who stammered so badly I couldn't understand his questions, and returned depleted to St. Paul's. A week later when the names of scholarship winners were announced in the *Times,* mine was not among them.

In early January, I made a similar trip to Oxford, to sit for a history scholarship at Oriel College.

Oriel was a small college, founded in the fourteenth century, with a reputation, held over from the nineteenth century, as a training ground for theologians—Cardinal Newman had been a long and significant presence. It also had a small but distinguished history faculty, including William Pantin, the mediaevalist, and the recently appointed Regius Professor of Modern History, Hugh Trevor-Roper, whose chair was traditionally held at Oriel. It was because of its present distinction in history, not its former glory in theology, that Mr. Whitting, the senior history master at St. Paul's, had selected Oriel for me.

I was given rooms in the second quad, on the ground floor. The quad, an immaculate eighteenth-century addition to the main quad, was charming, but the rooms, with their stone floors, were very cold. I slept nervously in the long cold bed and the next morning, with a hundred other young men, called from the history departments of a hundred other top schools, I trooped into the Great Hall. The first paper, on modern European history, was set out, neatly printed, on the long dark wooden refectory tables, beneath the wonderful long dark wooden refectory ceiling, a complete place setting together with paper, inkwell, and simple wooden-handled pen with nibs. "Answer three of the following questions," and for the next three hours a hundred hands took up a hundred pens and dipped and scratched and scribbled and blotted, and when the end of the allotted period was announced, took up a hundred reams of paper, carried them to the High Table, and deposited them before the somber proctor in the long black gown.

At the end of the afternoon paper—on classical languages—I felt queasy. I went into dinner in the same Great Hall with all my fellow historians but I couldn't eat. After the meal, I went back to my rooms to prepare for the following morning, but I was chilly and I couldn't concentrate. I put a shilling in the meter and turned the gas up as high as it would go. I made some tea on the hot plate, wrapped myself in a blanket, pushed the dilapidated sofa close to the fire, and huddled over my notes. But it was no use. I kept drifting off. The tea grew cold, the gas died out, and sometime after midnight, half-sleeping, half-waking, I took myself into the bedroom, slid between the ice-cold sheets, covered my head, and went to sleep.

At 7:30 there was a knock on the bedroom door, and the scout, a kindly and distinguished-looking elderly gentleman in a white service jacket, coughed discreetly: "Good morning, sir. 7:30, sir. Breakfast at eight."

"Oh, excuse me," I said, and as I removed my head from the covers I saw my breath misting in the frigid air, "I don't think I'm quite well. I seem to have a sore throat. And I think I may be running a temperature."

"Well, you just stay put, sir. And I'll bring you breakfast to your rooms."
"That's very kind of you. But I'm taking the exams."
"Oh, so you are, sir. Well, I'll ask the steward to come and see you."
"Thank you."
"Not at all, sir."

The scout withdrew, I climbed out of bed, put on my dressing gown and slippers, and went into the living room. It was a little warmer, but not much. I was unsteady on my feet. I hadn't the faintest idea what I was going to do. I had four more days of exams. I could hardly think straight. I gathered my washing things from the bedroom and shuffled along the stone floor to the washroom. I made my ablutions and shuffled back. Presently the living room door flew open and the steward appeared.

"Now, now, now, we can't have this. Taking ill while you're with us, that'll never do. Now, open wide." And from his breast pocket, in one swift movement, he produced a thermometer and thrust it into my mouth.

The steward was the senior domestic officer of the college, a Dickensian character in a three-piece suit, who attended to the college wine-cellar, organized the kitchen and the dining room, and commanded a considerable force of scouts, one to a staircase, who ministered to the needs of the young gentlemen in their domain and also served meals in the Great Hall.

"Derek, lay out breakfast for Mr. Hirsch, will you, on the table by the window."

Behind him, the scout had come in, bearing a huge tray.

"Well, let's see what we've got, then. Eggs and bacon and kidneys and kippers and toast and marmalade and tea. Well, that's not bad. Bet you feel better already, eh?"

I nodded and mumbled incoherently.

"Well, let's see what you've got, then." He whipped the thermometer out of my mouth. "Ooh, I say, we're going to have to do something about this. Alright, Derek, you'll be bringing Mr. Hirsch's meals to his room until further notice. And tell Mr. Pantin I want a word with him."

"Very good, Mr. Burton," said the scout, and then to me, "I hope it's nothing serious, sir." He slipped quietly out of the room.

"Well, you've got quite a little temperature, young man. I don't think it advisable for you to go out. And I don't want the other young gentlemen exposed to you. I'm going to arrange with Mr. Pantin for your papers to be delivered. Derek will bring you your meals. I'll send the doctor by at lunchtime just to make sure it's nothing serious. And if there's anything at all you want, don't you hesitate to ask, alright?"

"Thank you. Thank you very much."

"Now, you eat your breakfast. Derek will clear away. And then get ready; at nine o'clock somebody will be by with pens and paper and your exam. What is it this morning?"

"Modern English history, I think."

"Well, I don't know anything about that. But good luck. And I'll pop in on you and see how you're getting along."

"Thank you very much. Um, there is one thing."

"Yes?"

"It's, er, rather chilly in here at night. I wonder whether I could get a hot water bottle."

"I'll see what I can do. Now, eat your breakfast."

The steward left and I picked disconsolately at the cold food in front of me.

At nine, the scout returned and with him a small friendly roly-poly man whom I took to be the assistant steward.

"Heard you were ill. Too bad about that. I've got pens and paper and ink for you, and an exam on," he looked at the front page, "Modern European History—does that sound right?"

"No, that was yesterday."

"Oh, I'm sorry," and he riffled through his papers, "How about Modern English History?"

"That sounds more like it."

"Well, here it is. I'll be back at twelve to pick it up."

He disappeared. The scout loaded up the breakfast tray, winked, and followed him out.

At lunchtime, as promised, the doctor came by and announced I had the flu. In the evening the steward popped in with an enormous porcelain flagon with a cork. "Just top this up with boiling water and slip it in the bed before you turn in, you'll be warm as toast."

The next three days slid by in a haze. Four times a day the roly-poly man arrived to deliver or collect. Three times a day the scout arrived with food and three times to clear away. Outside, during the day, while I wrestled with French political thought in the fifteenth century or Luther's debt to Erasmus, workmen were repaving the quad. Every so often I would pad out in my dressing gown and slippers, and over the roar of the pneumatic drills shout something to the effect that this was only my life, my future, my career they were destroying and could they possibly, just possibly, fuck off. Actually, I never got as far as fuck off, since we were both exceedingly polite and they realized by my distraught air and ink-stained hands that I was in the midst of inspiration and obviously inspiration counted for something, at least a tea break.

On Thursday lunchtime, my fourth day and the third day of my illness, the roly-poly man, collecting my three-hour General Essay on Conscience, informed me that I was not on the shortlist, but that the committee wanted to interview me anyway. The committee understood that I was ill and that, since I was unable to come to them, they wondered whether they could call on me. They would come that evening, if that was alright. It would be alright, I said.

* * *

News of my confinement had spread. Not that I had a host of friends at Oxford. Indeed I knew no one. But some of the other boys from St. Paul's, my fellow historians whom Mr. Whitting had judiciously parceled out one to a college, had heard the news and on Thursday evening after the eighth exam decided to pay me a visit. There were four of them, one for each of the other colleges in this particular grouping. They arrived with fruit and chocolates and a bottle of sherry. They made tea and we sat around and compared experiences. Stedman-Jones was on the shortlist at Lincoln.

"What did they ask you?"

"Oh, you know, history stuff."

"And the extent of his sexual experience," Aukin chimed in.

"Oh, shut up, Aukin."

"What do you mean, shut up—it's a perfectly legitimate question."

"Well, I'm glad it's not *illegitimate*, poor little bugger."

"*Little* bugger—I understand buggers are big up here."

"Ooh, buggers are big, are they, how would you know?"

Slowly the terrible tension of four days of ferocious exams began to dissolve and the five of us who had for so long convinced ourselves we were grown-ups reverted to being schoolboys. We made terrible jokes, we rolled on the floor with laughter, tears streaming down our faces. Suddenly there was a knock on the door.

"My God, it's them. You bastards, you've got to get out of here. They're coming to interview me."

Aukin jumped into my dark blue duffle coat and made for the door. My God, what was he going to do? What was *I* going to do?

He opened the door a crack and we froze. I was almost peeing with the deadly combination of hysterical laughter and hysterical fright.

"I regret to have to inform you," Aukin intoned, "that Master Hirsch passed away half an hour ago."

"Aukin. Aukin," I could hardly get his name out.

There was some indistinguishable muttering on the other side of the door, then Aukin closed it and turned round. I was ashen. Even the others were stupefied.

"Judelson wants to know if he can borrow some sugar."

"What?"

"It was Judelson from upstairs. He wants to borrow some sugar. Ha ha. Fooled you."

"Aukin, you bastard, you creep, you one hundred percent rotten son of a slimebucket . . . Out! Out!"

And with my last feeble strength I bundled them out into the hall and closed the door. I collapsed on the sofa. The door opened. Aukin had turned his collar around and was chanting.

"It'll be a wonderful funeral."

"Out!"

They were gone.

I had no idea how I was to receive my impending visitors. Should I change? Would I be expected to offer them sherry? What were they going to ask me about? I heard the shuffle of feet outside and jumped up, sweating. When the familiar knock came, I opened the door querulously and there stood the roly-poly man.

"Oh, hello," I said, "I didn't expect you."

"Well, you know, I *am* on the committee. I'm Dr. Pantin."

"You're Dr. Pantin? Oh, I'm sorry, I had no idea."

"Well, maybe we should come in."

"Oh, of course."

Five men in black gowns came into my living room. I closed the door behind them.

"I don't know where you'd like to sit . . ." I offered timorously.

"Well, why don't you sit over there by the fire, since you're not well, and we'll sort of gather ourselves around you."

I sat down on a hardback chair by the fire and the five men in gowns draped themselves on the sofa and arm chairs.

"Well, gentlemen, as you know, this is R. M. D. Hirsch from St. Paul's. And as you have just discovered, I am Dr. Pantin. This is the Provost, Mr. Turpin."

"How do you do?"

"How do you do?"

"This is the Dean, Mr. Brunt."

"How do you do?"

"How do you do?"

"This is Professor Trevor-Roper."

"How do you do?"

"How do you do?"

"And this is the Chaplain, Reverend Crater."

"How do you do?"

"How do you do?"

"I've asked the Chaplain to join us because he looks after the people who read English here and there was some intimation from your school that you might be interested in reading English."

"Well, it wasn't possible to specialize in English at St. Paul's. You could only take it as a subsidiary to history. I switched around a bit. From classics to science and finally history."

"I see. A checkered past. James?" Dr. Pantin turned to the Chaplain.

"Yes. In your General Essay Paper, where you chose to write on Conscience, you wrote a poem. Why?"

In truth I had written a poem because I hadn't the faintest idea how I could write prose for three hours on such an abstract subject.

"Well, er, I didn't think the term *essay* necessarily meant prose, and . . ."

There followed some intense exchanges on the subject of poetry, of creative writing in general, of drama, in which I had become more deeply involved at the Phoenix.

After some twenty minutes on drama and literature, the Provost cleared his throat and inquired in the discreetest tone imaginable: "Tell me, Mr. Hirsch, are you *interested* in history?"

"Oh, yes, of course I'm interested in history . . ." and I tried desperately to recoup.

Pantin gamely picked up the ball, Trevor-Roper asked a couple of searching questions about one of my European history papers, but the interview had clearly run out of steam. Brunt, the Dean, sat through the entire thing without opening his mouth. Finally the Provost cleared his throat again and Pantin asked whether anyone had any further questions. No one did.

"Well, it's been very kind of you to allow us to visit."

"It's been very kind of you to come."

"Gentlemen."

The five men in gowns rose to their feet.

"I do hope you're on the road to recovery," said the Provost.

"Oh, yes. The steward even said I could take tomorrow's exams in Hall."

"Well, that is good news. Good-bye."

"Good-bye."

Each of them in turn wished me good health and good-bye, and finally the ordeal was over.

After the scout had removed my dinner, I boiled water for my porcelain hot pot and prepared myself mentally for the next day. If I was lucky they would judge me on the first and last days when I was compos mentis and give me the benefit of the doubt on the middle three days, and perhaps they would admit me as a commoner with some of the boys who did well but not well enough to win a scholarship.

I went to bed early and tried to compose my mind. At 11:30 I switched out the light and lay in the long narrow bed, trying not to think about the next day. Slowly I brought my mind to rest and slowly I arrived at the edge of sleep. Something rustled. I tried to put it out of my mind. It rustled again. I came back from the brink. Something was rustling. Slowly, heavily, I reached for the light and switched it on. The sudden light was shocking. When my eyes grew accustomed, I realized there was an open bar of chocolate on the dresser and that in the faint breeze that percolated through the cracks in the window the curtain was brushing against the silver foil. I got out of bed and removed the chocolate. I looked at my alarm clock. It was almost midnight. I switched out the light again and tried once more to fall asleep. In the darkness and the silence the old building seemed to be breathing with me. The floorboards creaked. In the distance a bell tower chimed the twelve strokes of midnight. Silence and darkness followed. Silence and darkness and the floorboards creaking. Silence and darkness and the floorboards and something rustling. Like lightning I switched on the light. Nothing. I switched off. Nothing. And then a rustling. Wide awake I switched on and jumped out of bed. Nothing. Nothing for a long time. And then a rustling. I banged on the dresser. Silence. I sat on the bed. Silence. Silence for a long time. I switched off. Silence. And then a rustling. I switched on, jumped out of bed and looked under the dresser. There was a rat the size of a dachshund.

I ran into the living room and slammed the door. Pale moonlight filtered through the diamond panes. I held my head in my hands and shivered. I opened the front door and stepped out into the cold stone hall. Not a sound. I walked into the quad. Everything was peaceful. Moonlight dappled the hedges and the elegant stonework. The new path was almost finished. The workmen's tools lay neatly in a corner, gleaming softly. I looked at the other staircases. Not a light. Everyone soundly asleep. My breath misted in the night air.

I was up all night. I built an elaborate runway for the rat, from the dresser to the bedroom door, from the bedroom door to the front door, and I banged on the dresser but nothing happened. Finally I closed the door to the bedroom, lay down on the sofa in the living room, and tried to lure myself to sleep. But every time a floorboard creaked it went through me like a pistol shot. Once there was a growl so close I screamed—it was my stomach. I picked up a novel from the shelf of the regular tenant of these rooms and began to read—Christopher Isherwood's *The World in the Evening*. I read furiously. By the time daylight began to creep in through the window I had finished it. I went to the washroom, washed, and, for the first time in four days, dressed.

When the scout arrived to wake me, he was shocked. "My goodness, sir, what are you doing up?"

I explained about the rat.

"My goodness, sir, how awful. I'll tell the steward."

I took the morning exam in Hall, but I was so tired I couldn't concentrate and I kept nodding off. When the time came to hand my paper in, I stumbled to the High Table and fainted at the feet of the Chaplain, who was proctoring. He knelt over me.

"You'd best take the afternoon exam in your room, don't you think?" he said when I came to.

"I suppose I better," I said.

He helped me slowly to my feet and called for the steward.

"Ay, ay, ay, what's this?" the steward threw my arm around him and walked me out into the cold air. "Back to your room with you, my lad," and he walked me down the steps and into the second quad and back to my rooms.

That afternoon, the last, I could think of nothing but going back to London, of the bosom of my family, of catching an early train, of spending a little time with my cousin, Ellinor, and her new husband whom I had yet to meet.

Ellinor was the daughter of my mother's sister. When my mother had fled Germany for England, her sister, Herta, four years older, with two growing children, had escaped to Uruguay. After the war she had settled in Buenos Aires. Her children, born in Berlin, raised in South America, were my only cousins. The older one, Gert, I had never met. He was old enough to be my uncle. Ellinor was the younger one. My mother called her *Püppchen*, little doll, from Berlin, but she was still ten years older than I. She had passed through London on her way to Israel, when I was still at Arnold House. She had stayed up all night, helping me to assemble a boat for the handicrafts competition at school. Now, living in Israel and recently married to another Jew from Argentina, she was passing through London again; they were on their way to America, where Herman was to take up a fellowship in plant physiology at some big American university. He was a scientist.

Now, with the rain beating down and my last paper staring up at me, I could think only of London and of getting on a train the next morning for my first holiday in two years, skiing in Switzerland. The paper was on modern languages and I dozed fitfully and saw the Alps. There was a knock on the door and I thought I was in a hotel. But outside it was raining, not snowing. "Come in," I said.

Two men in raincoats came in.

"Oh, don't worry about the noise," I said magnanimously.

But it wasn't the workmen.

"We're from St. Edmund Hall," said the first man, opening his raincoat and revealing a dog collar. "We were rather interested in one of your history papers and we wanted to have a chat. Would you mind?"

"No, no, of course not."

"Awfully sorry to interrupt you like this," said the second man. "We looked for you in Hall, but the Chaplain told us about your predicament. Awfully sorry."

"Perhaps we could sit over here by the fire. It's beastly wet out there."

Their laid their raincoats close to the fire and settled in. For the next hour they chatted amiably about methods of finance during the Wars of Religion. I scarcely contributed a word. When the rain had abated they thanked me and made their adieus.

I had nothing left. I wrote a note on my paper thanking everybody for their care and attention, explained about the rat and the lack of sleep and the unexpected visitation and the early train, packed my case and took a last look at the rooms. Then I stepped out into the drizzle and the dull gray afternoon.

There was no one around. I walked through the elegant main quad, turned inside the portico to take one last look at Oriel, nodded to the porter in the porter's lodge, touched the massive wooden door that closed off half the archway and stepped through the main gate into Oriel Square. On the High Street I caught a bus to the station. I arrived just as the train for London was pulling in. At Paddington for the first time in my life I took a taxi.

"*Ach, mein Dicker,* you look awful," said my mother.

"What, you didn't finish the language exam," said my father. But in him, too, beneath the gruff exterior, there was palpable concern. "Tomorrow, before the train, we take you to Dr. Cohn. *Penizillin.*" It had been discovered by an Englishman and developed at Oxford but he still couldn't pronounce it properly.

I had to recount every moment.

"More potatoes, more *Gemüse,* more *Fleisch,*" said my mother.

"*Ruhig,*" said my father, "let him speak."

"Oh, my God," said my sister.

"Poor boy," said my cousin.

My cousin's husband didn't say anything. He spoke almost no English. He ate.

The next morning the entire family drove me to Dr. Cohn, who pulled down my trousers and pumped me full of penicillin. Then we piled back in the car and drove through the rain and the rush hour traffic to Victoria Station. Barbie and I and Ellinor and Herman were squashed in the back seat. In the slow crawl of traffic on Finchley Road my father would forget to let in the clutch and the car would stall. "*Verdammt nochmal.* Wipe the window." And my mother would take out a tissue and wipe the window. The car would stall again. "*Ach, kannst du nichts tun?*" (Can't you do anything)?

"*Onkel* Herbert," said Ellinor, always helpful, "can I wipe your behind?"

"*Was?*" said my father, ever suspicious.

"Can I wipe your behind?"

"Ellinor," said Herman quietly, "that's really going too far." It was the only complete sentence I heard him utter.

At Victoria it was touch and go. I was piled on the train, with my bags and skiing equipment thrown in after me.

"Good-bye."

"Good-bye."

They all waved and the train pulled out, through the grimy south of London, past the endless housing tracts, semi-detached upon semi-detached, and then spots of green creeping in, and eventually Kent and the lush rolling rich green countryside and Dover and the ferry and a rough crossing and Calais and the hideous scarred northern French towns and the express to Zurich, chugging through the night, blissfully asleep in a couchette, my third bed in three nights.

The next morning blue skies, the indescribable hygiene of Switzerland, the train to Zermatt, and the ravishing bewitchment of the Alps. I had a room at the Victoria Palace. I unpacked, registered with the ski school, rented equipment, and plunged full-bloodedly into the physical aban-don of careering down mountains. Breakfast, ski school, lunch, the Gor-nergrat railway up to eleven thousand feet and then down in the after-noon to dinner and rum punch and dancing and stumbling home, drained, drunk, and mindless, to sleep the aching sleep of the virtuous and the exhausted.

On the fourth day, making a steep and icy traverse, I fell badly and tore the ligaments in my thumb. The instructor skied me down to the village and took me to the doctor. When I got back to the hotel I was late for lunch.

"Mr. Hirsch, there was a telephone call for you from London."

"Oh, my God, what happened?"

"It was your father. He will ring you again this evening at six."

My thumb and wrist in plaster, I spent the afternoon out on the slopes regaining my confidence and worrying about London. At 5:30, changed and washed, I sat in the foyer and waited. People I knew from the hotel or ski school stopped and commiserated with me about my accident. The minutes passed very slowly. I could pay less and less attention to anyone. Finally, at ten past six, the concierge nodded to me and I went into a booth and picked up the phone.

"Hello."

"Hullo," came my father's voice, distant, crackling, but unmistakable.

"Daddy, Daddy, what's wrong?"

"Hullo? Robin?"

"Yes, yes, Daddy, it's me. What is it?"

"Robin, I have to inform you," he said in his most funereal voice, "that you have just been awarded an Open Exhibition in Modern History to Oriel College, Oxford."

"Oh, my God, how terrible! What did you say?"

"You have just been awarded an Open Exhibition to Oriel College. It says so even in the *Daily Telegraph*."

Oxford was a million miles away, a million years ago, another world.

"*Nu,* you have nothing to say?"

"I don't believe it."

"That's all you can say? This costs money."

"It's not true."

"*Komm,* Robin, you can say better than that. You are a scholar."

"It can't be true."

"*Mein Gott.* And where were you at lunch?"

"Oh, I tore the ligaments in my thumb."

"*Was?*"

"I tore the ligaments—I broke my thumb."

"Why?"

"Skiing."

"How?"

"Come on, Daddy, this costs money."

"Well, at least have a bottle of champagne. I will pay."

"Thank you, Daddy."

"Not French. German will do."

"Alright, Daddy."

"Well done, *mein Sohn.* Now, here is your mother. Käthe," he bellowed.

"I'm here. I'm here." She was on the extension. "Ach, Robin, we are so proud of you." She was almost in tears. "Daddy is going to open a bottle of champagne."

"I don't believe it."

"No, not champagne. *Sekt.* I have it cold in the *Kühlschrank.*"

"Ach, Herbert."

"But you, you can have French."

That night at dinner I ordered a bottle of German *Sekt* and invited the strangers at my table to join me.

At St. Paul's when the new term started I was like a lame-duck president. As an Oxford Scholar I was allowed to parade around in my gown. I was accorded a great deal of respect. But I had nothing to do. There were no exams to study for. The immediate purpose of life—the taking of exams— had evaporated and the future stretched out before me as vast and insubstantial as a cloud.

Ars Longa

I spent the early spring working on a play I'd helped to write. It was a play with music and mime and song and dance and it grew out of our experiences at the Phoenix.

The play concerned just such a youth group and the decision of its members, which springs from a combination of youthful exuberance and endless committee meetings, to adopt a refugee boy. The members, of course, being thirteen to seventeen years old, attempt to carry all this out in secret.

It had a cast of thirty-five, played by children of all ages dragooned from the various youth groups of the congregation, it ran for two weekends to packed houses, and it received the sponsorship of the National Council of Christians and Jews. It was every bit as important to me as my Oxford Exhibition. I was in it, I had helped to write it with my friend Herbert Levy, and I had helped him produce it. It put a seal on my adolescence, it summed up all the years of growth and striving and laughter and the first stirrings of love and sexuality and the first yearnings of the spirit, all the important things that had happened not at St. Paul's but at the Phoenix, my Eden, my secret life, about which my parents knew little and my schoolmates at St. Paul's knew less.

Looking back on that play now, I can understand why grown men, who had escaped Auschwitz and Maidanek and Bergen-Belsen, who had survived the war in a foreign country, who had established themselves and their families, very often from scratch, who had seen their children begin to take root in an alien culture, why such men, watching their children now, in unaccented English, in the new hall of the Belsize Square New Liberal Jewish Congregation, with all the energy and high spirits and humor of youth, reenact the symbolic journey of the refugee—the escape, the hiding, the betrayal, the knock on the door, the flight—why such men should weep.

My father came to the play the second weekend. When it was late in starting, out front, in the middle of the audience, he began a slow hand-clap. After it was over, when people congratulated him on my performance, he told them about my scholarship.

Exodus

"What news on the Rialto?" sang in my head like a bell. *Venice.*

The first time I had ever set foot on a stage, at the Phoenix, it was as the Duke in the trial scene from *The Merchant of Venice*. I was thirteen. I had a white beard and a huge hat and sat on a dais, motioning the principals to begin their debate. Shylock, Portia, Antonio, and the rest were children also—my sister played Nerissa and, when she could get them out, had even fewer lines to say than I. Here, on the *bimah* of the Belsize Square New Liberal Jewish Congregation, under the direction of a refugee, the children of refugees first came to grips with the glories of the English language. Here, in our tiny voices, we first framed the great issues of justice, mercy, and revenge. And here for the first time we encountered the strange ambivalent figure of the Jew of Venice and the very English Italians in whose midst he is condemned to live.

Now, five years later, with St. Paul's behind me and Oxford a few months ahead, I stood on the Rialto and looked at Venice for the first time. Below me, the Grand Canal danced in the evening light. Vaporetti sped by. Gondolieri poked their slender boats through the water with that extraordinary one-sided motion that trembles on the brink between grace and disaster. And somewhere to the north, in the darkness, lay the remnants of the Jewish ghetto, the first ghetto, the ghetto that gave the name *ghetto* to all the ghettos of the world.

I had arrived in Venice by train with a rucksack and a copy of *Exodus*. I was to board a Greek boat for Haifa, a bargain my father had picked out for me in London. But, as with many of my father's bargains, there turned out to be a catch. The Typaldos brothers, who had salvaged their ship from a South American shipyard where it had lain rotting for thirty-two years, had not yet managed to make it seaworthy. Its first three projected sailings had been canceled. This time, the purser assured me, the boat would make it. Not on time, of course, but then, this was a maiden voyage and we couldn't expect miracles. If I cared to leave my luggage in the cabin, I could spend the evening in Venice, and sometime late that night we would sail out.

In the company of a young Moroccan Jew, a young French Jew, and a young Israeli, all of them in the same plight, I went out to explore the city.

Venice was full of music. Wherever we went small bands were playing. The song of the moment was a captivating Greek melody, which seemed to follow us everywhere. Later, on the boat, when it was played to death by the ship's orchestra, I discovered it was Theodorakis's music from *Never on Sunday*. Now it just seemed warm, exciting, Mediterranean, filled with sunshine and laughter and heady as wine. As we came into the great square of San Marco, with a little band leading the way, we broke into a kind of cosmopolitan *sirtaki*. With the freedom and intoxication of boys who are not yet ready to become men, and with a whole civilization at our feet, we danced and danced. Passersby joined us, tables and chairs went flying, people handed us drinks, and the little band urged us on. Louder and louder. Faster and faster. Drunk on the night air, the water, the lights, the music, and the Byzantine splendor of Venice, we caroused our way through the Piazza, past the Campanile, saluting the four great horses high above us, and arrived on the dock at the gangway to our boat. The *S/S Athinai* was bedecked with lights and we were sailing for the Promised Land.

I had had very little exposure to Jews outside England—and even then it was mainly to the rather cloistered community of German Jewish refugees, subdued, serious, sober, set apart by their language, the terrible upheaval in middle life, and the pervasive, if rarely spoken, sense of loss. Here, suddenly, in this magical city on the Adriatic, stalled by a pair of dilatory Greek shipbuilders, I found myself in an easy fellowship with Jews from other countries: with Zvi, the Moroccan, quiet, dark, uneducated, to whom dancing came more naturally than talking; with Chaim, the bearded Frenchman, a gentle filmmaker, blond, scholarly, anxious to put his delicate hands to work on the land of his fathers; with David, the Israeli, easygoing, good-natured, a tiny yarmulke perched incongruously on the crown of his head, a young man to whom religion seemed a second skin, not something to be denied or dismissed contemptuously or even defended, but a living, breathing tradition that inhabits every pocket of one's daily life. I had never seen a yarmulke worn so unselfconsciously. In London, on the High Holy Days, gathered in clumps in our suits outside the Odeon Swiss Cottage, the incongruous venue for the New Liberal Jewish Congregation's overflow services on Rosh Hashanah and Yom Kippur, we might still keep them on, but not on the street, alone, a marked man for passersby to gape at.

*   *   *

There were two classes on the boat, plus steerage. The people in first class were for the most part on a luxury cruise through the Mediterranean, one week of wining and dining and touching off at Brindisi, Piraeus, Rhodes, and Nicosia before arriving in Haifa and then turning round for a second week of steaming slowly back to Venice. Steerage was mainly occupied by students, mostly on their way to Israel. I was supposed to be in second class, but apparently, in readying the boat, the Typaldos brothers had not yet excavated to the lower decks, so by a stroke of good fortune I was assigned to a first-class cabin for sleeping, with second-class eating and drinking privileges. I could also use the swimming pool freely; the students in steerage, Zvi and Chaim among them, were allowed up only for an hour at dusk, when the first-class passengers would be preparing for dinner and would therefore not be disturbed.

A steward took me to my cabin. My companions for the voyage were a middle-aged Austrian Jew and his twelve-year-old nephew. The boy, Fritzl, was one of those obnoxious show-offs with a leering smile whom one immediately wants to kick in the teeth. His uncle, Herr Lewy, a balding, fey busybody, reveled in the accomplishments of his fat little charge and encouraged him to make conversation with me: "Show the young Englishman how good English you speak." And show me he did. Every time I made an appearance in the cabin the little bugger would buttonhole me and spout off about the weather or the food or the sea or Vienna or his uncle, whom he couldn't abide.

They were traveling with a larger party two cabins down, the brother-in-law of Herr Lewy and thus, I presume, although I never finally established this, the father of Fritzl. He was the Chief Cantor of Vienna and every morning at the crack of dawn he would hold services in his cabin. Herr Lewy was always trying to cajole me into making up a minyan and I was always, as politely as I could, declining. The only topic on which I was ever likely to see eye to eye with Fritzl was the sheer lunacy of crawling out of a warm bed at six in the morning to stumble down the corridor of a swaying boat and mumble together with a handful of strangers phrases in a language I didn't understand. But Fritzl was off the hook—he was not yet thirteen; he had a year to go before he counted in a minyan.

There was a reason that Herr Lewy was so importunate with me. Because of the previous cancellations and the uncertainties of the present departure, the boat was empty and ten good men were hard to find. I would see him on deck in his checkered shorts wheedling, pleading, entreating. I would see him at meal times in the dining room leaping from one sparsely populated table to another, apologizing to the women and then entering into negotiations with their husbands and sons. Evidently there was a critical mass—the Chief Cantor of Vienna, his brother-in-law (Herr Lewy), a handful of Hassidim in their long black coats and earlocks, David the Israeli, and so on—but never a quorum. And it was those last two or three places that Herr Lewy had taken upon himself to fill. It was a ceaseless struggle, and for six days he labored.

On the evening of the second day I ventured into the bar. It was virtually empty. At one table two young American couples, scarcely older than I, sat surrounded by luggage.

"Order ouzo," one of the boys said to me, "it's the only thing they have anyhow." I ordered ouzo.

"We're getting off at Brindisi," one of the girls said, gesturing at the bags. We had left Venice twelve hours late, so we were now due to arrive at Brindisi not at lunchtime as advertized but at midnight.

"You're from England, aren't you?" the second girl said. "I can tell by the accent."

I nodded.

"Where are you getting off?"

"Haifa."

"Oh, are you Jewish?"

I nodded again.

"Jewish and English?"

"Well, . . ."

"We're American."

"Yes."

"The Midwest. Kansas. Do you know Kansas?"

"No, I've never been to America."

"Lots of corn in Kansas," the boy said. "Not too many Jews."

"Oh."

"Have another drink," he offered.

I hesitated.

"Go on, it'll make you blind."

"Well, in that case . . ."

The steward brought another drink.

"*L'chaim*," I said, raising my glass.

"Bottoms up," said the boy.

I opened my copy of *Exodus*.

"Great book," said the second boy, who had been silent.

"Is it?" I said. "I'm only just starting."

"Boy, I envy you, starting," he said.

I alternately drank, read, and engaged the Americans in conversation. Slowly, as the hour got later and later, the realization began to creep in through a kind of ouzo-laden fog that we were not in any way heading for port and that perhaps the ship's captain had decided to make up for lost time by leaving out a scheduled stop or two. Finally the Americans summoned the steward. There ensued a kind of elaborate international dumbshow replete with maps drawn on the backs of Typaldos brothers napkins from the bar:

What time do we get to Brindisi?

Brindisi?

Yes, Brindisi.

No, no, signorita, tomorrow Piraeus.

But we're supposed to get off at Brindisi.

Shrug.

But my parents are meeting us. What about my parents?

Are they in a car?

Of course they're in a car.

Well, then, they can drive back up the leg of Italy—like so—to Venice—and then down through Yugoslavia—like so—to Greece. Of course, they'll never make it . . .

By the time I left the bar for the bosom of Fritzl and Herr Lewy, the boys had commandeered the bottle, the girls were staring glassy-eyed into their matched luggage, and the napkins had been transmogrified into little paper aeroplanes.

Ah, Brindisi.

Things were in a state of chaos on the boat. The crew was mainly Greek, with one or two Italians to leaven the mixture. Very few of the passengers, polyglot amalgam though we were, spoke either Greek or Italian, and very few of the crew spoke anything else. The dining room, of which beautiful pictures appeared in the brochure, was unfinished, and the kitchen apparently even further behind schedule. Food, which for the first-class passengers at least, was a major feature of the voyage, would appear cold, lumpy, uncooked, late, or not at all. We consumed a great deal of bread. Passengers began to whisper to each other. We formed alliances. Rumors spread. People would approach you furtively on the deck, look around, and then ask if you had heard the latest.

After our failure to stop at Brindisi, panic set in. Rumors escalated. "There's no more food on board." "We're not stopping anywhere." "There's an epidemic and no medical supplies." All of these issued covertly, in a variety of languages and with absolute conviction.

A Viennese dentist told me: "Do you not know? The boat is heading for

Alexandria. It's a Nazi boat. Full of guns. In Alexandria all Jews will be taken off. Of course," he whispered confidentially, "nobody knows I'm a Jew"—it hardly required a Himmler to identify him—"and my wife here is Irish Catholic."

"How do you do?" I said.

"How do you do?" she beamed back.

"My wife," said the dentist, "is a nurse. We met after the war. Of course, we don't have children," he patted his wife's arm affectionately, "we're too old. We came on this boat for to cruise, not to go to . . . ," he looked round stealthily, then whispered, "Israel."

They had taken under their wing a tall and beautiful young French girl, Nicole, who was not feeling well. "She is not Jewish," the dentist assured me, "a shiksa like my wife, but for some reason she is going to Israel." At that moment, he told me, she was lying in their cabin. She was supposed to be in steerage, but the conditions down there were so bad, he said, they had taken her into their own cabin. "You must come down and meet her," he said earnestly, and his wife beamed. I would be happy to, I said.

The cabin of the voluble Viennese dentist and his wife became a sort of home away from the inhospitality of the ship proper. Nicole was indeed beautiful but also, evidently, quite sick. She lay in the lower bunk, pale, sweating, and breathing painfully, while the good dentist's wife wiped her brow and sang to her quietly in her soft Irish lilt. The cabin was tiny, without a porthole, and, had I been the only visitor, it would have seemed crowded, what with Otto pacing and Mary wringing out towels, and Nicole moaning plaintively on the bunk. But generally I wasn't. There were friends of Nicole's from steerage, gabbing away in French, a couple of crew-cut Canadian boys whom I had met swimming, and all sorts of strays whom Otto had acquired in his rumormongering and brought to the cabin to discuss the present and hatch plots for the future.

"Did you ever hear such a thing? We didn't stop in Brindisi. If we don't stop in Piraeus, we will have to do something," Otto said ominously. "You boys are strong"—this to the Canadians—"we will have to work out a plan."

Fortunately for the Typaldos brothers, the boat stopped in Piraeus. Otto and Mary stayed on board. I saw the Americans, disconsolate and hung-over, carry their baggage down the gangplank and disappear, bewildered, into the throngs in the harbor.

Somehow, spontaneously, the little band which had formed in Venice reconstituted itself, acquiring a few new members.

Night had fallen, sailors of every nationality filled the streets, music throbbed from every doorway, and everywhere there seemed to be women beckoning and cheap liquor.

Zvi seemed to know his way instinctively. He led us from one bar to another, never saying anything, but always somehow welcome. Long after midnight, in a tiny café, with drinks on the table and two grizzled Greek men dancing, he made some kind of assignation with a woman and disappeared.

The rest of us—the Canadians, an American boy, a young Jew from Hamburg, David, Chaim, and I—made our way back to the boat, drunk, played out, and, most of us, a little in awe of the ease with which Zvi had sailed through this harbor.

The only one who seemed unaffected was Chaim, his tall, thin frame patiently climbing the gangplank, his sad, studious face seeming to register the night as just another facet of the remarkable diamond that the watchmaker takes out to examine before going to bed.

The next morning, without Zvi, we rented a taxi, raced into Athens, rushed up the Acropolis, rushed down, raced back to the boat, and set sail for Rhodes.

On the way to Rhodes, Nicole's condition deteriorated steadily. That night, in the cabin of Otto and Mary, a conference was called. No one felt terribly confident about the medical authorities on board, but it was decided to alert the purser and see what happened. In about half an hour a young Greek nurse arrived in a spotless white uniform carrying a thermometer. We looked at each other in astonishment. She placed it in Nicole's mouth and left. Five minutes passed. No nurse. Mary leaned over and removed the thermometer. "Oh, no, she put it in the wrong way round."

The nurse returned smiling. Otto launched into a long tirade on the nature of medical responsibility and did she not know what she was doing and where was the ship's doctor and did she not know what would happen to her when he reported her to the authorities.

To all of this the nurse responded with the same pleasant uncomprehending smile.

"And furthermore," said Otto in his fervid English, the language of the sea, of commerce, and of the International Dental Association, "zis girl most hef a betpen." He took her by the neck and shook her, "Betpen. Betpen."

Still smiling, the nurse left the room and returned immediately, bearing a tray with a pot of tea, a cup and saucer, and a slice of lemon.

"Betpen!" shrieks Otto wildly. "Betpen!" And seizing the pot of tea from the tray, he sits the poor bewildered nurse down on it, grabs the plate with lemon and sticks it between her legs. "Betpen! Betpen!" he yells, forcing her up and down with the pot, her tray balanced immaculately on her hand, the fear of Olympus in her eyes. Nicole is moaning, Mary is trying to restrain her husband, the two Canadian boys are rolling on the floor with laughter, and I am holding the door.

All of a sudden the light dawns and the nurse rushes out, returning now with an old-fashioned bedpan, an ornate brass bowl with a lid and a long mahogany handle. Otto, spent with the effort, collapses into the chair, Mary hands her back the thermometer, the nurse stands at the door, beams at each one of us in turn and leaves.

In the silence we hear, very quietly, a female voice singing a Hebrew melody: it is Nicole.

"Sh . . . sh," says Otto jumping up immediately.

"Sh . . . sh," says Nicole wanly from the bed.

It turned out there was indeed no doctor on the ship's staff, so a call was put out amongst the passengers. This produced a Dutch doctor and a German surgeon.

Immediately, friction. The Dutch doctor refuses to work with the German surgeon because he had clearly been a Nazi during the war. The German surgeon takes immediate umbrage—he had of course been in the Resistance. Each of them thereupon examines Nicole independently. Each comes to the same conclusion: appendicitis. The Dutch doctor insists that the captain radio for a helicopter to remove her to a hospital. The captain demurs and sends a message saying it can wait till Nicosia. The German surgeon offers to attend her in the meantime. The Dutch doctor withdraws. Nicole is moved into the luxury cabin of the German surgeon.

The next morning, as we arrive in Rhodes, Otto corners me: "Can you believe it? The Hollander was right. That Nazi bastard tried to rape her during the night."

"Rape her?"

"*Jawohl.* But now she is back with us. Robin, we cannot leave the boat. Bring us back some cherry brandy. It is a speciality of the island."

Rhodes. The whitewashed houses gleam in the heat of the day. Donkeys pull carts along dirt roads past cultivated fields and orchards filled with fig and pomegranate trees.

Chaim says: "I have something I want to show you. We just have time." We climb in the back of a battered taxi and head south. "It's called the Valley of the Butterflies."

Under the cool moist shadow of a million trees, we walk through a forest and come to rest. A strange, alert quiet.

"Look," says Chaim.

On each tree a second bark, the shroud of a battalion of butterflies, wingtip to wingtip, not a crack between them; and on the floor a blanket over every rock and crack and hollow, a living breathing forest waiting to take off.

"Is it not something?" says Chaim.

"Yes," I reply, "it is something."

In the harbor I buy a bottle of cherry brandy.

"Cherry brandy?" Chaim looks at me.

"It is a speciality of the island," I tell him.

He shakes his head. "It is terrible," he said.

That night, chez Otto, we break open the bottle and toast Nicole; the next day in Nicosia she is to be removed and taken to the British hospital.

Otto lifts his glass. "You know, some of us who are a little older have seen terrible things. It is why we are so frightened. It is for you, who are young, to struggle on, to conquer fear. Nicole, you are young and brave. Tomorrow you will need all your courage. Here, we drink to your recovery and to your good health, but we drink also to your youth and to your courage. *Santé*," and he makes a little bow.

"*L'chaim*, Otto, *l'chaim*," Nicole toasts him from the bed.

"Sh . . . sh," I say.

We laugh and drink.

That night as I make my way back to the cabin I see the cabin steward turning the lock in my door. As he passes, he nods but there is a strange look in his eye. I go in but nothing seems to be amiss. Herr Lewy is asleep as usual on the bottom bunk. Fritzl is awake on the bunk above him and gives me his usual leer. I raise my hand to him halfheartedly, go to the sink and make my ablutions.

I lie in my bunk, a little tipsy, the boat rocking gently in the warm dark water of the Mediterranean, starlight glittering through the porthole, Herr Lewy snoring quietly across the cabin. I think of the Valley of the Butterflies and I think of all of us on this Greek boat—Herr Lewy, Fritzl, me; and down the hall the Chief Cantor of Vienna; and on the deck below Otto, Mary, and Nicole; and David and the Canadian boys; and somewhere, with their black coats hung up for the night, their prayer shawls ready for the morning and their earlocks floating out across the pillow, the Hassidim; and, down in the hold, stretched out on the floor, the students, Zvi and Chaim among them. I think of all of us together in the belly of this boat and I think of all the Jews who have sailed this sea before us, those who made it and those who didn't, I think of my Uncle Georg in the twenties, and I feel safe.

"Herr Robin," Fritzl whispers from across the cabin, "are you awake, please?"

"No, Fritzl," I say, "I'm asleep."

"Herr Robin, I was wondering, when we arrive in Israel, will I still see you again?"

"Yes, Fritzl," I say.

"And will we be still friends, Herr Robin?"

"Yes, Fritzl," I say, gritting my teeth.

"Thank you, Herr Robin. I can sleep now better. Good night."

"Good night, Fritzl," I say, "sleep tight." And despite all my efforts, a tear begins to form in one eye. "By the way, Fritzl, you can cut the *Herr* stuff out, O.K.?"

"O.K., Herr Robin."

I laugh and turn my face into the pillow. In a moment, it is damp with tears.

The next morning I discover the reason for the cabin steward's strange look the night before. We are due to arrive in Nicosia and over the loudspeakers in four languages our cooperation is requested for a fire drill. We are all to report to our cabins where our steward will give us further instructions. Since our steward speaks no language that any of the three of us can understand I find this hard to believe. Still, I make my way down to the cabin and the steward is waiting in the corridor. He nods to me and opens the door. Inside, Fritzl and his uncle are sitting on their bunks. The steward motions me to do likewise.

"What's all this?" I ask.

Herr Lewy shrugs.

Fritzl gives me a leer.

The steward motions me again.

I sit down on my bunk.

The steward stands in the doorway, looks at us almost apologetically, then leaves and locks the door behind him.

I can't believe it. I go to the door and try it. It does not give. "Herr Lewy," I turn round. "This is unbelievable. What's going on?"

"Herr Robin, don't get excited. They know what they are doing."

We have arrived in the harbor and out of the porthole I can see the very rickety ladder that is lowered to small visiting boats. Descending it, supported by an officer, and seemingly in constant danger of slipping and plunging into the water below, is a tall frail figure wrapped in a scarf. I pound on the porthole until it gives.

"Herr Robin, don't get so excited."

"It's not that," I say. "It's a French girl. She's very sick. Oh, it doesn't matter. You wouldn't understand."

And indeed it didn't matter. The ladder was being hauled up and she was in a little motor boat, a solitary figure in the afternoon sun speeding off towards the shore.

The ship was moving very slowly now. Apparently we were being towed into the harbor. Over the cabin loudspeaker in four languages came an explanation: "This is the maiden voyage of the *S/S Athinai*, a ship of the Typaldos line. We are arriving in the Greek island of Cyprus. We are very honored to welcome aboard the Greek Prime Minister of Cyprus, His Holiness Archbishop Makarios, and one thousand of the leading citizens of Cyprus. We regret that for the duration of their visit, passengers will remain in their cabins for fire drill."

Ah, that explained the scampering, the furtive preparations after lunch, the strange demeanor of the crew.

And sure enough, striding along the quay at the head of a gaggle of Greek Orthodox bishops and a procession of citizens, came the archbishop. "*Komm' ma', Fritzl, guck heraus, es ist doch historisch*" (Look outside, Fritzl, it's historic), and Herr Lewy pulled his nephew onto my bunk and pushed his head through the open porthole.

"They look like your Hassidim, Herr Lewy," I say, trying to ease Fritzl gently into the sea. "Perhaps you can use them for your minyan."

"Ach, Herr Robin, you English have such a sense of humor."

The party lasted most of the afternoon. Strains of "Never on Sunday" drifted down the corridor. I lay down on my bunk and began to read. Herr Lewy thought this would be a good opportunity for Fritzl to practice his English. I thought this was a terrible idea. Fritzl began to cry. His uncle began to reprimand him. Fritzl climbed up on his bunk and continued to cry. Herr Lewy lay down on his bunk and fell asleep. I poured myself some cherry brandy and tried to concentrate on what I was reading: in *Exodus*, the boat was being held up and they were threatening to sacrifice the children one by one. My sympathies were not entirely with the children.

Eventually there was a hullabaloo on the quay. A band played. Cannons were fired, the archbishop and his gigantic entourage descended, and dusk swallowed them up. Slowly the boat began to move and over the loudspeaker in four languages came the announcement that fire drill was now over but dinner would be delayed. The key turned in the lock, the door to the cabin opened, and the steward appeared, a slight grin on his face.

"*Gott sei Dank*," said Herr Lewy, "*alles in Ordnung. Komm, Fritzl,*" and nodding politely to the steward, he hustled his nephew out of the cabin.

The steward began to straighten up.

"Tomorrow," I said, "Haifa—right?"

"No, no, signor," he said pleasantly, patting his chest, "Venezia. Venezia."

After dinner that night, our last dinner, I went down to steerage and drank with some of the students. For them, our stay in Nicosia had been little different from most hours of the day when the barriers were down and they were not allowed out of their quarters. They had spent the time singing and now, as the end of the journey loomed, spirits were high, carefully hoarded bottles were produced and passed around with abandon, someone played a harmonica, people embraced and kissed and exchanged addresses. The kitchen crew contributed some precious fruit, and a candle or two, and grinned and sang along with us. And in the soft light, pitching and rolling with a rough sea, we made our good-byes. Quite tipsy at midnight, with the kisses of a dozen strange girls on my cheek, I made my way back to the privileged sections.

The boat appeared to be pitching quite heavily. I wondered how tipsy I really was. Perhaps I was more than tipsy. I arrived at the cabin and opened the door. I almost fell into the cabin and then almost fell out. The boat was really pitching. I switched on the light. Fritzl was awake on his bunk, surrounded by vomit. He had vomited all over himself, and all over his sleeping uncle below him.

"Fritzl," I said, "why don't you take my bunk. I'll find somewhere else." Poor Fritzl, he looked so forlorn. And his uncle, oblivious, covered in vomit.

There were empty cabins that the Canadian boys and I had discovered. We'd had visions of Nicole recovering and seducing us there, of making great conquests amongst the students in steerage and bringing them there. None of that, alas, came to pass. However, there they were, still empty, and, thankful, I tumbled into one and fell asleep, dreaming a dream of the Promised Land.

Very early in the morning, with the first faint light of the new day creeping through the porthole, I awoke. I made my way back to the cabin and with some trepidation opened the door. Fritzl and his uncle were gone and in their place was the steward, cleaning up. We exchanged our usual greeting, he finished and left. What a relief. For one of the very few moments of the entire voyage, the cabin was all mine. And on this morning, the morning we were due to arrive. What good fortune.

I undressed, took a leisurely shower, washed the sleep out of my eyes, and prepared for the moment of arrival. In my stomach was a tiny knot, the thrill of anticipation mingled with fear and tiredness. I dried off.

As a going-away present, my mother had taken me to Marks and Spencer and bought me a pair of shortie pyjamas. The thigh-length trousers to these pyjamas I now pulled on, lathered my face up, and began to shave.

I had taken one swoop with the razor when the door burst open and in rushed Herr Lewy. "Ach, Herr Robin, you are awake. We need you for the minyan."

And without further ado he seized me by my free arm and dragged me, half-naked, the razor still in my hand, into the cabin of the Chief Cantor of Vienna. There, shivering, lather slithering down my chin, blurting out protests and apologizing profusely, I was received as though I were Archbishop Makarios himself. A yarmulke was clamped on my head, cold hands clapped me on my bare back, and congratulations were passed around in Yiddish and Hebrew.

Dimly, I recognized David and, sober in a corner, in a jacket, of all people, Zvi. I sidled in and took up the most inconspicuous position I could devise, my back to the wall. Nobody, however, seemed much interested in me any more. There was a huddle by the door which included a couple of Hassidim, a couple of elderly Jews I hadn't seen before, and, to judge by the beautiful tallis and the white four-cornered hat he was wearing, the Chief Cantor himself.

I looked around. There were two single beds with a porthole over the right one. The cabin seemed more spacious and better appointed than ours. But that was surely in order for the Chief Cantor of Vienna. Zvi was standing quietly to my right, a little ahead of me. A little to his left was David. Herr Lewy, the *shamas* of this particular shul, was fussing about, tugging at the coverlets of the beds and consulting with the earnest group of five men, who seemed to be coming to some sort of agreement.

As I began slowly to regain consciousness, it seemed to me that I was not in fact the tenth man and that the welcome I had been accorded must have been in error. There were only nine men in the room and perhaps that accounted for the speed with which my presence had been forgotten. I began to suspect that the earnest consultations of the five men had something to do with this unhappy predicament and that their coming to an agreement meant that the Law offered some solution.

All of a sudden the huddle broke off and all five men began counting.

Each of them began counting with himself, counted the rest of us, and then ended with himself. A great shouting of "Ach!" as each of them realized he had now indeed counted ten and how stupid to have miscounted before, and, with an appreciative nod from Herr Lewy, who couldn't have been happier if Fritzl had thought this up himself, they all took up their positions and the proceedings got under way.

The Chief Cantor of Vienna stood between the two beds facing the wall, his tallis covering his shoulders. The others stood ranged behind him. I stood at the back, almost naked, but, as far as this nine-man minyan was concerned, impeccably dressed.

The Chief Cantor of Vienna began to daven, swaying back and forth with each mention of the holy name of God, and the other men chanted back at him, swaying in response. I held on to my razor and said nothing.

Suddenly out of the porthole, Zvi catches sight of land. He edges over to the bed and peers out. One of the Hassidim sees him and nudges his companion. "*Eretz Yisrael*," he sings into his ear, interpolating it into the rhythm of the chant. The two of them, still swaying, still chanting, sidle over to the porthole, climb up on the bed and each one in turn, still davening, peers out. "*Eretz Yisrael*," each one interpolates, banging the crown of his head against the top of the porthole and then his bearded chin against the bottom. "*Omein*," chants the other one, climbing down and resuming his place.

Before the morning prayers had ended, each one of the men, with the exception of the Chief Cantor who remained oblivious, had made the trip over to the bed, had climbed up, had peered out, had banged his head against the porthole twice, once at the top and once at the bottom, and had resumed his place. By the time the Chief Cantor of Vienna had concluded and turned round, it was as though nothing at all had happened.

Everybody shook my hand and thanked me. David looked me over and smiled. Zvi took me by the shoulders and shook his head. "Ts, ts, ts," he said.

Herr Lewy followed me back to the cabin. "You see, Herr Robin, you made it. Without you we couldn't have done it."

"Any time, Herr Lewy," I said, washing my face.

"Ach," he said, and there was a tinge of envy in his voice, "What a mitzvah. To make a minyan in the Promised Land."

I took off his yarmulke and began to dress.

The Promised Land

In Israel, for three months I traveled the country, staying with friends and distant relatives, mostly of my father's, and working on kibbutzim. In Ramat Yohanan I picked bananas, in Maayan Zvi I farmed fish, in Kfar Yedidiah I dug trenches. In Masada, where no road had yet been built, for hours in the broiling midday sun, I moved rocks. And everywhere I shoveled shit—chicken shit, cow shit, every conceivable kind of shit, even pig shit, which was of course called zebra shit, wet shit straight from the trays in the chicken hatcheries, dry shit piled high in barns and loaded in sacks and spread on the fields as fertilizer, shit of every texture, density, proportion, weight, and smell.

I slept in a police station in Dimona, I slept on the beach in Eilat, I slept on a rooftop in Nazareth.

And I hitchhiked the entire country.

And at every footfall the echo of history, the echo of '48, thirteen years earlier, during the War of Independence, when on this spot Shlomo the kibbutznik with dozens of others in the dead of night had rolled empty oil drums filled with stones down the hills of Haifa, driving out the Arab inhabitants and capturing the city for the Jews. And if you listened longer, beyond that, the echo of David and Solomon and Saul, and Rebecca and Ruth and Sarah, and the patriarchs Abraham, Isaac, and Jacob, all the dead names from Sunday school, all the dead voices, calling up through the blood-soaked ground. And for some the mysterious echo of Jesus walking in Galilee or entering Jerusalem or carrying his cross to Calvary. And for others the echo of Mohammed, astride his legendary steel el-Burak, ascending from the Dome of the Rock through the seven heavens into the presence of the Almighty.

In August, on the same mad boat that took me out, I sailed slowly back to Venice, where my parents were on holiday. They took me to the Lido and then flew home. I took the long train ride to Paris and after a couple of days the train and ferry back to London.

In September I went up to Oxford to have tea with Dr. Pantin and the Reverend Crater in Mr. Crater's lodgings. There was a good-natured tussle between them over what I would be reading, Dr. Pantin shaking his head over the impending loss of another historian, but in the end it was amicably settled. I would read English. In the absence of any don teaching English at Oriel, Mr. Crater would become my moral tutor, the equivalent of good old C. M. C. Hendtlass at St. Paul's, and would guide my future welfare.

When I arrived for the Michaelmas term, I was assigned, for the duration of my academic life, to the tutorship of B. D. H. Miller at Brasenose. The Reverend Crater had spoken to him about me, they would continue to confer, and for the next three years B. D. H. Miller would preside over my study of English language and literature.

B. D. H. Miller was a very tall, very thin, very stiff young don with horn-rimmed glasses and a strangulated voice, who invariably wore, summer and winter, a dark brown corduroy jacket, to which was incongruously pinned a CND button. CND was the Campaign for Nuclear Disarmament, and in the late fifties and early sixties this was a grassroots movement which involved thousands of people, most of them young and serious, but few of them as serious as B. D. H. Miller. It was the only human trait I ever discerned in him. He spent three years guiding me through the linguistic thickets of Old English, Middle English, and eventually, for a brief halcyon interlude, Modern English, but not one nonacademic word ever escaped his lips. Every so often I would see him striding awkwardly down the High Street on his way to the Examination Halls for the latest installment in his lecture series on Mediaeval Handwriting, his head cocked to one side seemingly about to fall off, and he would nod curtly. But that was the extent of our human exchange. Rumor had it that as a child he had been caught up in a scandalous divorce case and his picture had been plastered over the front pages of the tabloids. Perhaps, I thought, that had had something to do with it.

At Oriel, Mr. Crater was the adviser to the College Dramatic Society and I became involved in the college play. It was a production of *The Strong Are Lonely*, a play about the Jesuits in Paraguay during the eighteenth century, by the Austrian playwright Fritz Hochwälder. Conveniently, it was an all-male cast, so no women had to be imported. The director played the Inspector-General who presides over the big trials at the beginning and end of the play. He had a tremendous proclivity for drink so that every night the fate of Paraguay hung in the balance a little more precariously than Hochwälder had perhaps intended. One night, in fact, he skipped directly from the trial at the opening of the play to the trial at the end of the play, leaving out most of Act I, most of Act III, and all of Act II. I was playing Querini, the legate from Rome, and, sitting on the dais, powerless to act, paralyzed with suppressed laughter, I saw not just Paraguay but the whole Jesuit mission coming to an end. Suddenly, the Serjeant at Arms, a distinguished classical scholar with no lines to say, came to attention and left the chamber. The Inspector-General looked momentarily puzzled, hiccoughed, and careened drunkenly on. In a moment the Serjeant at Arms returned, came to attention, saluted, and said, "Important message from Rome, sir," marched up to the dais, and launched into a torrent of Latin. Then he slapped a piece of paper down in front of the Inspector-General on which was written, "Go back to Act I" and the cue. The mission had been saved. It was a great day for the classics.

The part of Querini had been played at the Old Vic by a friend of Mr. Crater's and as a result, I think, he was doubly pleased at my involvement.

One night after the play I went over to the professional theater, the Oxford Playhouse, where they were doing Harold Pinter's *The Caretaker*. There was to be a discussion after the performance that night with the actors and the director. I had seen the original production in London and hadn't understood it. But in this production, which I had seen before our play began, everything came together. There was a moment in the third act where the two brothers, who are rarely on stage at the same time and who scarcely exchange a word, pass, one leaving, one entering. They look at each other without saying a word, and then continue on their way. In that look, on the stage of the Oxford Playhouse, had been the whole unspoken emotional life of the play, the unarticulated and inexpressible love of those two very different men for each other. It had been profoundly moving. I went back and, since it had started later than our production, I caught the last few minutes of the play and stayed for the discussion. Mostly I wanted to see what real actors and a real director were like, in ordinary clothes, in an ordinary situation, talking like ordinary people. But somehow, even in ordinary clothes, up on the stage talking, they still retained an aura, and the magic of the play and the theater never quite disappeared. I was much too shy to ask a question. I just sat and listened and when it was over, I left.

As I entered Oriel Square I bumped into Mr. Crater.

"Oh, hello, I've been meaning to tell you, that's quite a wonderful performance you're giving."

I blushed.

"When my friend, Robert Eddison, did it at the Old Vic, it was a different interpretation. I'm not sure I don't like yours better."

"Thank you very much."

"Why don't you come up and have a drink?"

"Well, Mr. Crater, it's getting rather late. It's twenty to twelve." Curfew was at midnight, when the great wooden door swung to. Every college had an alternate means of entry, albeit unofficial, after midnight, over a wall with a strategic stone or two pried loose for handholds or through a window with a removable bar, but there were not insubstantial penalties if you were caught. In my case, however, the issue was somewhat academic since I had been allotted rooms outside the main gate on Oriel Square and Mr. Crater occupied rooms in the adjoining building.

"Oh, you don't need to worry about that."

"Well, as a matter of fact, Mr. Crater, I need you to sign an exeat for this weekend." My birthday was coming up and in order to leave town during the term one had to have permission from one's moral tutor.

"Well, come up and I'll sign it for you."

He led me into his building and pressed the light button on the ground floor. The light came on and the timer started ticking away. By the time we got to the first floor, the light had gone out, but Mr. Crater didn't press the light switch on the first floor. We climbed to the second floor in darkness. On the second floor he unlocked the door to his flat.

"Go on in," he said, pointing down the corridor to the living room. He didn't switch the light on in the corridor. He followed me into the living room and switched on two table lamps, one on either side of the sofa. "Sit down, don't stand there looking so forlorn."

Every seat except the sofa was filled with books.

"I really need that exeat, Mr. Crater."

"Yes, yes, I know, we'll get to that." He went over to a cabinet by the wall. "How about a drink?" He poured a tumbler full of brandy and handed it to me.

"Oh no, about a tenth of that."

He poured a little off and handed it to me again. I took the glass with the little bit poured off. Mr. Crater took the other one. "Now, do sit down."

There was only the sofa. I sat down.

Mr. Crater came over and sat down next to me. "Now, I want you to tell me how everything's going."

"Well, . . ." I began to talk about Mr. Miller and Anglo-Saxon and how I felt my considerable ignorance compared to other boys who had specialized for years in English before coming up. I talked rapidly, to keep from thinking, to keep whatever was about to happen from happening.

Mr. Crater put his hand on my thigh. "Don't worry," he said.

This couldn't be happening. Mr. Crater was the chaplain of the college and my moral tutor. Maybe I was misinterpreting. Maybe it was just a friendly gesture.

I crossed my leg and leaned forward, talking faster and faster, not making any sense.

Mr. Crater threw his arms around me and pulled me back on the sofa.

I disentangled myself and got up. I was shaking. "I'm sorry, Mr. Crater, I have to leave now."

There was a pause. "But what about your exeat?"

"Well, if you would sign it."

"How long is it for?"

"Just Saturday and Sunday."

He crossed to the cabinet, took out a pen and signed the form. "Here," he handed it to me without looking.

"Thank you," I said.

Still shaking, I retreated down the corridor, fumbled with the door, raced down the dark staircase and out into the light of Oriel Square.

I couldn't believe it. What did I do now? Was all Oxford like this? It was midnight. I climbed the stairs to the adjoining building and unlocked the door to my rooms. For an hour or more I walked around the living room in a daze, unable to think. I sat down. I stood up. I sat down. I stood up. There was no one to talk to. The only person I could think of was a third-year theology student called Wright whom I had spoken to at a sherry party for Mr. Crater's moral pupils. All night I sweated and the next morning at breakfast I sought him out.

"Could I have a word with you?"

"Certainly."

"It's a rather touchy subject."

"Well, come over to my rooms."

We went over to his rooms.

"Coffee?"

"Thank you."

"What is it, Hirsch?"

"Well, I don't know. I don't even know how to put it. It's about Crater."

"Yes?"

"Well, he invited me up for a drink last night."

"Yes?"

"And he, um, he, er, he tried to, um, he, er, put his arms around me."

"Oh, my God."

"Well, I don't know what I do now."

"Well, I'd expect you might want to change your moral tutor."

"Oh, is that possible?"

"Yes, it is. Mr. Brunt, the Dean, handles that."

"Well, I don't want to go around making accusations."

"Well, why don't you just talk to him, like you talked to me."

The Dean lived on my staircase. He was a little man with an egregious forehead, taciturn. He had been on my interview committee but hadn't said a word. I passed him sometimes on the stairs and he would mumble an incoherent greeting. Just before lunch I knocked on his door.

"Come in. Oh, you. What can I do for you?"

Well, Mr. Brunt, it's a rather delicate matter. It has to do with my moral tutor."

"With Mr. Crater. Yes?"

"Well. I wonder if I can talk to you in confidence."

"Certainly."

"Well, I want to lay some facts before you so that if, in the future, I should request a change of moral tutor you will know why."

"That sounds very cumbersome. What do you have to say?"

I told him what had happened.

"These are serious charges."

"Mr. Brunt, I don't know. It might still be possible for Mr. Crater to remain my moral tutor. I just needed to let someone know."

"Alright. Well, you go off and have lunch now and we'll give it some thought."

"Thank you, Mr. Brunt."

I was beginning to sweat furiously. After lunch I went to the Bodleian Library and tried to study. I was getting feverish. I couldn't concentrate. Nothing made sense any more. At five o'clock, feeling faint, I packed up my books and stumbled out, down the steps, across the High, into Oriel Square. As I was entering my building, the steward, breathless, caught up with me.

"Oh, Mr. Hirsch, I've been looking all over for you. The Provost wants to see you."

"The Provost? What for?"

"I don't know, sir. But you'd best get over there. Right away."

"Alright."

The steward accompanied me across the square, through the gate, past the porter's lodge into the main quad and took me to the front door of the Provost's Lodgings. He let us both in and told me to wait. He walked through the elegant reception room and opened a door at the far end. "Oh, Mr. Turpin, sir, Mr. Hirsch is here now." A pause. "Very good, sir."

He left the door open and came back to me. "You can go in now. They're having tea."

"Thank you."

I walked along the edge of the carpet and came to the door. Inside was a huge living room. Late afternoon light was coming in through the windows. Seated around the fire having tea were the Provost, the Dean, and the Chaplain.

"Come in, Mr. Hirsch. Close the door. Why don't you sit down by that table over there. Good. Cup of tea? No? Well, now, the Dean tells me that you have leveled some rather serious charges against the Chaplain. Isn't that so, Peter?"

"Yes, he came to see me at lunchtime to request a change of moral tutor."

"And did he give you a reason?"

"He said that James—forgive me, James—had made improper advances to him."

"Well, Mr. Hirsch, what do you have to say?"

I was speechless. I sat there in my duffle coat, sweating, unable to look at any of them.

"Well, Mr. Hirsch, does Mr. Brunt report you accurately?"

Finally I stammered out: "I didn't expect this. I didn't want any of this. I just wanted to acquaint him with the facts."

"Well, that's what we're here for, Mr. Hirsch, to determine the facts. Now perhaps you would tell us what happened yesterday evening."

And step by step they led me through the events of the previous night—the encounter, the staircase, the lights, the corridor, the room, the books, the brandy, the sofa.

"And then, Mr. Hirsch?"

"And then, er, he, er, . . ."

"He did what, Mr. Hirsch?"

"He, er, put his hand on my thigh."

"James, is that true?"

"Of course not."

"You didn't, for example, reach over and pat him on the thigh—to reassure him?"

"Well, Kenneth, he was very upset. I felt badly for the young man, first term, lot of catching up to do, I don't know, I may have, just to reassure him."

"Very well. Go on, Mr. Hirsch."

I felt I was about to be sick. "I moved my leg. I leaned forward. I spoke very rapidly."

"Yes?"

"And then Mr. Crater threw his arms around me."

"Oh. Nonsense."

"James, are you saying this didn't happen?"

"Of course not."

"Alright. Peter, more tea?"

"Thank you."

"Jim?"

"Just a drop."

"Well, Mr. Hirsch, Mr. Crater doesn't seem to agree with you. According to you, what happened then?"

"I got up, I excused myself, Mr. Crater signed my exeat. I left."

"Alright. Thank you. Peter, do you have any questions?"

The Dean shook his head.

"Jim?"

"Yes, Kenneth, as a matter of fact I do. Tell me, when you came up last night, in the living room, were the curtains open or closed?"

"I—I don't remember."

"Well, as a matter of fact, they were open. Now do you think I, do you think anyone, would be likely to do what you have been alleging I did with the curtains wide open onto Oriel Square?"

I didn't say anything.

"Kenneth, I don't think I have anything else to say."

"Mr. Hirsch, thank you for coming. By the way, the Dean and I very much enjoyed your performance the other night. I expect you probably have to go and prepare now."

"Yes, I do."

I left the three of them in the failing light, talking quietly around the fireplace, their tea cups still in their hands.

That night Mr. Crater came into the dressing room before the show. I was sweating so badly the makeup wouldn't stay on my face. The director asked Mr. Crater if he could help. Mr. Crater with thick firm hands applied a base to my face, penciled in my eyebrows, lined my eyes, powdered me down. Neither of us looked at the other. Neither of us said a word. I hardly breathed. "There we are," he said to the director. "That should fix him."

The next morning I went down to London on the train.

"*Ach, mein Dicker*, you look awful," said my mother.

"I am awful."

"What happened?"

I told them what happened.

My father got very angry. "It's *eine Unverschämtheit*. It's immoral, it's disgusting, it's outrageous."

Every so often, when I was ill or when I was in trouble, the sureness and swiftness of my father's reactions were a great comfort.

"I will ring the Provost."

"No, Daddy, please."

"I will ring the papers."

"It's not necessary."

"I will break his neck."

I assumed there was an unwritten code amongst the bachelor fraternity at Oxford. I certainly realized that the Reverend Crater, who was in the line for the Regius Professorship of Ancient Hebrew, was of rather greater value to Oriel than this little Jewish interloper who had had the gall to switch from history to English, after all the trouble they had taken and all the faith they had shown. I imagined that as in the Snow novels there would be some subtle and elegant way of letting me know I wasn't wanted. When I returned to Oxford on Monday morning there would be a note in my mailbox from the Provost saying my request for a change of moral tutor had been denied and I would be honor-bound to pack my bags and leave.

When I returned to Oxford on Monday morning, there was a note in my mailbox from the Provost. It said: "Your request for a change of moral tutor has been granted. Your moral tutor will be Mr. Seton-Watson."

For the remainder of that year, I trod the college grounds with diffidence. Every so often Crater and I would pass each other, on the way to dinner or in the square. It was always a moment I dreaded. There was no getting out of it. Each of us pretended the other didn't exist. And with the Dean and the Provost I felt a terrible awkwardness. Even with B. D. H. Miller, who dined regularly with the Chaplain and whom I saw weekly, the shadow of my encounter hung in the air.

At the end of the year, Crater's Fellowship at Oriel was not renewed. He accepted a post as Chairman of the Theology Department at a red-brick university. The next two years at Oxford were a little easier. The shadow lifted, although it never fully disappeared.

In 1964, after three years under the awkward tutelage of B. D. H. Miller, I graduated. White bow ties, black gowns, mortarboards high in the air. Champagne. Fireworks. Freedom.

Years later, living in America, a friend of mine sent me a cutting from the *Oxford Mail.* It was about a sensational trial that had held both town and university in its grip, and it involved, as the central witness, my former tutor, B. D. H. Miller. He had for years apparently been the victim of a violent homosexual blackmail operation. Now, all these years later, he had come forward at the Oxford Assizes to testify against his tormentors.

Grown-ups

My parents were not given to big celebrations. They made considerable efforts for our birthdays, there would be the occasional gala in the Jewish community for which they would dress up, they would generally do something elegant in evening dress with friends on New Year's Eve, but that was about it. So it came as a surprise to Barbie and me when in January 1964 they announced that next month we were all going to Mallorca. The 16th of February, we vaguely knew, was their wedding anniversary—it was not a date they made a big fuss about—and after we worked at it we realized this year was their Silver Wedding Anniversary.

We looked forward to and at the same time dreaded the trip. Even small expeditions with my parents tended to end in disaster. We'd go to a restaurant to celebrate some event—my getting into Oxford, for example—and even before we got there, the promise of an easy night out would have evaporated. My mother wouldn't be ready on time. My father would be furious at my mother. My sister and I would be embarrassed at having to be out with our parents. We wouldn't be able to park. My father's initial generous impulse would give way as soon as he saw the menu. "You can have this, this, or this. And here they give a lot of bread—eat bread."

By the end of the night we would be driving home in silence.

"Thank you, Daddy."

"Thank you, Daddy."

"Good night, Daddy."

"Good night, Daddy."

"*Ja*, good night."

The trip to Mallorca was a package tour. My parents were going to be in a first-class hotel in Palma, and Barbie and I were going to be in a little *pension* a few miles out of town.

After we'd landed and gone through customs we were shepherded onto a bus by the local courier. The members of the tour were going to be dropped at their different hotels.

"You are stopping at the Imperial first?" my father wanted to know.

The reply was not to his satisfaction.

"We are staying at the Imperial Hotel, we have paid a lot of money for this holiday. They assured me that this would be the first stop."

Barbie and I start to cringe. This is a scene we can play in our sleep. The courier is unfailingly polite. My father gets angrier and angrier. The courier explains that there are people transferring from one hotel to another and that unfortunately we will have to pick them up first. My father refuses to hear of such a thing. The bus has now been held up for a good fifteen minutes and people are beginning to get upset.

"Come on."

"Get on with it."

"We paid a lot of money too."

"Who do you think you are?"

Some compromise is eventually worked out, but Barbie and I are too overcome to know what it is. We can only wait for the moment when my parents are deposited at their hotel. After a year, it arrives.

"*So*," my father says to me, "you will ring us at the hotel at six o'clock and tell us if everything is alright."

When they get off there are cheers and whistles. "That dreadful man," somebody says.

Barbie and I bury our heads.

Our *pension* is the last stop on the bus and we are the only ones staying there. It actually turns out to be fine. Barbie and I share a simple room. "My God, it's like being five years old again," she says. We haven't slept in the same room since we moved out of Grove End Gardens when I was eleven and she was nine.

At six o'clock we call the Imperial Hotel.

"Happy anniversary, Mummy. Happy anniversary, Daddy."

"*Ja, ja.* Everything is alright?"

"Yes. Wonderful."

"In your *pension* everything is compris, so you can have what you want."

"Thank you for a lovely holiday."

"It has not yet started, so what are you thanking."

"Well, thank you anyway."

"*Nichts zu danken*" (Nothing to thank).

Our parents have been married for a quarter of a century. It is still the minor portion of both their lives. What were their lives like before us, what were their lives like before they met, what had they given up, what had they lost, what out of the turmoil and the violence and the displacement had they managed to salvage, what, now, in the shadow of this history, did they feel they had accomplished.

We have no time for such thoughts. We are free. We go down to the tiny restaurant. We order beefsteak and wine. And for a brief and halcyon moment we feel like grown-ups.

Part II

<hr>

The Man Who Danced with Marlene Dietrich

<hr>

(1964—1973)

On the Road

I met him three times altogether, each time in a different country: the first time in Hamburg, the second time in London, and the last time, a few months before he died, in Los Angeles.

I had known about him all my childhood. Every so often, once or twice a year, a finely textured envelope addressed with a flamboyant hand would slide through the mailbox of my parents' flat in London. It always bore an American stamp and it seemed impregnated with the perfume of a rich and romantic land. Inside would be a letter to my parents, not just wishing them the customary formal greetings for the holidays, but sending them love and kisses, kisses too to the dear children, whom the author had yet to meet, but for whom he cherished a deep and abiding love already, and one that would only grow from year to year. My father would shrug and give a snort, somewhere between amusement and derision. My mother would laugh too, but there was a softness to her laughter, something almost girlish. Taking up most of the second page, underneath the Xs, in the same flamboyant hand, would be the signature— Jochem.

Jochem had been married to my mother before the war, in a different country, in a different time, almost in a different life—Berlin in the twenties, before the inflation, before Hitler, before the concentration camps, before the *Auswanderung*. My mother, when she talked of him and her marriage and that distant time, talked as one talks of an errant child, fondly, but trying to muster disapproval. "He was a bohemian. We were so young. He was so irresponsible." And then a sigh. And that sigh was supposed to indicate how inadequate a provider Jochem would have been in those terrible years that followed and how lucky we were to have the firm hand of my father to shepherd us through the troubled early years in England and how one must make choices in this life and how ultimately one chooses responsibility. But I always thought that sigh was also a sigh of regret.

When I was eleven or so my father had gone to America. He had climbed the Empire State Building and made a record saying hello to us. He had been driven in a car at eighty miles an hour. And he had brought me back a cowboy outfit. On the West Coast he had also apparently sought out Jochem. What that meeting was like I don't know. I do know that Jochem was one of the few figures in the family's mythology whom my father did not immediately dismiss out of hand. Indeed he regarded him with what amounted to tolerance, an almost unheard-of commodity in my father's arsenal. I assumed that meant that Jochem operated in a different orbit, that he was not to be taken seriously, that he was, in that word my father reserved for the most negligible of the species, harmless.

I knew one story about him and it spanned the decades. In the early twenties, in Berlin, at a masked ball, he had danced all night with Marlene Dietrich. She had refused all other invitations. They did not see each other again. Forty years later, living in America and making a livelihood as a traveling salesman, he was passing through Las Vegas selling art reproductions. He found himself having to spend the night and noticed that in one of the big hotels Dietrich was appearing. On an impulse he sent her flowers with a note which said, "From the man who danced with you at the Doctors' Ball." At four in the morning the phone in his room rings. It is Dietrich. "You cocksucker," she says, or words to that effect. "You didn't even say which hotel you were in. I've called every hotel in Vegas." And they talked for hours.

While Jochem was talking to Marlene Dietrich I was at Oxford and only dimly aware of either of them. I was preparing for Schools, that rigorous series of final exams in which for six hours a day, every day for a week, dressed in a black suit and a white bow tie, wearing a gown and carrying a mortarboard, you write down everything you've ever learned or thought or wished you knew, about the field you've spent the last three years pursuing. A month or so later there were Orals, in which, before a panel of distinguished scholars in my field, I was supposed to defend the hasty opinions I had come to on *Gawain* or Chaucer or the Metaphysical poets or Matthew Arnold. They were extraordinarily polite. I was numb with terror.

After it was over, drunk with relief, I rushed down to London, said good-bye to my parents, and joined forces with a friend of mine to hitchhike to the Continent. Gerry was a friend, not from Oxford, but from my youth group days in London, from the congregation in Belsize Square to which his parents and my parents both belonged, a congregation of German Jewish refugees who had banded together during the war, praying and quarreling in German and being bombed in an alien land by planes whose pilots spoke the same language as the rabbi. Gerry had just finished at London University as a budding psychologist and we were both ready for a change of air and a taste of the road, two young men on an adventure.

There were a couple of fixed points on our itinerary—Amsterdam, where my uncle lived, and Berlin, where Gerry's parents had a friend who had gone back after the war; apparently he was now a political figure of some consequence in East Berlin. I also had a friend, a young professor, in Cologne, with whom I had struck up an acquaintance a couple of years before in a theater queue in London. Otherwise our plans were to hitch north into Scandinavia, which neither of us knew.

In Amsterdam we dined with my uncle and aunt in their elegant apartment and spent the night. They had no children of their own and I always felt a special warmth from them. My sister, Barbie, always found them remote. They had left Germany in the mid-thirties, long before my parents, and settled in Amsterdam. During the occupation they had gone into hiding. They had made an agreement that if they were separated, and if they survived, they would meet after the war at the house of their friend Professor Heringa. One day, in 1944, they were betrayed. They, together with my grandmother—the mother of my uncle and my father— were shipped to Westerbork, a holding camp in the northeast of Holland, and then to Auschwitz. They were separated. My grandmother was exterminated. My uncle, however, survived, and in the last confused days before the liberation escaped from Auschwitz and with a broken leg made his way back to Amsterdam, to the house of Professor Heringa. Six weeks later the doorbell rings. He goes to answer it. There, weighing fifty pounds, is my aunt. She too had survived. They were one of only five Dutch couples to survive the camps intact.

Now, almost twenty years later, they lived in an immaculate apartment on Michelangelostraat in the south of Amsterdam. My uncle was the head of a refugee organization, my aunt was a well-known fashion designer. In both of them it seemed to me, behind the luxurious appointments of everyday life and behind a kind of acquired Dutch reserve, a special light shone, a special reverence for life. It explained for me both the remoteness and the warmth.

"Where are you going?" Uncle Georg asked.

"Well, we're going briefly to Germany, and then north to Scandinavia, but we have no real plans."

"You have no itinerary?" There was a note of incredulity in his voice.

"No," said Aunt Bertel, "they'll make it up as they go along."

"I see," said Uncle Georg. "And how will you travel?"

"Well," I said a little hesitantly, "we're hitchhiking."

"Ach, no," said Uncle Georg, "*Komm,* let me give you money for the train."

"Don't be silly, Orgi," said Aunt Bertel, "that's the whole point of it."

"I see, *Liebchen,*" he said, not very convinced, and then he shook his head gravely, "*Nein, nein, nein.*"

But the next morning, he took us in his gray Lancia to the edge of the city and waited in the car until we got a ride.

There is something exhilarating about being on the road in all kinds of weather, not knowing when your next ride is going to come or with whom or how far it will take you. A certain trepidation overtook me as we crossed the border into Germany, but on the road you are in a kind of international corridor and the prism through which you see a country is a little distorted—you judge it by the speed with which people pick you up and how far they take you. By this token, England is great, Holland is quite good, Germany is not bad, and Scandinavia is terrible.

In Helmstedt we were forced to take the train. The road to Berlin went through East Germany and border control was extremely strict. Drivers making the trip were nervous enough to begin with and didn't want the added complication of unknown passengers. As it was, precautions on the train were pretty grim. We waited for hours at the border. Somber guards with rifles patroled the platform. Compartments were searched, passports removed for inspection. As the train rolled slowly through the East German night, passengers shivered and grew quiet. No one exchanged greetings. We spoke only when a guard threw open the door and asked a question.

West Berlin was a glittering island set in a Communist sea. There seemed to be a conscious attempt to revive the glitter of the twenties, the excitement, the intellectual ferment, the theatrics. But it seemed forced. It was as though, in the surrounding gloom, the citizenry felt the need to burn more brightly. Ironically, the relationship it most immediately brought to mind was that between Israel and her Arab neighbors.

Three times we made our way to Checkpoint Charlie, submitted ourselves to the friendly scrutiny of the Americans, walked the dismal stretch to the Soviet inspection post and waited till their grim conference was over and we were permitted to enter the Soviet sector. Berlin, the city in which my parents had been born, had grown up, had conducted their very different and promising lives, had been destroyed. The buildings in which their families had lived had been torn down, the streets paved over. Berlin was a city arbitrarily divided. Ironically, in this respect, the city it most closely resembled was Jerusalem.

In East Berlin, Herr Sachs, the friend of Gerry's parents, had sent a government car to fetch us. He was a deputy mayor and had recently made a speech in favor of the wall, which the Soviets had only just completed and which was a subject of enormous sensitivity in the Berlin we had just left. Here the streets were almost empty, there was scarcely a car on the road, and the buildings were large, drab, and uniform. We were given a tour of some of the municipal offices, of the war memorial, and Herr Sachs himself took us to the cemetery where Gerry's grandparents were buried. At one gravesite a solitary figure in a shawl stood in contemplation. She left as we approached. It was Helene Weigel, said Herr Sachs, the widow of Brecht. Apart from her and us the cemetery was deserted.

In the evening we had a light meal in the simple bungalow that Herr Sachs and his wife occupied on the outskirts of the city. We drank. He outlined to us the economic difficulties which had led to the decision to erect the wall. The West, he told us, had flagrantly disregarded the currency agreements that had painstakingly been worked out between the two governments, the West German mark had been arbitrarily inflated to a value five or six times that of the Ostmark, and the Bundesrepublik had been systematically trying to buy out East German workers when there was free access back and forth. The DDR was being undermined and sabotaged and had to defend itself. We drank some more, a hard transparent liquor.

"And your parents, Gerald, how are they?"

"They send you their best. They are well. They also send you this." And he handed over to Frau Sachs a tin of Nescafé.

"Thank you, Gerald. Of course, not everything is in plentiful supply here. We are grateful."

"Herr Sachs," I said, "my mother was married to a man named Sachs in the twenties. I was wondering if by any chance you were related."

"Where is he now? Is he alive?"

"He lives in America."

Herr Sachs shook his head curtly. He had no patience for America. He had fled to Sweden during the war. Like Gerry's parents he had been a Communist. He had known Rosa Luxemburg. He had kept the dream alive. When the war was over he had made his way back to Berlin and helped to bring the Communist regime into being.

"Your parents, Gerald. Why did they never come back?"

"I don't know. It wasn't easy in England. But my grandmother was still alive, and they had me. And . . ." He hesitated.

"Yes, Gerald?"

"They don't altogether approve of what you are doing."

"Oh, I see," Herr Sachs said. "I thought as much."

"Well, the wall. And the shootings."

"They don't know the whole story. They don't know the facts." And he expanded in great detail on the economic arguments.

"But none of that," I said, "justifies the shooting. Surely."

"Tell me," he said pleasantly, "in your country you don't shoot traitors?"

"Yes," I said, "but . . ."

"But these people are not traitors," he finished the sentence for me. "They are just trying to escape."

I nodded.

"To us, they are traitors. They are undermining the system. They are destroying it. We don't build for ourselves. It takes time, a generation, maybe two. We build for the children." He looked at Gerry for a long moment, and then he turned to his wife. "Hannah, let's have coffee."

The limousine brought us back to the border. Twice more we made the crossing. There was nothing seductive about the East, but there was nothing frivolous about it either. It was the other side of the moon, the dark side—ravaged, gray, depressed. In West Berlin we would sit in a café on the Kurfürstendamm and watch the pretty girls in their high heels clatter by; in the East we would order the single available dish in a cavernous basement restaurant and watch the elderly waiter limp morosely down the empty aisle. The third night we spent again at the bungalow. As curfew approached, we raised our glasses with the harsh liquid one last time.

"To the future," said Herr Sachs.

"And the facts," we added, good students that we were.

The next day we canvassed the line of cars waiting to make the journey through the East German corridor to Helmstedt. We found a ride with a dignified elderly lady who took us as far as Hanover. We hitchhiked north through Schleswig-Holstein into Denmark. In Copenhagen we slept in the station because none of the hostels had room. We took the ferry to Malmö and headed up the coast of Sweden towards Stockholm. One day, on the road, after walking six hours in the rain without a ride, we quarreled and split up. With the rain pouring down we stood for an hour a hundred yards apart, two Jews alone amid the Aryan corn, each with our thumb out, not looking at the other. We met briefly in Stockholm, more by chance than design. Gerry decided to go on to Oslo, where there were other family friends. I had run out of money, so I stayed on in Stockholm, washing dishes in a fancy Italian restaurant and making friends with other overqualified aliens who kept the Swedish restaurant business alive. By September it was growing chilly. I had kroner in my pocket. I decided to head south.

I got a ride with three excitable Frenchmen who had driven their Citroën all the way from Moscow. In the middle of the night on the deserted road to Malmö these world travelers ran out of gas. Worse, they had only Russian and French money, neither of which was welcome tender to the proprietor of a small gas station, whom we managed to rouse out of bed shortly before dawn. With the bulk of my earnings as a dishwasher we filled the Citroën, spare tanks and all, and it got us all the way to Hamburg.

Compared to Sweden, Hamburg felt almost like home. I still shivered at the thought of Germany, but I understood the language, Gerry and I had spent a couple of days here on the way up, and so the city was not unfamiliar. We had stayed in a *Studentenheim*. I found it again and the *Wirtin* remembered me. She told me there was a vacancy in the room occupied by Herr Schmidt and I could have it if I agreed to stay for a month. I was tired of traveling, I had enough money left over from Stockholm and the Citroën to pay the rent for a week, and the rest I was confident I could earn. One of the virtues of not having an itinerary is that you can make snap decisions like this. It is of course one of the drawbacks too.

I found work on the night shift at Axel Springer, a newspaper publisher. Not every night, but frequently enough to pay the balance of the rent and keep me fed. I started at eleven in the evening and worked through till seven the next morning. There were hundreds of others, men and women, in huge halls. Sections of the newspaper would come off the presses and it was our job to fold them correctly, or to put two parts together, or occasionally to slip an insert in. Inserts were regarded as a prize, because they were printed up beforehand and so the ink was dry: the women mostly did the inserts.

We worked at great speed. Rhythm was the key. Sometimes the presses would run unchecked for an hour or longer and only if you had developed an appropriate rhythm could you keep up. The shunting of the presses, the rolling of the conveyor belts, the whole complex of machinery which deposited identical loads in front of you like the ticking of a clock, compelled you to keep time. Nonsense songs would arise spontaneously and form themselves on my lips and when the presses shut down for a few minutes or sometimes, blessedly, for an hour, I would still be singing. In the sudden silence it was alarming. Some of my fellow workers would be amused, some would be annoyed. The foreman, however, would be infuriated. He called me *Sänger* and whenever he had some particularly unsavory task he would yell out, "*Sänger, komm ma' her.*"

When the presses shut down and if we could finish our load before they started up again, we had a respite. But it was always a respite with an edge to it, because you never knew when the machinery would start again and you could never wander from your place. In shifts, staggered over a four-hour period from twelve till four in the morning, we would get a half-hour break. The men would generally drink beer and eat a sandwich which they had brought from home. The women kept themselves apart. At seven in the morning we would troop into the washrooms, rub our hands with white abrasive powder, remove our overalls, and surge out into the daylight. Our hands would still be black with ink. I would generally still be singing.

I made one acquaintance at the plant, an unlikely one. His name was Sami and he was a young Israeli. His parents, like mine, had been born in Germany and had left at the last moment. Unlike mine, however, they had spent years on the run and, shortly before the war ended, had arrived in Israel. He had been born there. After independence, the parents grew increasingly dissatisfied with their standard of living. Finally they decided, for business reasons, to return to Germany. Hamburg, because of old associations and new prospects, had been the logical choice.

Hamburg had of course changed. Surprisingly, it had a not insubstantial Jewish population—about four hundred families. But the composition was unusual. A large proportion—a lop-sided proportion, some felt—was made up of Syrian Jews, whose chief interest in the city derived from its importance as a market for Oriental carpets. The rest were German Jews who had drifted back fitfully after the war, as Germany began to reestablish itself during the *Wirtschaftswunder.* Sami's family was unusual in that they were German Jews, but they dealt in Oriental carpets.

One Friday evening after services, Sami invited me to join them at the synagogue. It was a huge old building which had been ransacked in the thirties but which now had been almost totally refurbished with restitution money from the German government. The old division between men and women was no longer observed. Instead the congregation divided, by informal agreement, along national lines. The Syrians had the downstairs and the Germans occupied the balcony. However, the balcony was large and comfortable and had the air of a spacious café. I joined

Sami's family at a table by the balustrade. The Syrians seemed to be in charge of the festivities, the Germans more spectators than participants, though there was clearly nothing to prevent them joining in, and no animosity at all between the two camps. The whole occasion had about it an air of celebration, of excitement. There was food, there was music, there was laughter. There was also easy access up and down, and from time to time we would descend and join the dancing.

Shortly after ten I made my excuses, went back to the *Studentenheim*, put on my work clothes, and went to work. Sami stayed. He didn't work on Shabbas.

Slowly my life in Hamburg developed its own routine. I got used to falling asleep at eight in the morning, to getting up in the afternoon, to eating the oddest things at the unlikeliest hours— *Currywurst* from the stand on the corner for breakfast at four in the afternoon; occasionally, when I felt profligate, half a chicken. Generally that was my meal for the day.

Some of the students supported themselves, at least partially, by working one or two nights a week at Springer, and I got to know a few faces. They all looked older than me and somehow worldly-wise.

There was a Hungarian with a fine open face and clear blue eyes, who rarely spoke and never to me; he had escaped during the invasion of 1956 and it was rumored he had killed two men in the sewers getting out; it was also rumored that he carried a gun and feared he was being hunted.

There was Rosemarie, who studied English and had befriended me as a fellow *Anglist*. She was from Leipzig in the East and could never return; all her family still lived there. She wore butterfly glasses and a look of seriousness and resignation. Sometimes she would make me tea and talk about Shakespeare, Coleridge, or A. J. Cronin, and I would talk about the theater. She predicted a great future for me. She was the only person whom I called by her first name. It was probably because we spoke in English.

There was Herr Hahn, stolid, powerful, balding, with a hint of the repressed homosexual about him. He and I would occasionally walk to Springer together and he would talk intensely of Berlin, his home, a divided city administered by foreign powers, an island, half of which he couldn't visit. I had been there, I told him. It was the price of war, he said, the penalty for a mania which had seized the German people, the heart of a nation torn out and cut in two. If I ever came to Berlin again, I should visit his family.

Herr Schmidt, with whom I shared a room, I never saw. He lived on the other side of a bookcase divider and he would generally be asleep when I came in from Springer in the morning and not yet in when I went out at night. We rarely exchanged a word.

One morning I came back as usual at about 7:30, my hands still dirty. I opened the heavy door, walked gingerly across the cold cement floor past the sleeping body of Herr Schmidt, slid into bed and fell asleep. Almost immediately, it seemed, the room buzzer started ringing and I woke up. It wouldn't stop. Finally, I knelt up on the bed and looked over the bookcase for Herr Schmidt. He wasn't there. I looked at my watch. It was nine in the morning.

Infuriated, I got up, put a towel around me, and rushed out into the hall. I picked up the phone.

"*Herr Schmidt ist nicht da,*" I said.

"Herr Hirsch?" said the *Wirtin.*

"*Ja.*"

"*Ein Gespräch für Sie.*"

A call for me. Impossible, I thought, I don't know a soul in Hamburg, except Sami, and why would he call at this hour? Did I know a Herr Sachs, the *Wirtin* asked me.

Herr Sachs. Half asleep, I remembered my mother had written that Jochem was in London. She and Olga, another old flame of his, had given him a party. All his London friends had been invited. He had wept.

"Yes," I said hesitantly, "I know a Herr Sachs."

"Just a minute," she said.

Presently a man's voice came on the line, English with a German accent, somehow made palatable by an American patina.

"Mr. Hirsch? This is Jochem Sachs. Do you know who I am?"

"Yes," I said, "you used to be married to my mother. Where are you?"

"I'm in Hamburg. I arrived yesterday. I'm staying with an old friend of mine, Charlotte von Langenstein. She would like you very much to come for dinner."

"I'd love to. But I'm working at night. How long are you going to be here?"

"Just two days. I was hoping you could come tonight."

I gripped my towel. "I'll come."

"I'm so glad. I'm longing to meet you. Your parents were wonderful to me. Your mother is unchanged. She and Olga—do you know Olga?— gave me a party with all my old friends. It was beautiful. I wept."

"Oh," I said.

"Your mother is as beautiful as ever. She was always the most beautiful woman in the world. And your sister, I met your sister. She is *bildhübsch*, beautiful as a picture—do you understand German?"

"A little."

"Well, your family is very well. They would like to hear more often from you. I am supposed to tell you that."

"I know. I'm a bad letter-writer."

"It doesn't matter. What matters is in the heart. So, you will come tonight. Charlotte will give you directions. She is a remarkable woman. Her husband is in Bremen for a couple of days looking after his ships. That's why I'm here. She has a daughter, Ulla, a beauty—*bildhübsch*—she's a model here in Hamburg. We'll make a night of it, the four of us. I can't wait to see you."

"I'm looking forward," I said.

He handed me over to Charlotte, who spoke to me in English. They lived in Othmarschen. I was to take the train at five. It was the last stop. They would pick me up at the station.

"I'm looking forward," she said.

"So am I. It's very good of you to have me. Thank you."

"We'll see you this evening," she said.

I hung up the phone and went back to the room, shivering. I had one major problem. I had nothing I could possibly wear to meet for the first time, at the house of someone whose husband was a shipbuilder, the man who had been married to my mother. Apart from my summer hitchhiking ensemble, I had a shirt, a tie, and a hopelessly creased jacket. This was clearly an occasion which called for a suit. I asked around the *Studentenheim*. No luck. I set out in search of Sami.

I walked to Springer. I knew occasionally he worked a day shift. The plant was unfamiliar in the daylight. I didn't recognize a single face. No one knew me. At the entrance I was stopped. I didn't have a day pass. I tried to explain the situation in my halting German. I showed my night pass and my dirty hands. Eventually they let me in. I made my way to the main hall where I was stopped again. I wasn't in overalls. I explained again. Looking around the hall I saw Sami at one of the conveyor belts. No, I could not go over to him. He had his back to me. I waited. After twenty minutes the presses stopped, and I slipped in.

"Sami."

"*Sänger*, what are you doing here?"

"Sami, you said if ever I needed anything I should contact you."

"What do you need?"

"My mother's former husband is in Hamburg. I need a suit."

As luck would have it, he had a suit that was ready to be thrown out. If I could catch his mother before the charity collection, it was mine. He gave me the address.

His mother recognized me from the synagogue. The suit was all ready, wrapped in brown paper, tied with string.

"It's not . . . ," she hesitated.

"It's alright," I said, "I'm sure it'll be fine."

She shook her head, more in sorrow than in contradiction. I thanked her, took the parcel and left. I didn't think it appropriate to unwrap it in her presence.

Round the corner I tore the paper off. It was a dark brown suit with pinstripes. Couldn't be helped. I took my coat off, held it between my knees, and tried the jacket on. A little tight, but it would do. The curious stares of onlookers persuaded me to wait till the *Studentenheim* to try the trousers on. There I discovered why the suit was being thrown out. Every normal pocket—in the trousers and in the jacket—had a hole in it. The only functioning pocket was the outside breast pocket of the jacket. Everything would have to go in there.

Rosemarie pressed the suit. At four I set off for the station with an unfamiliar lump on my left breast composed of keys and coins and folded money and a comb, all topped off with a fashionable handkerchief. Every time I touched my right side for my wallet it took me a moment to remember that it wasn't there.

The Othmarschen station was the end of the line, so the train disgorged its entire load and hundreds of us streamed towards the exit barrier, mostly commuters ending their day's work in the city of Hamburg and returning to their comfortable homes in the suburbs. I walked up and down looking middle-aged men in the eye, not sure at all whom I was seeking. Presently I saw a man of more than middle height in an elegant dark blue overcoat and I had a presentiment it must be him. At that moment he turned around.

"Robin," he said.

"Jochem," I said.

"Come," he said, "Charlotte is waiting with the car."

We walked towards the station exit.

"Charlotte is an exceptional woman. Every week during the war she put flowers on my mother's grave. Do you know what kind of a risk that was?"

I nodded.

"Her husband we won't speak about. He's playing with his ships in Bremen."

What did that mean, I wondered. Was her husband a Nazi?

"Ulla you will meet later. *Bildhübsch.*"

There was something elegant about Jochem, but also, surprisingly, something withdrawn. I hadn't expected this. A distance, a detachment. It was something I recognized in almost all my parents' relatives and friends, the shadow of history. For some reason I hadn't expected it to loom over Jochem too.

In the quiet station yard, amongst the Volkswagens, the Audis, the BMWs, an incongruous beast was purring—a huge immaculate English Bentley. Jochem steered me towards it. "Don't be afraid," he said and put his arm around me.

At the wheel was a striking middle-aged woman who reached her hand out of the window to me and said, "Robin, I'm glad he found you. Or did you find him?"

"How do you do," I took her hand. "We found each other."

"Good," she said, "I'm delighted you could come."

"So am I," I made to open the back door.

"No, no, no, come round to the other side and sit with us."

I held the door open for Jochem and followed him in.

"I'm sorry about the car," Charlotte said. "Hans has the Rolls in Bremen. So we have to make do with this. Also he took Willi."

"Willi is the chauffeur," Jochem explained.

"So you've got me."

"That's quite alright," I said. My right hand, I noticed, was enlarging the hole in my jacket pocket.

As we drove, Charlotte asked me what I was doing in Hamburg. I explained, as delicately as I could, that I was passing through, that I didn't know how long I would stay, that I was giving occasional English lessons to German businessmen during the day and, um, working at the newspaper plant at night.

"Oh, Springer," she said. "Terrible man. Right-winger. No good."

"Yes," I said, "I know."

"It's alright." She laughed. "I don't hold you responsible."

"Oh," I said. "Good."

She turned to Jochem.

"So this is the beautiful Käthe's beautiful son. Well, Jochem, he could be yours. He has your eyes."

Jochem smiled. "Keep your eyes on the road, Charlotte. You don't want this beautiful car in a ditch." He patted my leg. "Him we'll save for Ulla."

"Oh, he's much too good for Ulla."

"He works in a newspaper plant. How can he be too good for Ulla?"

"She just knows how to spend money."

"Well, she earns it."

"As a model!" Charlotte snorted.

"You mustn't mind us," Jochem said, turning to me. "We're just having fun."

The car pulled into a private road lined with trees. "Here we are," Charlotte said. After half a kilometer or so the road opened up into a large circular drive with a huge house above it on a clump of rock. "Ulla's not back yet," Charlotte said as the car crunched to a halt on the gravel. "Everybody out—and mind the dogs." We climbed the steps to the house. On the terrace two Great Danes leapt at us. I reeled back, terrified. "Down, down," shouted Charlotte, and then, over her shoulder, to me, "My husband's idea."

We entered the house, followed by the two enormous animals. "Make yourself at home," Charlotte said and flung open the doors to a gigantic living room. I thanked her and entered gingerly. She and Jochem went into the kitchen. The two dogs followed me in.

I looked around warily. If the dogs sat down I would sit down. They stood breathing heavily between me and the entrance.

"Help yourself to a drink," Charlotte's voice came from the kitchen.

I tiptoed over to the bar. The dogs followed me. I reached for a bottle. The dogs growled. I gave up. I stood behind the armchair and looked around the room for clues. There were none. The room was very well appointed but it was impossible to figure out who lived there. It was as if all human history had been obliterated.

I heard voices from the kitchen.

Charlotte's voice: "We should go out to the lake and have lobster, the four of us—he'd enjoy that."

Jochem's voice: "I'd just as soon stay in and have *Würstchen.*"

Charlotte's voice: "Whatever you think, darling, he's your son."

Würstchen, I thought. My God, I spent all day rustling up a suit, I've had no sleep, I spent a considerable amount of my night's wages getting out here, and we're going to have *Würstchen. Würstchen* I can have at the corner stand by the *Studentenheim.* What am I doing here, anyhow, in the house of the mistress of my mother's first husband, who's probably married to a Nazi anyhow, with two huge dogs pinning me behind the armchair, and Jochem and Charlotte arguing in another room, and all for *Würstchen.*

Suddenly the dogs turned away. Through the entrance I saw the front door open and a tall young woman enter. The dogs leapt up at her. "Down, down," she said, "Sit, *verdammt nochmal.*" And miracle of miracles, they sat.

"Hello," she said, coming towards me, "you must be Robin."

"You must be Ulla," I said, coming out from behind the chair.

"Have they left you all alone in here?"

I shrugged.

"Poor boy," she said. "Let me make you a drink." She poured some whiskey into a glass and added a dash of soda from an old-fashioned siphon. "Mutti," she cried out, "I'm here. Where are you? You've left the poor boy all alone in here."

"We're coming," Charlotte called back, "we're just deciding what to do about dinner."

Ulla sat down. I sat down. The dogs remained outside.

"Crazy, huh?" Ulla said. "But she's in love with him, I think. Funny, no, him coming to visit while my father's in Bremen. What do you think of him?"

"Well, I don't know. I've hardly had a chance to meet him, except briefly in the car."

"But I thought he was almost your father."

"Well, he was married to my mother. But that's long before I come on the scene."

"He's a nice man," she said. "I like him. He's sexy. And he has laughing eyes."

Charlotte and Jochem came into the room.

"Well," said Jochem, smiling, "Charlotte won. I wanted to stay home, be *gemütlich*, make some *Würstchen* in the kitchen. But she wouldn't hear of it. Ulla, you know the restaurant on the lake?" Ulla rolled her eyes heavenward.

"What's wrong?"

"It's so stiff," she said. "The waiters are like stormtroopers."

"Darling," said Charlotte.

"It's alright," said Jochem. "We'll have fun, the four of us. Ulla, don't make such a face." He went over to her and stroked her hair. "Such a beautiful young woman. You will have them all at your feet."

"Alright," said Charlotte. "Drink up. We're going."

"I'm not going in your car," said Ulla.

"Alright, darling, you take Robin in yours—and see they give us the table by the window."

Jochem went into the kitchen to take a pill.

Charlotte went upstairs.

Ulla reached in her bag. "Stormtroopers," she muttered. "Here," she threw me the keys, "you drive."

I started to protest.

"No," she said, "I've been shooting all day. I just drove in from the studio. I've had it with driving."

We went to the door. The dogs growled. "Shut up," said Ulla. They growled, but stayed seated. "*Verdammte Hunde*," (Damned dogs), she said, opening the door.

Outside I was overcome with a mixture of emotions: relief at having left the house and the dogs behind and apprehension at having to escort this tall elegant headstrong young woman to dinner, let alone drive her car. Parked with its nose up against the rear bumper of the Bentley was a low, sleek, green open sports car.

"I'm sorry, we have this thing for English cars."

"That's alright."

We got in.

"Why do you park like this?" I asked.

She shrugged.

"Where's reverse?"

She leaned over, put her foot on the clutch and put the car in reverse.

"Thanks," I said.

I reversed, put the car in first, and roared off down the drive.

"Right at the bottom."

On the road I said, "How do you drive this thing? Everything's on the wrong side for you."

She looked at me as though I were a moron. "You just drive."

The restaurant was idyllically set jutting out over a lake, entirely surrounded by forest, the only building in sight. When we entered, the middle-aged man at the door came to greet us. Taking Ulla's hand in his, he clicked his heels discreetly and inclined his head. "Fräulein von Langenstein, how wonderful to see you, what an honor, allow me to show you to a table, how many will you be?"

Ulla swept past him and held up four fingers.

"Ah, yes, of course, *gnädiges Fräulein*, your parents are joining you."

"No," she turned on him, "my mother is coming with her lover. Now stop this groveling and get us the table by the window."

"But of course, *gnädiges Fräulein*. Of course."

And he issued a stream of orders to waiters and other flunkeys. "If you would be so kind, to have a seat at the bar, we will have the table ready at once."

Ulla led the way to the bar and ordered Campari for both of us. The manager sailed over to the window table and made some explanations to the elderly couple sitting there. After some expostulations and a glare at us, they rose and followed the remainder of their meal to a less desirable location.

Charlotte and Jochem came in. More bowing and clicking and in an instant the four of us were seated by the window, looking out over the lake, the water sparkling in the light from the restaurant, candles and glassware glittering before us and starched white linen at our elbow.

Jochem put his arm around me, leaned over, and whispered in my ear: "I just threw up. Now we'll have a wonderful time." And then, aloud to all of us: "I'm sorry. I was still recovering from the plane. Now I'm much better. *Herr Ober!*"

The waiter sprang to his side.

"Champagne."

The manager himself brought over the champagne and poured it.

"Tonight," said Jochem, "I am sitting with two of the most beautiful women in Europe. I drink to you." He raised his glass. "Robin, tell me. Are they not both beautiful?"

"Yes," I said.

"You see," he said, beaming, "I am not alone." And he clinked glasses with me and we drank to two of the most beautiful women in Europe.

"Beautiful women," he said. "They have been my downfall. All my life. The source of all my happiness and the source of all my misfortune. This boy," and he indicated me, "is the son of a great beauty to whom many years ago—before time began—I was married. She is still beautiful. She is a wonderful woman. And she has two wonderful children. We drink to her children."

So we clinked glasses and we drank to me and Barbie.

"Now, Ulla, I was in love with your mother. You are not as beautiful as she, of course, but that will come. A brave woman, a courageous woman, a woman who did things that you should never have to know about. And she too has produced a daughter, a fine young woman with fire and spirit, like her mother. And we are all here together round this table, so many years later, after so many things have happened, and we are still alive. We drink to life."

"Come on, Jochem, let's order," said Charlotte. And she motioned the waiter over.

As dinner progressed, I told them about my adventures, about Oxford and hitchhiking through Europe, and my uncle and aunt in Amsterdam, and Berlin, and the sense of history that hung over all my steps in Germany, and my stay in Hamburg and how I felt that perhaps there was a new generation in Germany that was trying to come to terms with the past and that I was touched by that.

After the main course, Jochem turned to me and said, "Come, we call London." The manager directed us to a quiet wooden booth and made the connection from the main telephone. Presently the phone rang in the booth. Jochem picked it up. "The call is going through," he said, and then, "Käthe. Here is Jochem. I am sitting with your son by the lake in

Othmarschen. We have just had dinner. He is a wonderful boy. I love him already like my own son." He laughed. "No, he is not too thin. Käthe, you should be proud. Here, I give him to you." He put his arm around me and handed me the phone. My mother wanted to know if I was eating enough— well, if I ate like this every day it would be fine, I said—and why I was working in a factory and when I was coming home. Then she put my father on. He wanted to know if I was alright with money, how his brother was in Amsterdam, and why I didn't write. He then handed me back to my mother, and I handed her back to Jochem. "We are having dinner with Charlotte and her daughter Ulla. *Bildhübsch*. She and Robin make a wonderful couple. I'll see what I can do. *Mach's gut.*"

"Wasn't that nice to do?" he said.

"Yes," I said, "thank you."

When we got back to the table, Ulla had had enough. She fished her car keys out of the lump in my pocket and shook my hand. "Good night," she said. "Learn to drive." Then she turned on her heel and flew out.

Charlotte and Jochem drove me back to Hamburg in the Bentley. This, I thought, I want them all to see—the Hungarian, Herr Hahn, the *Wirtin*, Rosemarie. But there was no one up when we arrived, except the night porter, and he was asleep at the desk. In the car, Charlotte invited me to visit any time I wanted: she would welcome the diversion and even Ulla might be persuaded to join us. I said I would ring.

Jochem got out of the car and took me to the door of the *Studentenheim*. At the door he embraced me. "I am so happy that I called you. And I am so happy that you came. Charlotte means what she says. Any time."

"Thank you," I said, "and please thank Charlotte."

"I will see you again," he said. "Somewhere. Sometime." And he leaned over and kissed me on the cheek. As he turned away, I saw there were tears in his eyes. At the car he stopped and waved. Then he got in. Charlotte honked the horn and they disappeared.

"My goodness, what are you all dressed up for?" said the porter, as I fumbled in the pocket for the key.

"I just arrived in a Bentley, didn't you see?" I said.

"Oh, come off it," he said, rubbing his eyes. "A Bentley. You must be dreaming."

And he locked the door behind me.

In the Shadow of History

I never returned to Othmarschen, not because I wasn't invited, but because the following week I received a telegram from my father telling me that Aunt Bertel had had a stroke and instructing me to finish up in Hamburg and take a train to Amsterdam.

I was almost relieved. There was by now no compelling reason for me to stay on, but equally, with no itinerary, and with the November cold approaching, no compelling reason to leave. The news from Holland made the decision for me.

I gave notice to the *Wirtin,* finished out the week at Springer, packed my rucksack, and, in the company of Herr Hahn and Rosemarie, took a bus to the *Hauptbahnhof.*

"Come back and visit us," said Herr Hahn, "come and visit my parents in Berlin."

"I will," I said, "soon."

They walked me along the platform, found me an empty compartment, and saw me safely inside. I put my rucksack on the luggage rack and pulled down the window.

"Thank you," I said.

"Nothing to thank."

"Thank you for bringing me down here. Thank you for everything."

Herr Hahn's broad shoulders gave the tiniest of shrugs. Rosemarie looked up at me through her butterfly glasses. "We shall miss you," she said.

The train began to lurch forward.

"Good-bye," I said. And then as the train began to pick up speed, "Don't read too much A. J. Cronin."

But the words were lost in the roar of the wheels, and the figures on the platform were obliterated by smoke from the engine. When they reappeared they had grown small in the distance, two shrinking figures waving white handkerchiefs. I fished in my pocket for my own but with alarming suddenness we entered a tunnel and Hamburg was left behind me. I closed the window and sat down.

I sat for a long time alone in the compartment. These strangers, these people who had taken me to the train, had become friends. Would I see them again? I didn't know. Would I send them a postcard from Amsterdam? Perhaps. Were they really friends? Who could tell? And what was it about Germany that raised such questions?

I thought about my aunt. She had had, over the nineteen years since the war ended, a series of mild strokes, a result of the camps. But each time the slight paralysis had left her, the slight impediment of speech had disappeared. This time, obviously, it must be different. Was she at home? Would I even see her? What good could I possibly do in Amsterdam? Why wasn't my father going over?

The door to the compartment slid open and a uniformed official of the Deutsche Bundesbahn stood in the doorway. "*Fahrkarte, bitte.*"

As I reached for my ticket I realized I was still holding in my hand the handkerchief I had been unable to wave.

"*Machen Sie es ein bischen schneller, ja*" (Move a little faster, will you)?

I produced the ticket.

"*Ach, Sie fahren bis Amsterdam.*" He clipped the ticket. "*Sie müssen in Utrecht umsteigen.*"

I nodded.

"*Gute Reise,*" he said and the door slid shut behind him.

At the border I produced my passpoort, in Utrecht I changed trains, and in the early evening I arrived at the Centraal Station in Amsterdam. I rang my uncle.

"Georg, I'm here."

"You know how to come by tram? Take the 27 to Minervaplein."

"How is Bertel?"

"We will talk when you get here. Are you alright?"

"Of course I'm alright, how are you?"

"*Nun, mach es schnell, ja?*"

"*Ja,*" I said and hung up the phone.

At Minervaplein I bought flowers, as I always did, from the flower stall by the tram stop.

"*Deutsch?*" enquired the old lady.

"No," I shook my head, "English."

She smiled. "For a girl?" she asked in English.

"No," I smiled, "for my aunt—I mean, my uncle."

"You're a good boy," she put an extra flower in the bunch.

I thanked her, paid, and walked through the deserted square with my rucksack and my bunch of chrysanthemums. When I turned into Michelangelostraat, it seemed quiet, dark, and peaceful. Cars were parked neatly on a diagonal. Nothing stirred. Under a streetlight I noticed my uncle's Lancia.

At No. 61 I climbed the stairs to the second floor and rang the bell. "*Ach, mein Junge,*" said my uncle as he opened the door.

"Georg," I said and handed him the flowers.

He seemed startled, and then he took them and shook his head sadly. "*Nein, nein, nein,*" he said softly. Then he touched his cheek to mine, put his arm around my shoulder, and guided me inside. "Bertel is not here," he said as he closed the door. "Come, you are in the study, and then we find some water for the flowers."

I put my rucksack down in the study.

"You are exhausted from the journey?"

"No, no, really, I'm fine. I just need to wash."

"Ach, yes, of course," he opened the door to the bathroom. "That towel is mine. But you can use the other one." He touched it absently. "It is quite clean."

The immaculate apartment was still immaculate but life seemed to have gone out of it. The quiet was palpable. I walked on tiptoe. In the kitchen the flowers stood in a vase on the sideboard.

"Here." My uncle had made me a sandwich and a pot of tea. "Eat, *Junge.*"

"And you?"

"No, I have no appetite."

"At least have some tea."

So he brought another cup and we sat down at the kitchen table and I ate my sandwich.

"It's not good. This time it's not good."

"Where is she?"

"She's in the hospital in Hilversum. I will go out again tomorrow. You can come with me, but you don't have to. Only if you want."

"Of course, I want."

"It's not pleasant."

"I can imagine."

He shook his head and lapsed into silence.

I drank my tea from the beautiful white cup and replaced it quietly on the saucer.

"*Komm,*" he said at last, "we go in the other room and you tell me about your trip."

We walked through the dining room into the living room, the elegant gray living room where a few months before Gerry and I had outlined our hitchhiking plans.

"You came on the train now, yes?"

"Yes, yes," I laughed, "I came on the train."

"Now, after the dinner," he smiled apologetically, "you will have a drink?"

"Well, if you have a cognac . . ."

"Yes, yes I have a cognac," and he went over to the liquor cabinet. "And I will have a whiskey."

He poured our drinks.

"Whiskey," he said, "I find it wonderful. A wonderful drink. *L'chaim.*"

"*L'chaim.*"

We raised our glasses.

"*L'chaim,*" Georg repeated and he drained his glass. "To life," he said in English. "Ah, that tastes good." And then he questioned me about my trip, particularly about Germany and how I found the Germans, and about my plans.

I told him I had intended to go on to Cologne, where I had acquaintances.

"So, we cut you short."

"Don't be silly."

"And to Köln you will go also by train?"

"Yes, I suppose so. My hitchhiking days seem to be over."

"Well," he sighed, and it was a sigh both of sadness and of relief. "Tomorrow in the morning we ring London and then if you want you drive with me to Hilversum. Now you have a nightcap and you go to sleep."

"And you?"

"I have a nightcap too." And he poured us each another drink.

"*L'chaim,*" I said.

He looked at me and nodded slowly. "*L'chaim,*" he repeated and then he shook his head. "*Nein, nein, nein.*"

The next morning in the rain we drove the flat black glistening road to Hilversum. My uncle was silent. I didn't interrupt him.

After an hour or so he said suddenly, "We are here," and we turned off the road through an impressive entranceway onto a cobblestone driveway and pulled up in the courtyard before an imposing building. "I will go up. If she will see you, I will come down again."

"Alright."

"You do not mind to stay in the car? I'm sorry."

"I understand."

In the back seat under a blanket was a suitcase.

"I bring something every day," he said.

I opened the door for him, he took the suitcase, nodded at me, and walked across the cobblestones up the stone stairs to the front door. At the door he rang the bell and wiped his shoes on the mat. The door opened. I could just make out the white headdress of a nursing sister. My uncle removed his hat, inclined his head towards the sister, and went inside. The door closed behind them.

The rain had abated a little. I needed to stretch my legs. I left the car and walked aimlessly across the courtyard. The light drizzle felt good against my face. My body was tired from the train and I realized I was shaking. I leant against the balustrade and felt the hard wet stone under my hand. Everything was silent, everything was orderly: the gray slate roof of the old building and the two new wings stretching symmetrically into the distance, the dull red chimneys, the perfect rectangular windows with the tidy white curtains and the dull shining glass reflecting the dull gray day, the silent cars sitting in perfect formation around the perimeter of the courtyard, the implacable squares of the cobblestones with their gentle coving and the tiny rivulets running between them, and the dark earth of the flower beds with their careful borders, but no flowers. No flowers. Damn, I hadn't brought flowers.

There was a hand on my shoulder and my uncle's voice said, "*Komm' ma', Kind, wir gehen rauf*" (Come, my child, we're going up).

We walked through the long silent hallway. Silent nurses in starched gowns appeared and disappeared wheeling trolleys and wheelchairs and stretchers. No sound but the occasional rustle of skirts, the well-bred squeal of rubber on tile, and our own footfall. At the end of a corridor we paused before a door. My uncle squeezed my arm and then reached for the handle and opened the door.

"*Guck ma', Liebchen, heute gibt es eine ganz grosse Überraschung*" (Look, darling, today we have a really big surprise).

The room was entirely white. White curtains, white walls, white sink, white table, white screen, and behind the white screen a huge white bed with white sheets, white blankets, white pillows and on the white pillows a white face with black hair.

"*Liebchen, der Robin ist hier.*"

I leaned over the bed towards her face. She strained to speak but no words came out. Half her face was frozen, saliva trickled from the corner of her mouth. Suddenly she turned her face away. I leaned down to kiss her. Her face was wet with tears. Her hand came up and held my head to her. She wound her bony fingers in my hair and wept.

"*Es ist doch schön dass der Kleine gekommen ist*" (Isn't it nice that the little one came to see us?), said my uncle. And she sobbed and sobbed.

When I disentangled myself, my uncle was massaging her feet through the bedclothes. "Tomorrow we start exercises, next week you come home, and next month we go to the country."

My aunt nodded.

"It is nice, no? The three of us here in your room and you having court—is that the right expression?" My uncle looked at me.

"Holding court."

"Holding court, of course. All the way from Hamburg—*ist doch schön, nein, Liebchen?*"

My aunt looked at me, her eyes shining. Then she tugged at the bedclothes and motioned towards the bedside table.

"What do you want, my darling?" said Georg.

On the table were two framed photographs, a hairbrush, and a box of jewelry.

"Oh, you want to look beautiful for your nephew," he picked up the hairbrush.

She looked at him and shook her head. Then she looked at me and rolled her eyes as much as to say, "He's crazy, that husband of mine."

He picked up the jewelry box and she nodded. He opened it and put it on the bed beside her hand. She fumbled inside and pulled out a single strand of pearls. Georg took it from her and put the box back on the table. Then he leaned down to fasten the pearls around her neck, but she shook her head vigorously.

"What is it, *Liebchen?*"

She looked at me and pointed at Georg, then she slowly raised her finger and tapped it twice against her temple.

"*Meshugge?*" said Georg.

She nodded and there was a half smile on her face.

Georg roared with laughter. "What, then?"

She looked at me again and tried to form a word.

Suddenly I realized what she was trying to say. "For Barbie?" I said and she nodded violently.

"*Ach, Süsse,*" said Georg.

She motioned him to surrender the pearls.

"It's alright," I said, "I trust him." And I bent down and kissed her.

She tousled my hair. Then she pointed to the window. We looked. Outside the sun was coming out.

My aunt lived for six more years. My uncle gave up his job to nurse her. A nursing sister, Sister Marie, an ample woman of good Dutch peasant stock, strong as an ox, moved in with them. The flat on Michelangelostraat grew colder, but the little country house in Ruurlo which they had just bought together with a friend began to blossom. My uncle and Sister

Marie and their friend Mart, who had known them during the war, before they went into hiding, before they were betrayed, worked on the little property around the house, turning the earth, making the grass and flowers grow, fetching milk and eggs from the farmer down the road. And my aunt would sit in her wheelchair with a blanket over her knees and gaze out of the window at the garden and point at a bird or a flower or a bee with bright shining eyes. And my uncle would laugh and joke with her and wheel her round to face the dying light. And at five after a day of clomping around in clogs in the mud of the garden he would bring out a bottle and a little bowl of nuts and they would sit and have a drink. "Ach," he would say, "whiskey. It's a wonderful drink." And he would raise a glass to his wife in the wheelchair. "Isn't this a wonderful life?" he would say. And she would nod, her eyes shining, and smiling her little half smile. "*L'chaim*," he would say and she would mouth the word with him, "*L'chaim*, Orgi, *l'chaim*."

When I left Amsterdam for Cologne my uncle looked in his liquor cabinet and found a half bottle of cognac. He also insisted that I take with me an old leather suitcase, a family heirloom. On it in black were embossed the letters M.H. "It belonged to my father, your father's father. It survived two wars. It will serve you in good steed. Is that right?"

"Stead."

"*Ach, ja, natürlich*, stead."

My hitchhiking days were now indeed over, for with this heavy old piece of equipment and my rucksack I could hardly stand in the road and expect to be picked up. The essence of this kind of travel is to be light on one's feet and my uncle had seen to it that I was now weighed down. I suspected that it was not entirely without premeditation.

In Cologne I was going to see a man I had met in London a couple of years before. It was one of those chance encounters that can change the direction of your life.

I had, for each of his last three performances at the Aldwych, tried to get in to see Paul Scofield as Lear. Each day I had turned up earlier in the hope of acquiring a returned ticket. On the final day I arrived at ten in the morning. There were already a dozen people forming a queue. The man directly ahead of me, and thus my conversation partner for the bulk of the day, was a young professor of English from West Germany, Tilman Westphalen. I had had all of a year at Oxford and was of course by this time quite virulently anti-academic. An entire year studying Milton! Not one, but two, dead languages—Latin and Anglo-Saxon! Anglo-Saxon grammar, which had been painstakingly constructed by a nineteenth-century philologist since the Anglo-Saxons themselves had omitted to develop one—could there be anything more absurd? So from ten in the morning till 7:30 at night we had a lively conversation about the nature of English and pedagogy and the study of Milton and, of course, Shakespeare. The Germans, it soon became apparent, made the English look like dilettantes and my nineteen-year-old fervor must have struck Dr. Westphalen with all the charm of a bomb-thrower.

Just before 7:30 he and the man ahead of him, a charming elderly teacher from Portsmouth, got a pair of seats in the stalls, and as the final performance of Peter Brook's revolutionary production began, I found myself, on my third successive day of trying, straining at a red velvet rope, the cutoff person. The queue began to disband. Suddenly an usher approached, waving one ticket in a box. I plonked down more money than I had ever spent on a theater ticket, raced up the stairs in my jeans and pullover, and, apologizing profusely, joined the glittering dignitaries in the Royal Box. For the two hours until the interval I looked down on Paul Scofield's towering performance from the delicate perch of a spindly gold-painted chair covered in petit point. I had a perfect view of the top of his head.

Every so often I would gaze out over the audience and recognize from the intensity of their concentration other devotees from the daylong queue. Down in the stalls, seventh row center, I saw Dr. Westphalen and the elderly teacher from Portsmouth. We acknowledged each other and at intermission they waved frantically at me to come down.

It turned out that the last train to Portsmouth left an hour before the final curtain and the poor teacher, having come up at the crack of dawn, would have to leave now, halfway through, before the mad scene on the heath, before Cordelia's return, before the great redemption, before the final agonizing deaths. "But it was worth it," he said, his eyes glowing with a kindly fire. "Now you come down from up there and sit with our German friend and look at this performance from the front, where it's meant to be seen from, you understand me?"

It was as a direct result of his intervention—and of the unfortunate timetable between London and Portsmouth—that I now found myself, two and a half years later, heading for Cologne. Til and I had continued our discussion after the play was over, we had continued to correspond while I was at Oxford, he had even stayed with my parents on occasional trips to London. And when I started out on my travels he had invited me to stay with him if my itinerary should take me via Cologne. I had no itinerary, I wrote from Hamburg, but after a brief stay in Amsterdam I would like very much to pop in.

I spent the weekend with Tilman and his wife Hildegarde and their son Gernot, good German names all. They drove me round the city in their little red Volkswagen, taught me to say Köln instead of Cologne, showed me the cathedral and the tremendous devastation wreaked by the bombing. On Saturday night after Gernot had gone to bed we polished off my half bottle of Martell and discussed Germany, England, literature, the war, his dissertation (six hundred pages on the first eight lines of *Beowulf*), my career. Til was involved in setting up the English department at the new University of the Ruhr in Bochum. On Sunday morning he asked if I would be interested in teaching there.

"Could I begin this week?"

He laughed. "The university is not yet built. You couldn't possibly begin in Bochum until next September. But I could perhaps in the spring offer you a job with us in Münster. We are assembling the departmental library and you could advise us, maybe, on twentieth-century acquisitions. I wouldn't want to assign you to Milton."

If I could have started immediately I would have had no question, but to have to think about it for several months, to have to actually address the question of whether to choose to take up residence in Germany, that was another matter entirely. And what about my heavy leather suitcase? Was I going to schlepp that around with me until the spring? "I'll have to think about it," I said.

At the *Hauptbahnhof*, where they dropped me off at midnight, I bought a liter of Asbach-Uralt, carefully decanted most of it into my empty Martell bottle, kept myself warm with much of the rest, and took the only train going anywhere at three in the morning.

"So, you finally decided to come home," said my father. "May I enquire why?"

"Well, it was getting cold. And Georg gave me this suitcase. And besides it's my birthday."

My mother of course was overjoyed. I gave them each the prescribed number of duty-free cigarettes, tipped for my mother, untipped for my father. I handed over my half bottle of Martell. My father examined it carefully. "The seal has been broken," he said.

"Georg gave it to me. I drank it with Til. I refilled it with Asbach-Uralt."

"Asbach-Uralt is not cognac."

"I know. It's the German version."

"How many times have I told you to bring cognac."

"I'm sorry."

It was my twenty-second birthday. Thanks to St. Paul's and Oxford and my recent travels I hadn't lived at home since I was sixteen. The prospect of moving in with my parents now was unsettling. And the questions hovering in the air didn't help.

"Where do you propose to live?"

I didn't know.

"How do you propose to pay for it?"

I hadn't the faintest idea.

"And what do you propose to do with your life?"

The first two were easy.

A friend from Oxford had taken a flat in Linden Gardens, off Notting Hill Gate, and was looking for someone to share it. With some trepidation I volunteered. It was my first independent venture in London, my first thoroughly independent living arrangement, not connected with school or university or the temporary independence of the road. And to pay for it I would need a job.

My sister's boyfriend, with whom she had been involved since the age of twelve, whom she knew from the Phoenix, and whom she later married, had worked the previous summer for friends of his mother, who owned a butcher's shop-cum-delicatessen on West End Lane. They were a family of Czech Jews, two brothers and their wives, the other side of the tracks, of course, as far as my parents were concerned. They were going into their busiest season—Christmas. They needed an assistant. I applied and, to my relief, I was accepted.

As a result I spent three of the happiest months of my life, driving a van round London delivering meat, working in the basement with Martin, the single full-time employee, a Czech too but not a Jew, stuffing sausage skins and breaking the legs of turkeys. This grisly business, to which I quickly became inured, we accomplished over suspended meathooks, one holding the feet, the other wrenching the body so the broken shins would separate from the meaty thighs and take the tendons with them. It took the two of us. We worked hard. Our turkeys were much in demand. Christmas was getting closer.

At the Sporting Club of Knightsbridge, to which I delivered the largest order, the finest meats, the manager, a small balding Hungarian in a suit and glasses, took a liking to me, and, perhaps because my bosses, the Kesslers, were generous patrons of the establishment, donating a considerable portion of their profits to one of the premier gambling clubs of

London, invited me to the Sporting Club's Members Only Sunday Night Buffet.

Since I was making nine pounds a week delivering meat part-time and since a Notting Hill Gate address—or half of it—cost a fair amount to keep up, the Sunday night buffet became the highlight of my week. I would put on my suit and bicycle down, having generally not eaten for the entire weekend. At the door elegant women in furs and men in evening dress would alight from large limousines and be ushered inside by an obsequious flunkey. I would slip in, sometimes with a girl, and the manager himself would take us to a table with a bottle of champagne in a bucket, an extraordinary moment for a delivery boy on a date.

On endless tables piled to the chandeliers would be astonishing works of culinary art, sculpted by a brilliant French chef they had lured from the Savoy. I would try to look nonchalant.

On the red velvet banquettes, braying and chomping, would be the regular Sunday night crowd of spendthrifts and toadies and well-heeled freeloaders. "I stood among them, but not of them," I would mumble with Byron. But with enough champagne I would blend right in.

One old lady who regularly confided in me and who dwindled away her inheritance at the rate of two to three hundred pounds a week would tell me how the place was changing: "Why, just last Wednesday, you should have been here, a Greek—imagine, a Greek—lost forty thousand pounds on a single throw of the dice. What is the world coming to?" And she would look at me and wait for an answer, her fork delicately poised in midair with some of the Kesslers' most exquisite filet on the way to her mouth.

But after three months of delivering meat and breaking turkey legs and consuming more than my fill on Sunday nights, my father's third question could no longer be put off. I wrote to Herr Professor Dr. Ulrich Suerbaum, head of the prospective Department of Anglistik at the prospective Ruhr-Universität Bochum, now temporarily housed in an apartment in Friedensgasse, Münster, in the province of NordRhein-Westphalen, and accepted his formal offer of a job as *Lektor*. I gave two weeks notice to the Kesslers. They understood and said it was the best thing for me. Down in the basement Martin shook my hand and wished me well. "But why Germany?" he asked.

As I had tried to explain to Jochem by the lake in Othmarschen, to my uncle in the cool gray living room on Michelangelostraat in Amsterdam, and to my parents after my return to London, my experiences in Germany had suggested that there was a younger generation trying to come to terms with the same overpowering history that shadowed me. Certainly the perspective was different. But it was the same shadow.

I had a more personal reason. Having been born at the tail end of the war, our first memories being tied to the Blitz, our parents' lives having been ravaged by the Nazis, my sister and I had grown up with an instinctive hatred of everything German. I don't think it was ever consciously instilled in us, it was something we absorbed with the air we breathed. Later, for example, at school, when it would have been possible to take German as a foreign language and we would have had something of a head start on our classmates, we both took French instead—when you have developed an instinctive hatred for everything German it is difficult to make a logical exception for the language. We hated the sound of it, its gutturalness, its harshness, its sense of order and suppressed rage. For me, as a child, I couldn't separate all the strands: I didn't know how much of what I feared was the bombing, how much was the language, how much was my father. I didn't know where Germany left off and England began. I didn't know whether to be a Jew meant to be persecuted. And to be a German Jew? That was the most unfathomable thing of all.

So part of my reason for going to Germany—though I could never explain this to Martin, let alone to my parents—was to dip a toe, at least, in the source. If there was indeed a new generation in Germany trying to come to terms with its past, did it not behoove me too to try to come to terms with mine? I didn't really expect any answers. Indeed, when I stepped off the train in Münster, my hair cut short at my father's insistence, I had barely begun to articulate the questions.

I was greeted by two *Wissenschaftliche Assistenten*—graduate students working in the department—Herr Lenz and Herr Anders. They were extremely polite, addressed me in excellent English—more fluent, more idiomatic, less accented than my parents'—and carried my luggage to Herr Anders's VW. They drove me through Münster, a city far less devastated by the war than Köln, retaining in its narrow streets and ancient buildings a great deal of its medieval character. The department had found me a room in a new building on the outskirts of town, where a cousin of Herr Lenz also rented a room. Herr Lenz introduced me to the landlady, a stolid, dour woman, who directed us upstairs and unlocked the door to a clean, simply furnished room. She gave me a key, told me there were to be no female visitors, and said she would come round to clean in the morning.

Herr Lenz and Herr Anders helped me unload my luggage and then drove me to the department. The flat on Friedensgasse was filled with books, shelf upon shelf, all neatly labeled according to period, genre, and author. On the desks were catalogues from booksellers all over Europe and the United States. The complicated process of choosing, ordering, receiving, cataloguing, and labeling was being masterminded by my erstwhile theater companion, Tilman, who greeted me warmly and introduced me to the other members of the department: Fräulein Sander, Fräulein Schaeffer, Herr Hess, Herr Rabeneck, Herr Brandenburg, Herr Toth, Herr Waldraff, all *Wissenschaftliche Assistenten*; Herr Ruppert, a quiet mouselike man, who would become the department's librarian once we moved to Bochum, and Herr Hamblock, who like me, held the rank of *Lektor*. Herr Professor Dr. Suerbaum was away and I would not meet him until the following week.

When we were alone I asked Til whether the formality was mandatory. "You're a bloody Englishman," he said, "you can do what you like. For us it's a bit more complicated."

Herr Anders had appointed himself my chauffeur. He was a tall, aristocratic-looking young man, about my age. He drove a much more impressive VW than Til, off-white, with a sunroof, a radio, and padded arm rests. It was his fiancée's, he told me. She was studying in Münster, but she was away on a field trip. I would perhaps meet her on the weekend. The department was very excited to have me. They hadn't expected me to be so, er, young.

He dropped me off at my lodgings and wanted to know if I would be able to find my way in the next morning. I assured him that I would, it would be a pleasant walk, and I thanked him for his concern and attention.

I climbed the cement stairs to the third floor and walked across the tiled landing to my room. Everything was new. It had that faintly acrid smell that I associated with fresh cement. This portion of the building couldn't be more than a year old. I wondered whether anything had stood there before. Had it been bombed? It seemed unlikely. The area was not well populated.

If there were other tenants I neither saw nor heard them. The landlady was certainly asleep by now. She evidently ran a tight ship. No one seemed disposed to laugh or talk or drink or make music. I unpacked and washed and went to bed. For a long time I lay awake, listening for sounds, for signs of life, thinking about the day, about the room, about what lay in store. Some of the most elementary things were a puzzle—what would I do for breakfast, for example? Some of the larger things I didn't want to think about. And how was I going to make this room my own? It didn't feel anything like home.

The next morning the sun shone in through the window, there was the sound of activity on the landing, and I arose with that feeling of emptiness in the stomach and excitement on the skin that is common to hunger and anticipation. I washed and just as I was beginning to dry myself there was a knock on the door.

"*Moment, bitte,*" I called out.

The door opened and the landlady stood in the doorway with a bucket and a mop.

"I'm sorry," I said, flustered, "*entschuldigen Sie,* I'm not ready." I pulled on my trousers.

She was a large presence in the doorway, her arms folded across her ample bosom, the mop stuck in the bucket at her feet. She did not move. I started to dry my hair with a towel.

"*Sie sind Engländer, nicht wahr?*" she said, more as a statement of fact than a question.

"*Ja,*" I said, "*aber bitte . . .*"

"*Sie sind mit der Universität beschäftigt?*" Again a statement rather than a question.

I nodded.

"*Der Uni.*" She spat. "The students are all immoral. I expect you think you can bring women up here. Well, young man, let me tell you, you've got another think coming. Cigarettes and music and parties and women." She spat again and took a step into the room. "*Wie kommt es eigentlich dass Sie so gut Deutsch sprechen, Engländer*" (How come you speak such good German)?

"I studied it at school."

"*Ach so.*"

"Now, please, I have to get dressed. I have to go." I reached for my shirt.

She took a step towards me. "You know, of course, that the English started the war."

"Come on. Surely you know that's not true."

"Thousands of bombs. Thousands of bombs."

"I know. There were bombs on both sides. Now, please, let me get dressed."

She took another step towards me. "How does it come that you have a German name, huh? Huh?"

"Well, my parents . . . ," I began.

"*Herr Hirsch,*" she sneered, "*Herr Hirsch . . . sind Sie vielleicht ein . . . Jude?*" And she spat the word in my face.

Trembling violently, blind, I grabbed my jacket and shoes and rushed past her to the door.

"*Jude, Jude,*" she started to scream.

On the landing I threw my shoes on the floor, jumped blindly into them and tore down the stairs.

"*Jude. Scheiss Jude.* Filth. Scum."

The mop sailed past my head and landed on the steps below me. I leapt over it.

"*Scheiss Engländer.* You murdered my husband."

The bucket with a tremendous roar clattered down the staircase spraying water.

"You Jews began it all. *Ihr Schweine. Ihr Schweine. Ihr Scheiss Juden.*"

Splattered with dirty water, tripping over my shoe laces, I banged open the door and ran wildly into the street. Her voice rang in my ears and I ran and ran to get away from the sound of it. Finally, panting, trembling, sobbing, under a bridge I came to rest.

At the department everyone was apologetic. Herr Lenz said his cousin had told him the landlady was not quite all there. Herr Anders offered to collect my things. Til said that for the moment, until I found another place, I could stay in the department—it was all set up for living, after all, if I didn't mind being surrounded by books. I asked him how this could have happened—they knew my background after all, hadn't they checked the place out?

He shrugged. "She's just one crazy old lady. You mustn't judge us all by her."

Herr Anders asked whether on the weekend, as a diversion, I would like to see an English film. Certainly, I said. Very well, on Saturday after work, we would drive in his car to Enschede where they showed English films with subtitles; in Münster, unfortunately, everything was dubbed.

On the road to Enschede I asked Herr Anders whether he had any objection to my calling him by his first name. None at all, he said. In fact, he was hoping that I would make that suggestion, because, being of senior rank, I had to initiate it.

"Wolfhardt," he said.

"Robin," I said.

Of course, in German it would be a little trickier, he said, because we would have to switch from *Sie* to *du*. I had no objection, I said. Well, he said, he might be a little uncomfortable with that, but he would see.

After some thirty or forty kilometers, he said, "Oh, by the way, you do have your passport with you, I hope?"

"What? You need a passport to see a film?"

"Enschede's in Holland. It's just across the border. In Germany all the foreign films get dubbed."

We turned round, drove back to Münster, collected my passport, and started out again.

"What masterpiece are we doing all this for?"

"Well, we won't get to see the whole film now. The border's seventy-four kilometers from Münster and we've lost more than an hour with your passport."

"Well, what is the film anyway?"

"*Sex and the Single Girl*, I hope it's not too risqué—it stars Tony Curtis."

"Tony Curtis," I said. "Well, then, I guess it'll be alright."

After a few more kilometers, Wolfhardt turned to me: "Herr Hirsch—I mean Robin—can I ask you something?"

"Yes."

"It's rather personal."

"That's alright."

"Well, er, is it true—you are Jewish?"

"Yes, of course, I thought you knew, I thought everybody knew—the um . . . ," and I gestured in the vague direction of my former lodgings.

"Well, we supposed, of course. But we didn't know."

"Well, yes, I'm Jewish. So?"

"It's terrible what we did to the Jews during the war."

"Mm-mm," I nodded.

"Of course, my father was in the Resistance."

"Of course."

"But that doesn't excuse anything."

"Mm-mm."

"I mean, one million dead."

"I beg your pardon."

"One million dead," he said, "it's terrible."

"Excuse me," I said, "the figure is six million."

"Impossible."

And in an off-white Volkswagen with a sunroof, on the road to Enschede, with a newly acquired first-name friend, on our way to see the last half of *Sex and the Single Girl*, staring Tony Curtis, I began to argue about the number of Jewish dead.

*   *   *

At the border we were stopped and I was taken away by the German police. Apparently the visa for East Berlin in my passport had aroused suspicion. They searched me, then they methodically searched the car. After half an hour they let us go. I apologized to Wolfhardt for having further delayed us and he forgave me handsomely.

By the time we had found the cinema and a place to park and persuaded the bewildered cashier to sell us a ticket at this late hour, we were just in time for the closing credits. When it was over and the audience surged out into the street it was eleven o'clock. There was a sense of spring and camaraderie in the air.

"Wolfhardt, have you ever had *Geldersche Wurst?*"

"No. It's some kind of Dutch sausage, I suppose."

"I can't be in Holland, if only for a few hours, and not have *Geldersche Wurst.*"

We surged with the crowd down one of the walking streets and into a square and found a place that served the sweet, pungent boiled sausage that my uncle used to bring over on his trips to England after the war. I bought a piece for each of us in greaseproof paper and we stood on the street and lapped it up.

"Isn't it wonderful?"

"Well, it's a bit messy."

So far our trip to Holland had not been a riotous success.

Wolfhardt decided to do something to redeem it. He stopped some likely-looking people on the street and asked them in German what there was to do on a Saturday night in Enschede.

They directed us to a club for cripples.

"Listen, Wolfhardt, perhaps I should ask in English."

"Very well, go ahead."

Three young people were sauntering down the street towards us and I stopped them.

"Excuse me, do you speak English?"

"Of course we speak English," said one of the two young men.

"We're looking for something to do on a Saturday night—what would you suggest?"

"Well, we just got kicked out of the White House—it's a bar—for not being dressed properly. The bartender is a friend of ours. So we're going home to change into the best clothes we can find and then we're going to go back and make him suffer. Why don't you join us?"

"Well, I don't know," said Wolfhardt.

"It sounds fine to me," I said.

"Well, it's settled then," said the young man, putting his arm in mine and leading us off down the street. They introduced themselves as we went—Lex and Marjanne Pauka were married to each other, and Guus was Lex's younger brother, who was here for the weekend from Amsterdam.

"I have an uncle in Amsterdam," I said.

"I don't know him," said Lex, laughing and disengaging his arm from mine.

Lex and Marjanne lived in one room in which they ate, slept, painted, and made love. From the tiny refrigerator they produced some ice-cold genever.

"Listen," said Lex, "I hope you understand. You have to take these two glasses and stand outside in the yard. Marjanne has to change into her long black dress. Guus can stay because he's family."

Outside in the yard, Wolfhardt turned to me. "What are you getting us into? We could be robbed."

"Don't worry. It'll be alright."

"Alright," said Lex, "you can come in now."

We went in.

The transformation was astounding. Marjanne was the most beautiful woman I had ever seen.

"What are you looking so funny for?" she said. "It's only a dress. Here, you want me to roll you a cigarette?" And with two flicks of her fingers and one flick of her tongue she produced an immaculately rolled cigarette.

"Thank you," I said.

"And you?"

"No, I don't think so," Wolfhardt shook his head.

When they were ready, after much drinking and laughter and smoking and banter, they led us back to the square and we clambered into Wolfhardt's fiancée's car and drove through a maze of streets. With a great honking of the horn we pulled up outside the White House. The entire population of the bar came out and cheered our arrival. Raising his pipe and acknowledging the roar of the crowd, Lex led us inside. Drinks were on the house.

Marjanne dragged me onto the dance floor. "Come on, English, let's see how you dance."

After two breathless numbers, I said, "Listen, Marjanne, I can't anymore."

"O.K. You go and talk to Lex."

At the bar Lex was smoking his pipe and talking to the bartender.

"Here. We have to teach you about genever." And he ordered two glasses from the bartender. "This is old genever. And this is young genever." I drank them both. "Now what about your friend?"

"Well, you better ask him."

"Tell me something."

"O.K."

"Are you Jewish?"

"What?"

"Are you Jewish?"

"Maybe," I said.

"Oh, *maybe*," he said, "you can do better than that."

"Well, what if I am?"

"Well, nothing, *maybe* I am too—or *maybe* I'm just a bit Jewish."

"Oh, I see," I said, "and your wife?"

"Well, *maybe* she's a sort of honorary Jew, O.K.?"

"I see," I said again.

"And what about your friend?" Lex asked, gesturing in the direction of Wolfhardt, who was now trying to waltz with Marjanne around the dance floor.

"Well, he's not exactly my friend," I began.

"It's alright, my friend," he put his arm round me, "I can figure out what's going on. You're among friends now, O.K.?"

The five of us spent the next twenty-four hours together. When the White House finally pried us loose we drove back to the little room on Haaksbergerstraat and talked through the night. In the morning, on the two electric rings, Marjanne made breakfast—eggs and bacon and fish and fried bread and tea. Then we all piled into the car and drove to Münster. We had lunch at the Rathskeller, we went boating on the lake, we ran around town ringing on doorbells and introducing our new friends to every member of the department. In the evening Elke, Wolf-hardt's fiancée, returned from her field trip and we gathered her up and roared back to Holland. Marjanne cooked dinner, Guus got on the train for Amsterdam, and somewhere around midnight Wolfhardt, Elke, and I clambered into the white VW, made our adieus, doffed our caps at the border, and chugged slowly back to Münster. In the morning Elke had a seminar and Wolfhardt and I had to resume the serious business of building a library.

That weekend set a pattern for the next eighteen months. Lex and Marjanne became my lifeline, my escape route, my closest friends. Virtu-ally every weekend I would slip over the border and take a respite from the stiff formality of the department or they would breeze into Münster and breathe some fresh air into the musty crevices of my life amongst the

Anglisten. Occasionally, on a break, we would go on a wild cavort to the beach or Amsterdam or even to Paris. Once, in Amsterdam, where Lex's mother lived, I introduced them to my uncle. I was a little apprehensive. But he was charmed by Lex and quite dazzled by Marjanne—"*Sie guckt so nett*," he said, a phrase I could never quite translate—"She has such a nice look," but that doesn't capture it.

Gradually Münster and the department broke down and the terror of that first morning receded. The impermeable facade presented by the department to the everyday world cracked a little at night—at cafés or *Kneipes*, in the dormitory rooms of single students, in the homes of married students or the faculty, at parties. And in the process I began to make friends.

Herr Hamblock, my colleague, who was married to an Englishwoman and who himself spoke virtually flawless English, approached me at a party one night. He took two beers, handed me one, pulled me outside onto the balcony, crooked his massive arm in mine, and said: "*Jetzt trinken wir Brüderschaft*" (Now we drink brotherhood). We drank. He said, "*Bruder*." I said, "*Bruder*." He said, "*du*." I said, "*du*." And from then on I called him Dieter.

The change from day to night, from last name to first name, from *Sie* to *du*, was sometimes subtle, sometimes dramatic. It was easier with women. Fräulein Schaeffer became Elsbet almost immediately, Fräulein Sander became Ursula, and both of them in their quiet studiousness reminded me of Rosemarie. With men it was like jumping off a cliff. There was never a right moment or a right way. And sometimes nobody jumped. Herr Ruppert never became anything but Herr Ruppert. Herr Brandenburg, however, became Wilhelm and, presto, from behind the sober-suited quotidian reserve, there emerged the anarchic humor and impeccable timing of a true vaudevillian. In the department, during the day, fueled by coffee, he would go quietly about his work. But at night, at a party, beer in hand, he would jump on a table and do a slow, raucous, and perfectly calibrated striptease, which consisted entirely of pulling off a sock.

Beer was the universal drink. It loosened tongues. It was the great liberator. The rigid hierarchical structure of everyday life receded after a few beers. Walls came down. People slipped more easily into the familiar. Intoxicated, the aspiration towards brotherhood seemed fulfillable. I remember one night walking back tipsy with Herwig Rabeneck to the flat that he and his wife rented from her parents in Dortmund, four o'clock in the morning, the sun just beginning to take the dark edge off the sky, Herwig with his perpetual cigar stuck in his cherubic face (the cigar he refused to remove even for the departmental soccer game) and crying out, "*Ach Gottchen,* Robin, *ich könnte die ganze Welt umarmen*"—"God, Robin, I could take the whole world in my arms." His heart was so full, his feet were dancing down the street. But in his voice was the tremulous joy of a tiny moment of free fall between the tangible past of freedom and young manhood and the intangible future of marriage and children and dark-wood paneling. As we unlocked the front door he turned and said, "Sh . . . we mustn't disturb the parents." And he put his head in his hands and led me silently up the stairs.

And so at night with beer, briefly, before the dawn of another day, the formality that held everything in check, the questions that hovered in the air, the pains, the sorrows, the unspoken weight of a terrible inheritance, were beaten back.

And of all the friends I made in Germany, no one beat them back more fiercely, or with greater élan, than Tilo Waldraff.

Tilo and his wife Ute had taken us boating that first weekend, and from the beginning they took me in and I became family. I became a kind of uncle to their four-year-old daughter, Oda—Lex and Marjanne became auxiliary parents—and Tilo, for the duration of my stay in Münster and even after the department moved to Bochum and I with it, became an older brother. We shared a kind of recklessness that sprouted at night and that was kindled almost immediately, a couple of days after he took us boating.

It was Marjanne's birthday. He suggested that we drive to Enschede and surprise her. We gathered armloads of orange gladioli, raced to Enschede in his dark blue VW, and promptly got lost. I couldn't remember the name of the street and Lex and Marjanne didn't have a phone. Eventually in desperation we drove to the police station and the police called round amongst their friends until they found someone who recognized the name. Then they insisted on coming with us, so, close to midnight, we pulled into the little courtyard with a full motorcycle escort and a back seat full of flowers. At dawn, with the sun rising to greet us, we drove back.

Tilo was always ready for a jaunt, a spree, a wild stab in the dark at the black canopy that obscured the stars. But he was also rooted in the soil of a Germany far broader and more variegated than the Germany I would have met in the ordinary course of my duties in the Englisches Seminar, a Germany to which he became my guide, a Germany of medical students and dance halls and beer gardens and horseback riding and cabarets and tall flaxen-haired aristocrats with double-barreled names and impenetrable southern dialects and dueling scars on their cheeks from their initiation into the fraternities at Heidelberg or Tübingen.

And yet, despite his roots, or perhaps because of them, there was something fundamentally incompatible about his relationship with the land of his fathers, something at odds, something out of place. His spirit was too unorthodox, too wild, too unconfined. Perhaps inevitably, not long after I left Germany, he moved with his growing family to Brazil where he became head of the Goethe Institut, bringing to that country of sunshine and music his own impetuous understanding of German culture and history.

Years later, when I was married and living in New York, he and Ute passed through on their way to Europe. The sun had turned Ute's hair completely blonde. Tilo was unchanged.

I saw him again, some years after that, also in New York. After a dozen years in Rio and São Paulo he had been posted back to Germany. It hadn't worked. He and Ute had split up. He was about to take up a new post as head of the Goethe Institut in India. His daughter, Oda, was now herself a mother. And Tilo, my wild cavorting brother who had carried the complicated message of his German forebears to South America and was now readying himself to bring it to a new continent, had become a grandfather.

One night Dieter and Heather Hamblock took me to a rally for Franz-Josef Strauss. Not that they were supporters of Strauss. On the contrary. Dieter was a Socialist and worked at a grassroots level for the SDP. Strauss was the leader of the CSU, the Bavarian party that had allied itself with Erhard's Christian Democrats and as a result held a critical balance of power. Dieter took me along to heckle.

Strauss was a large man with a beer drinker's belly and the common touch of a Bavarian peasant. He had been the subject of a serious scandal as Minister of Justice in the Erhard Government but had come bouncing back on the strength of his huge following in the south. There were thousands of us in a large stadium with guards posted at the perimeter. Dieter and Heather and I stood towards the back. Strauss spoke. His voice with its Bavarian accent took on a metallic quality as it crackled through the speakers. A man towards the front began to heckle and was silenced. Strauss said that Willy Brandt had deserted his country during the war and was a coward. Moreover he was a bastard—he didn't even know who his own father was. The man in the front protested and was silenced again. Strauss said that he himself had an impeccable military record and the man in the front started to shout. Strauss made a small motion from the platform and guards from the side moved in. Suddenly there were no more cries from the front. Strauss said that Socialism was bad for the people. Why, look at England, he said. Just the year before they had elected a Labour government and the price of butter had gone through the roof.

"That's not true," I said to Dieter and Heather.

"Say it, say it," said Dieter.

"*Das ist nicht wahr,*" I started to shout. "*Das ist nicht wahr.*"

People in front of me turned round. "*Ruhig.*"

"But it's a lie. I'm English. I know."

"You're a foreigner. Shut up."

That year Brandt again failed to win the election, the CDU-CSU coalition was again returned to power, Strauss with an overwhelming majority, and the disgraced former minister again took his place in the Cabinet.

At times like this the beast did not seem far from the surface. At Fasching the streets were awash with beer and a kind of thumping jollity seized the populace, and behind the masks and the makeup and the costumes I had the uneasy sense that a pogrom was in the offing.

And one night at a party, Wolfhardt, quite sober, taunted his fiancée, the quiet, studious, sweet-tempered Elke; he taunted her about the scar on her thigh, which he wanted us all to see; and then quite silently she raised her skirt and, covering her face, showed us the emaciated leg. Wolfhardt applauded.

Beyond the contrived excitement of public occasions and the intense reality of personal relationships lay the calm formality of everyday life in the department. My friend Tilman, apart from permissible excesses at times like Fasching and occasional gropings after some of the female *Wissenschaftliche Assistenten,* adopted the mantle of a kind of career diplomat, a sort of lady-in-waiting to the Herr Professor. I had no inkling of the leadership role he was to play in the student uprisings of the later '60's. But then, with a body of students dressed in shirts and ties and jackets and busy addressing each other as Herr or Fräulein So-wie-So, I hadn't the vaguest notion that there would ever be any kind of student activity, let alone uprising.

And the Herr Professor himself, the God of the department, in whose wake even the faculty touched its collective forelock? He was a tubby unassuming little man, young for a full professor and making quite a career for himself. He had been a young soldier at the end of the war and had acted as an interpreter for the allies. He had of course fought on the Eastern Front. Of course, of course. Hadn't everybody?

When the rigidity of everyday life grew too much, I would jump in my little Renault Gordini and drive to the border. Ruurlo, the tiny village where my uncle had his country cottage, was less than an hour's drive from Enschede, and every now and then I would trade the infectious exuberance of my friends for the slow measured tread of my uncle's clogs in the garden and the still, sad presence of my aunt, gazing out of the window from her wheelchair in her cardigan and blanket and brown-laced shoes. A couple of times I brought Lex and Marjanne to Ruurlo, but in the silence of the countryside their vitality and fervor seemed to grate on my uncle, and my uncle's reserve seemed to throw a pall over them. Or perhaps it was my imagination. Perhaps my uncle, in the autumn of his own life and the winter of his wife's, felt in our collective presence the stirring of spring and was silenced. And perhaps, in the fading glow of the embers at Ruurlo, we felt ourselves chastened and humbled and brought to a standstill.

At the beginning of the summer the department moved to Bochum in the heart of the Ruhrgebiet, the most heavily industrialized area of Europe, perhaps of the world. We took up residence on the top floor of one of the two huge concrete structures that had risen from the mud in the suburb of Querenburg. They were the first of a projected fourteen that were to be united by a concrete mall and would eventually make the Ruhr Universität one of the largest in Germany and a blueprint for the future of German higher education. Albert Speer's dream of heaven.

Over the summer we developed a curriculum and in the autumn we enrolled our first students. I, the least academic of all my contemporaries at Oxford, now found myself the object of considerable academic respect, conferred on me as a result of my title and the carefully nurtured obsequiousness of German students towards their superiors, no matter how young they might be.

And in November, when my birthday rolled around, I had a rapprochement of sorts with my old friend John Milton. For a seminar on literary analysis I took as the text for discussion Milton's sonnet on his twenty-third birthday, and across the centuries, in the presence of a dozen earnest but unwitting German Anglisten, the old blind poet and I commiserated with each other on the unhappy business of turning twenty-three. "How soon hath Time," we sighed together, "the suttle thief of youth / Stolne on his wing my three and twentith yeer!" Ah, I knew exactly what he meant. The old boy wasn't so bad after all.

I stuck it out till the end of the academic year, still making frequent forays into Holland. In the summer of 1966, Dieter Hamblock and I held a bilingual seminar on literary translation. We assigned as course work the stories of Hubert Fichte, a young German writer whose most persistent theme was the impact of the war on the children of Germany. With these lost souls, playing in bombed sites, laughing, taunting, fleeing, dreaming, creating a life in the rubble, I felt a kinship I couldn't articulate. They would be my age now, some of them dead, some of them drifting, some of them taking seminars on literary translation. Would they now, articulate, educated, thoughtful, determined, pause long enough to recognize in the adult that lost child from Dresden, from Köln, from Münster, from Berlin? And would they look up long enough to catch, if only for an instant, a reflection in their contemporary across the table, weighing with them now the nuances of their different languages, gazing at them across the gulf of this text, of *Sie* and *du*, of the terrible history that would eternally shadow and eternally divide them?

When all the translations were in, I spent a couple of weeks bringing them into some sort of stylistic coherence. Then I handed the manuscript to the departmental secretary, made my adieus, loaded up my faithful Renault with all my books and other possessions and drove furiously through Germany, through Holland, through Belgium, not stopping till I reached the ferry at Ostend.

In London, the High Holy Days were approaching. My parents had gone to Spain. They had left me their tickets to services at the Odeon Swiss Cottage in case I wanted to avail myself. My sister told me that Jochem was in London, but she didn't know where. He had asked after me.

On Yom Kippur, out of curiosity and the desire to renew old acquaintanceships, certainly not out of faith, I walked to the Odeon Swiss Cottage in the afternoon and presented my parents' tickets. Down on the stage before the huge panoramic screen, Kokotek, the rabbi, and Dollinger, the cantor, two tiny figures in white, were chanting. The long solemn day of prayer was coming to an end. I saw a lot of old faces and stood for an hour listening to the prayers and thinking about this congregation, a congregation of Jews from Germany, many now well established in London, many with children even younger than I, many of them friends I had known since childhood. The synagogue on Belsize Square which they had founded and built up was not large enough to accommodate everybody who became a Jew again for the High Holy Days. So here we were in this incongruous cinema at one of the busiest crossroads in northwest London, listening to a rabbi speaking English with a German accent and atoning collectively for our sins—we, who had survived.

After an hour, with my yarmulke still on my head, I walk out. As I'm crossing Finchley road, I see a familiar figure coming down Fitzjohn's Avenue towards the Odeon.

"Jochem," I cry above the traffic, "Jochem."

He is with another man, a friend of the family, Mr. Krotos. Krotos sees me and nudges Jochem. Jochem gives a start and the three of us make for each other across the six-way intersection. On the island in the middle, surrounded by the late afternoon traffic, we embrace.

"*Mein Sohn*," says Jochem, "how *are* you?" And then to Mr. Krotos, "Do you know Käthe's son, Robin?"

"Of course I do," says Mr. Krotos, "Good Yontif, Robin."

"Good Yontif, Mr. Krotos," I say.

"So, Robin, how has it been since I saw you in Hamburg?" says Jochem.

And I look at him and I think, "In Hamburg it was different. I was a young boy on an adventure. Since then a lot has happened." And I feel as though I have experienced a sea change and I will never be able to explain it. And I say, "A lot has happened, Jochem."

And he says, "Good, my boy. Now I must go in with my friend and say kaddish."

And Jochem and Mr. Krotos picked their way through the traffic towards the Odeon Swiss Cottage to contemplate the past and I made my way towards my parents' house to think about the future.

To the New World

The future, as usual, hinged on a chance encounter. I met an actress at a party. Out of work, of course. But a real actress. This was in itself thrilling. And compared to the girls from the Phoenix, essentially family, with whom any dalliance smacked of incest, or the young women at Oxford, intensely cerebral, for whom the idea of congress was more stimulating than the act, or the scarred and solemn graduate students I had just abandoned in Germany, it bordered on the exotic. Glennis had glorious blonde hair, the shortest skirt I had ever seen, the ability to radiate excitement and simulate an air of style, even elegance, with resources so limited as to border on the nonexistent. And then suddenly a job. For a year. In Sheffield. About as far away from London as it's possible to get without tumbling over the border into Scotland.

She was going to act on the main stage at night and help start a pilot project which would take theater into the community during the day. She had so impressed the director he had asked her if she could recommend anyone else and she had recommended all her friends.

"And what about me?"

"You're not an actor."

"Well, I've acted . . ."

Reluctantly she passed my name on and within a week, without an audition, I was a professional actor. Or, more precisely, a bee.

Traditionally the Sheffield Playhouse observed the Christmas season with a modern pantomime written by the playwright-in-residence. Currently this was Alan Cullen, responsible some seasons earlier for the enormously successful *Stirrings in Sheffield on a Saturday Night*, a musical about the union movement among the "grinders" in the Sheffield steel trade. His present offering, while inspired by Maeterlinck's *Life of a Bee*, was less lofty, its main purpose being to pack the Playhouse for six weeks during the holiday season. *John Willy and the Bee People* concerned the eponymous John Willy, a local lad, whose family washing machine, an almost unheard of luxury in Sheffield in the sixties, metamorphoses into a space ship and transports him to the land of the bees. I was hired to play a warbee, or, more precisely, the Second Warbee (out of a total of two), whose job was to leap onto the stage in concert with the First Warbee and to attend stiffly and in silence such principals as Queebee, Sweebee (the princess), and Humble (the faithful drone).

It didn't take the company long to discover that in me they had the perfect foil for that exquisite English actors' diversion known as corpsing. I had heard about this practice from an Old Boy of St. Paul's who had come back to visit the boarding house and talk about his career as an actor. He was in a long West End run of *The Masters*, an adaptation of one of the Snow novels about Oxbridge. The dons sat at a long table in their gowns having committee meetings for most of the play. In a long run, our distinguished Old Boy told us, even in the West End, boredom sets in, and certain actors, in order to keep awake, would drop down below the table and under the pretext of tying a shoe would in fact tie the long empty trailing sleeve of a rival's gown to a leg of the table or to the sleeve of another gown, so that when the time came for the Master in question to rise and make a dramatic exit, he would be helplessly trapped. This would of course lead to paroxysms of suppressed laughter, wild fury, and revenge.

If you stand at attention guarding a fake door for forty-five minutes dressed as a wasp, holding a stinger, and facing downstage, it takes considerably less ingenuity than the sophisticates in the West End had developed to make you crack up. Any principal could turn casually towards me in the middle of a speech, briefly unbutton and rebutton his fly before completing his turn, and leave me and my stinger trembling for what seemed like eternity. Even a wink would do it, or a roll of the eyes, or the insertion, unbeknownst to the audience, of a wildly inappropriate word or phrase or gesture. I was the perfect victim. And for this I was loved.

My popularity was further enhanced by the fact that of all the actors at the Sheffield Playhouse, mine was the most dramatic and precipitous fall from grace. I had been a scholar at Oxford, a lecturer at a German University, and here I was, after such heights, playing a bee. To seasoned actors, accustomed to an endless round of chilly bedsits and closing time at the pub, this was an incomprehensible, though laudable, descent. For me, of course, after the rigors of Oxford and the privation of Germany, it was heaven.

In the course of the year that followed my relationship with Glennis died on the altar of professionalism, but Theatre Vanguard, our pilot project for taking theater into the community, gathered momentum and I found myself acting, writing, and even directing for it. I played Goldberg in *The Birthday Party*, Young Mortimer in *Edward II*, and Cliff in *Look Back in Anger*.

And at night on the mainstage, after *John Willy* had run its course, my roles began to increase, in quantity if not in quality. Indeed, by the time we reached *As You Like It*, I was playing so many different small parts that I was terrified at every entrance of coming on as the wrong character. By the end of the play I was the missing middle brother who arrives to resolve all the play's loose ends in the famous "shilling" speech. Even so venerable an actor as Sir Lewis Casson, so tradition held, had started out his career stumbling over this speech. For the finale every last actor, technician, and assistant stage manager was thrust into costume to create the Duke's entourage in the Forest of Arden. The only two left offstage were the stage manager and me and between us we furiously turned the wind machine and rattled the thunder sheet and hallooed at the top of our lungs to indicate a crowd, and at the height of the frenzy I would be propelled onto the stage with the stage manager's hand giving me a final push and his voice yelling out the immortal line, "Here comes Robin Hirsch in another disguise." Emerging suddenly into the lights with the entire company ranged in front of me, kneeling before the Duke and attempting breathlessly to recite my speech, I found out how hard it was to earn a shilling. All twenty-two members of the company, including the Duke, Rosalind, Touchstone, Jacques, had their backs to the audience and nothing to do except try to corpse me.

This idyll was not to last. In 1967 the Fulbright-Hays Commission and the English-Speaking Union conspired to send me to America to undertake research.

To be truthful, it wasn't quite as simple as that. It wasn't as though Senator Fulbright himself sought me out in Sheffield and said, "You, come with me to a distant land." It was, as usual, the urging of my father, who had disapproved of my going to Germany in the first place, and who, now that I was back, disapproved of my return, that I had picked up the formidable application from the offices of the English-Speaking Union on South Audley Street and set in motion a process of which my mysterious benefactor in the U.S. Senate could hardly have been aware. There followed a year of intensive screening (every time a distinguished panel assembled on South Audley Street I would jump on a train in Sheffield and pray to get done in time to return for the evening show), of laborious essays on the Purpose of Life, of soliciting references from dons at Oxford, who, if they remembered me at all, required a decidedly imaginative leap to connect my name with any academic purpose whatsoever. Eventually my hefty dossier (ten copies of everything) was shipped over to the New World, where, replete with certification to the effect that I was free of syphilis, homosexuality, Communism ("for the purpose of this document the term 'Communism' is here understood to include fascism"), and the like, it was circulated discreetly amongst interested parties. It was like a computer dating service, only much slower. In June of 1967, a year after my first enquiry, I received an offer from a huge state university in the East to teach in the English department for eighteen hundred dollars a year and pursue a joint Ph.D in English and theater arts. In July, at the end of the season, I tearfully bade my fellow thespians adieu, and in August I found myself crammed inside the family car with an old steamer trunk my father had used in the twenties, a pair of wooden skis donated by friends of the family ("the skiing is wonderful in America"), assorted hand luggage, my father and mother quarreling in the front seat, my uncle (who had come over from Amsterdam for the occasion) sitting stoically in the back with me, on the road to Southampton, where the Fulbright Commission had booked me passage to New York in the belly of the Queen Elizabeth.

I had wanted to go down by train—which the Fulbright Commission would have paid for—but my parents, for different reasons, wouldn't hear of it. My father was glad that he had saved me from a life of drifting, in particular from the almost unspeakable embarrassment of being an actor. He was determined to see for himself the accommodations Herr Fulbright had arranged for his son. It was his achievement as much as, if not more than, mine, and they were his dreams that this huge liner—the biggest in the world—was taking with her across the ocean.

My mother, on the other hand, was sad to see me go—her only son, still not settling down, sailing off to some vast and terrifying country which had as many rats as people and where the people carried guns and sometimes bombs and where the cities exploded in violence and the countryside stretched out in desolation. She would have stowed away in the hold if she could. Certainly she wouldn't wave good-bye at the station when she could prolong the agony and wave good-bye at the quay.

"When are you coming back?"

"Oh, I don't know, Mummy, a year, maybe two."

"*Ach, nein*, so long?"

"Well, these things take time, you know."

"*Ruhig!*" my father shouted, clutching the steering wheel, as an impatient lorry swung out behind us and started to overtake. My uncle, next to me, stared wanly out of the window, contemplating the drizzle and the rich green countryside with the weary tranquillity of a Buddhist monk.

At the dock, in a huge hangar, passengers congregated by the letter of their last name and luggage not needed on the voyage, dutifully affixed in my case with a blue H, was whisked away. I tried to persuade my parents to make their adieus now. My uncle seconded the motion.

"*Ach, nein,*" said my mother.

"*Ausgeschlossen*" (Out of the question)! said my father.

So all four of us trooped up the gangway onto the boat.

"Herr Fulbright sends you tourist class. It's impossible."

"Daddy, I'm sure it's alright."

"I'm going to see the purser."

"Daddy, please don't make a fuss."

"*Ach Gott, nein,*" said my mother.

"My son is a Fulbright scholar and here it says tourist class. There must be some mistake."

"Let me see the young man's ticket. No. Everything appears to be in order. Four decks down. You'd best take the lift."

Four decks down a steward accompanied us to the designated cabin. Three young men were already ensconced on bunks. "Hello," one of them said cheerfully, "Are you another Fulbrighter?"

"Yes."

"Your parents brought you, did they?" asked a second, gesturing through the open door to my family mustered outside. I nodded glumly. My father stepped into the tiny room.

"Welcome aboard, sir."

My father stared at the young man, trying to determine whether he was being insolent.

"Not exactly luxury quarters, is it, sir?"

My father glared at him. Then he turned to me. "So, Robin, which bunk will you take?"

"Well, three of them are already taken, there's only this one left."

"But you should have an upstairs bunk."

"I should. Why?"

"So you are not disturbed at night."

"But they are taken."

"So, ask them to move."

"No."

"Ask them to move, I said," my father was starting to shout.

"No, I won't," I said, gritting my teeth.

"*Verdammt noch mal, ich sag' es nur noch einmal*" (Damn it, I'll say it only one more time).

"*Ach, Herbert, es ist nicht alles so wichtig,*" my uncle had come into the cabin, "*lass den Jungen allein*" (Oh, Herbert, it's not all so important. Leave the boy alone).

"*Ich hab' diesen Fulbright gewonnen. Ich will ein* upstairs bunk" (I won this Fulbright. I want an . . .).

"*Ach Gott,* Herbert," my mother was now in the cabin. "*warum muss es immer Krach geben*" (Why must there always be a row)?

The three of them were now arguing in the cabin. I was sitting on the vacant bunk.

"Excuse me," said the young man above me, "it's not so important to me. If it would help, I don't mind switching."

"No, it's alright," I said.

"Now there's a nice young man," said my father.

"Really, sir, it's no trouble at all."

"No, I wouldn't want my son to inconvenience you."

"No inconvenience at all, honestly, sir."

"Well, Robin?"

"I'm quite happy where I am."

At this moment a voice crackled over the loudspeaker: "All visitors are kindly requested to leave the ship." My father glowered at me, my mother sighed, and my uncle shook his head disconsolately from side to side, "*Nein, nein, nein.*" We were all standing now. Finally my mother gave me a kiss. "Why does it always have to end like this?" she said. I shrugged. My uncle shepherded them out of the cabin. In silence I escorted them down the corridor to the lift. It took an age to come. Finally the doors slid open, my father and uncle removed their hats and stepped in, my mother gave me a last embrace. "Thank you for taking me down to Southampton," I said to the crowd in the lift. My mother waved her handkerchief. The doors slid shut. They were gone.

I returned to the cabin and unpacked. My companions introduced themselves—Mark, Chris, and Jeremy, Fulbrighters all, one headed to Columbia to study politics, one to Cornell to study literature, and one to the Midwest to study agriculture. "Agriculture?" I said, "They have Fulbrights for agriculture?"

"Well, its formal name is Agricultural Economics. But it's really just farming."

Our conversation was interrupted by a voice in the corridor crying out, "Post. Post." They had postal deliveries on this boat? How big was it? There was a knock on the door and a steward with a bundle of letters poked his head in. "Any one of you gentlemen here Mr. Hirsch?" We looked at each other. "Mr. Robin Hirsch?"

"Oh, yes, er, me."

"Letter for you, sir."

"A letter? How amazing!" I looked at the envelope. On it was typed "Mr. Robin Hirsch, R.M.S. Queen Elizabeth, Port of Southampton, England." It bore an American stamp.

"Thank you," I said.

"Pleasure, sir," said the steward and left to continue his rounds.

"Should I have tipped him?" Nobody knew. I opened the envelope. Inside was a letter welcoming me aboard and enclosing one hundred dollars in cash so I could enjoy myself on the boat. It was signed Fritz and Ellen Schoenheimer.

Fritz and Ellen Schoenheimer were long-standing friends of my parents. Fritz had rowed with my father as a boy in a famous Jewish rowing eight in Berlin before the First World War. He and Ellen had left Germany in 1933 and moved to Paris where their son Pierre had been born. They had escaped to America by different routes when the Germans overran France. Pierre I knew had been seriously wounded in the neck as an eight-year-old boy fleeing with his mother towards Marseilles, but he had survived. In the fifties as a young man just out of college he had toured Europe and stayed with us briefly in London. My sister, now married, still had a crush on him from those days. Fritz was a year or two older than my father, one of the few men my father held in genuine regard. He had been successful in Germany, he had had even greater success in Paris, and now, so it was rumored, he had become many times a millionaire in the United States. I remembered him every so often passing through London, an imposing figure, tall, with a shock of white hair, the thumb on his right hand missing, shot away in the First World War. Ellen would pass through on other occasions. I remember my parents bringing her up to Oxford once, a quiet, strong, gentle, sensitive woman, slender, slight, graying, impeccably dressed, no makeup, no jewelry, with the ability to transform the most insignificant remark into a confidence. She had been so enchanted by the front quad at my college she had wanted to take it back with her. She had laughed. I had laughed. We had become conspirators.

I ran out of the cabin and caught the steward farther down the corridor. "Here," I said and handed him half a crown. "Thank you."

"Thank *you*, sir. No need to do that."

"Well, it was a wonderful letter. Here, go on, I insist."

"Very well, sir. Thank you, sir. I'm very much obliged."

My father, I knew, had made arrangements for the Schoenheimers to receive me in New York—I would stay with them for ten days or so before proceeding to Pennsylvania. If this was a taste of things to come, that strange, mythical country, as remote and forbidding as the moon, as seductive as jazz, might not be so inhospitable after all.

"Let me buy you all a drink. I'm suddenly rich." I explained the contents of my letter to my companions. But we had not left port yet and the bars would not open until we were beyond the three-mile limit. "Well, the offer is good for a bottle of wine at dinner. I'm going to explore."

The barriers between classes had not gone up yet, so I had the freedom of all decks and all parts of the ship. In first class I discovered squash courts and the Turkish baths. I had never had a Turkish bath before and I was a little apprehensive about what that might entail. But, being newly rich and independent and having but a few more hours in first class, I decided to give it a try. I was welcomed like royalty. My clothes were put in a locker, I was given a huge immaculate white fluffy towel and sandals and escorted into the steam room. There was dry heat and there was wet heat, a series of chambers where the temperature gradually but inexorably increased. Every so often one of the bath stewards would arrive with a tray of ice water. I was the only customer. The weight of London and the uneasy anticipation of New York drifted away and all that was left were clouds of steam and the thrill of the ice-cold glass. After thirty minutes the bath steward asked if I would like a massage.

"Well, . . ."

"It's all included, sir."

"Well, then, alright." Drained, I lay down on a massage table on a pure white cotton sheet and one of the stewards rubbed lineament into my body.

"First trip on the Queen, sir?"

"Mm-mm," my voice floated out from a thousand miles away.

"First trip to New York, is it, sir?"

"Mm-mm."

"Well, you'll have a wonderful time, sir. Young gentlemen always do." He applied a bit more pressure. "It's the accent, sir. They really go for the accent."

"Oh?"

"And the girls, sir. You'll have a wonderful time with the girls. They do what they call a back rub, sir."

"A what?"

"A back rub, sir. You know, it's a little like this, only a girl does it. They all do it in America, sir."

"Well."

"Well, sir, you just remember when you get to New York."

"I will. I will." New York sounded more and more promising.

"Just finish you off now, sir." He pummeled me, then coated my body with alcohol and, as the delicious cool liquid evaporated, draped my body with a towel. "Now, you just lie there, sir, and take a nap if you've a mind to."

"Mm-mm."

"You get up whenever you're ready, sir. I'll just draw the curtain." He drew the white curtain to the booth and disappeared.

I drifted off into a light and heady sleep: huge sea-creatures floated to the surface of the water and sailed serenely through the balmy air; the spray scattered into the sky for stars. Presently I awoke. My clothes had been neatly placed on a chair. Slowly I dressed. The clothes felt cool and fresh against my skin. I stepped out. "Thank you very much," I said. "That was wonderful."

"It's our pleasure, sir. Come again."

"Well, I'd like to, but, um," and painfully I explained that I was an interloper from tourist class.

"Oh, never mind about that, sir. Here, if you purchase one of these tickets—Good for the Whole Voyage—they'll let you through any time you want, sir. This way you'll be able to use the squash courts and no-body'll know the difference." He winked. Would they accept American money? They would be happy to.

Clutching my newly acquired passe-partout, exultant, dancing down the corridor, I picked my way back to the cabin. In my absence the huge ship had set sail and evidently dinner was now being served. I changed and took the lift up to the dining room. There was another cabin of Fulbrighters and the eight of us were placed together at one large table. I bought a bottle of wine and, eight bright young men, the cream of a highly competitive crop, we toasted the New World and the egalitarian society that lay ahead of us.

The days and nights drifted by, meal after heavy meal, one organized diversion after another, and everywhere—for thé dansant in the after-noon, for cocktails in the early evening, for ballroom dancing after din-ner, and for late-night rock-and-roll—the Neptune Trio, three sad and bleary-eyed young men carrying their tired instruments from one corner of tourist class to another, never at rest, but never completely awake. The Ineptune Trio we dubbed them, wags that we were.

On the second day, waiting for my fellow Fulbrighters to join me for a drink, I was writing a letter in the huge deserted ballroom when I became aware of two young girls standing shyly at the entrance several hundred yards away, whispering, giggling, nudging, egging each other on. Finally they plucked up sufficient courage and tiptoed over to my table.

"Excuse us," they said in unison. "Could we have your autograph, please?"

I looked round to see whom they were addressing but, apart from a discreet bartender, I was the sole inhabitant of this enormous room.

"Are you referring to me?"

"Yes."

"Who do you think I am?"

"Robin Hirsch."

"I beg your pardon?"

"You're Robin Hirsch."

"And how on earth do you know me?"

"We're from Sheffield. We're emigrating with our parents to America. We saw you at the Playhouse."

"How extraordinary. What did you see me in? *The Silver Box?*"

"No."

"*Ring o' Roses?*"

"No?"

"What, then?"

"*John Willy and the Bee People.*"

In Stockholm, when I was washing dishes, the Beatles had opened *Hard Day's Night,* and in the mania surrounding the premiere I had been mistaken for Paul McCartney and swept into the cinema on the shoulders of screaming teenagers. Now, for the first time in my life, in a deserted ballroom in the middle of the Atlantic, I was being mistaken for myself, and I had no witnesses.

"I wonder if you could do me a favor? I have some friends joining me in a few minutes—they're Fulbright scholars—and I'd love you to meet them."

Nothing doing.

I signed.

The girls vanished.

Various Fulbrighters arrived.

"You'll never believe this," I said.

They didn't.

On the third night, a bingo night, which magically produced out of nowhere eight hundred blue-rinsed bingo ladies, we, the cream of our generation, persuaded Mark, the Agricultural Economist, to have a birthday and the Neptune Trio to strike up the appropriate tune. Eight hundred blue-rinsed bingo ladies sang "Happy Birthday" to Mark, who hadn't had a birthday in months, the ship's photographer had a field day, and suddenly the entire population of tourist class was caught up in a giant conga, snaking its way along the deck, past the barricades, pulsating and chanting and swaying from side to side. In cabin class we interrupted a floor show in the night club and took a few revelers with us. In first class we trooped across the ballroom floor under the chandeliers while elegant dancers waltzing in formal attire recoiled in horror. Eight hundred blue-rinsed bingo ladies on the march and the Fulbright contingent fomenting social discord. It was a sight to behold. The next day the bulletin board had hundreds of photos—Mark's Birthday, a joyous occasion, with hundreds of celebrants—and the ship's newspaper published one of the eight of us hoisting the birthday boy on our shoulders and laughing uproariously.

At lunch the table steward told me I was wanted on the telephone. I was completely taken aback. They had phones on this boat? I was taken down to the purser's office and a receiver put to my ear. I was told to stand by. Presently a man's voice came over the line, a voice with a German accent. "Robin, welcome to our side of the Atlantic. This is Fritz Schoenheimer. We are in Montauk. We look forward to seeing you. Pierre's wife Janet will collect you from the boat. How is your trip?"

Everything was fine, I told him. I was having a wonderful time. I had put the money to good use.

"*Sehr gut,*" the voice said, "See you in a few days."

"Thank you. Thank you." But the line had gone dead.

I went back to the dining room but I couldn't eat and the high spirits at the table had somehow lost their appeal.

Three days later on a blistering August afternoon we sailed into New York harbor. Everyone had plans. Chris and Jeremy were staying at the Biltmore. Mark had lost the number of friends he was supposed to stay with and would be at the YMCA if he failed to make contact. I was being collected by Janet. We all agreed to meet the following day and make a ritual pilgrimage to the Empire State Building before scattering across the continent.

All American cars, I knew, were enormous. Janet's was white and open and sporty and didn't in fact seem so overwhelming. Indeed we had trouble piling my trunk, let alone the skis, into the boot.

"The boot?" She laughed. "We call that the trunk, dear."

"Oh, I'm sorry." I slid into the bucket seat on the passenger side, and we roared up the West Side Highway in the shimmering heat. "Gosh," I said, "American cars are enormous."

Janet laughed. "This is tiny. It's Ellen's. She loves it. It's a Mustang. Fritz and Ellen have the Lincoln out in Montauk so we'll drive this out on the weekend. Pierre has the Buick. I should have brought the station wagon, I guess, but this is so much zippier."

We went through a toll booth and into the Bronx and turned off the highway into a cool shaded tree-lined area with enormous houses set back from the street or perched on clumps of rock or entirely hidden by gardens. The road was appalling. The lid of the boot—the trunk—flew open, I turned round and caught my skis before they sailed out of the back seat. We lurched up to a roundabout.

"It's a traffic circle, dear."

"Thank you."

"We don't pave the roads here. It's sort of a private community and it keeps the automobiles—the cars—from running down the kids."

We turned a corner and pulled into a driveway underneath a huge rocky overhang.

This beautiful stone house in Fieldston, so spacious and so tranquil, so close to, and yet so far removed from, the thrum of the city, would be the nearest thing to home I had for the next several years. Pierre and Janet, who were a little older than I but infinitely more established, threw open their front door and their larder, lent me their automobiles and station wagons, allowed me to call collect from any part of the country. Their children became my kid brothers and sisters. I found myself all of a sudden with an extended family. It was, from the first moment, what I imagined having cousins must be like.

The next morning Janet drove me into the heart of Manhattan in the station wagon. We picked up Chris and Jeremy and a couple of other familiar faces at the Biltmore and Janet sped around New York, through the glass ravine of midtown into Harlem, across the Triborough Bridge into Queens, along endless highways in suburbia to Brooklyn, across the Verrazano Narrows Bridge into Staten Island, then onto the ferry and the slow trip across the bay past the Statue of Liberty with the majestic southern tip of Manhattan rising up to meet us. She dropped us at the Empire State Building in the early afternoon. "So long, kids, have fun."

In the stifling August heat we lined up to buy tickets. After forty minutes they allowed us to pay our money and line up for the elevator. In the elevator we were shot to the eighty-eighth floor where we were disgorged and lined up for the elevator to the observation deck. On the observation deck, packed shoulder to shoulder with people we'd never met and would never see again, we were shunted round four sides of a square staring out over the haze unable to make out anything distinctly, carried along in an inexorable tide, turning, turning, turning, turning, until we found ourselves back in the elevator and heading down for the eighty-eighth floor. After three and a half hours we tumbled into a kosher Coca-Cola joint on 34th Street and ordered a beer. New York had wiped us out.

Mark had not shown up at the appointed hour, either at the Biltmore or at the Empire State Building and we wondered whether he had ever found his hosts or was now stuck in the YMCA. I was deputized to call him. I went downstairs and thumbed through the huge directories. I tried to ring the Y but couldn't get through. I called the operator. She put me on hold. Finally a voice said "Hello."

"Hello, is this the YMCA?"

"Are you kidding?"

"Is this the operator?"

"No, honey, this isn't the operator."

"I'm trying to get through to the YMCA. I was asked to hold."

"Where are you from, sweetheart?"

"England. Why?"

"How long have you been in this city?"

"Twenty-four hours. Why?"

"Well, honey, it seems to me you've got a crossed wire. We're having a party here and if you fail to get through to the Young Men's Christian Association perhaps you should come up and join us."

"Well, that's very kind of you. But I'm with friends."

"Well, I don't know about that, darling, we're a little short on glasses."

"Well, thank you anyway."

"No, honey, you come on over. It's a summer party at the office, and we'd be real glad to have you. My name's Anna and I'll be wearing a green dress. Where are you now?"

"The Empire State Building."

"Well, you just come up Park Avenue till you get to Number 500 and then you take the elevator to the fifty-fifth floor and then you walk up one and you'll be there."

"Well, thank you. You're very hospitable."

"See you soon."

I tried the YMCA once more and failed again to get through. I returned to my companions. "I couldn't get hold of Mark. But I did get us an invitation to a party."

We walked up Park Avenue. The number 500 in gigantic figures was attached to the top of a skyscraper. We had in fact seen it as we shuffled round the deck of the Empire State Building and had hazarded a guess as to what the figure stood for—the building's height in feet, doubtless to alert the pilots of helicopters. Now we realized it was how the mailman recognized the building on his appointed rounds. In the lobby there were three banks of elevators, one indeed going to the fifty-fifth floor. I had been nurturing visions of some fat-thighed nymphomaniac with a cigar and the illusion of a party in the background—or perhaps it was a complete hoax and we young Fulbrighters abroad in the big city for the first time, a city of depravity and unimaginable guile, were being duped or set up or lured into a trap.

On the fifty-fifth floor there was indeed a stairway going up one more flight. I told my companions to wait for me on the stairway and come to my aid if anything untoward should happen. At the top of the stairs was a door with two names on it: Springbok Jigsaw Puzzles and Feedurite Cookery Recipes. From behind the door came the sounds of conviviality. I looked down at Chris and Jeremy and the others and they gave me a look of encouragement. I knocked on the door. It opened immediately and a man in a blue serge suit with a cigar in his mouth said, "Gee, you must be from Hallmark. Come in. Come in." He ushered us all in. "These are the guys from Hallmark."

The office was large and crowded. There was an abundance of food— shrimp the size of bananas and cold roast meats stretching into the distance. "What are you drinking, boys?" Fat tumblers crammed with ice and overflowing with hard liquor were thrust into our hands.

"Actually, Anna asked us to come."

"Oh, you're the boy Anna spoke to. Anna, come over here, your Englishman has arrived."

Anna in the green dress was immediately recognizable by the look of perturbation that crossed her face. "Gee, Harry, I'm sorry, I told him not to bring his friends."

"No, boys, you're all welcome. You all from England?"

We explained that indeed we were, that this was our first day in America, that we had come over on Fulbrights, that we were about to be scattered across the country.

"Well, boys, welcome to the States. Fill these boys' glasses." A bartender in a white jacket sailed over with a bottle of bourbon. "Now, boys, here's to you." And Harry in the blue serge suit raised his glass and toasted us.

Harry's wife, it turned out, was the brains behind Springbok Jigsaw Puzzles. They were art puzzles. She had started out renting a desk in an office owned by Feedurite Cookery Recipes. Springbok had grown. Feedurite had contracted. Now Springbok had the entire office and Feedurite occupied one desk.

"Barman, another drink for these boys."

Springbok was now being taken over by Hallmark Greeting Cards and this party was to celebrate the merger. "Well, here's to Hallmark," said Harry and we drank to Hallmark Greeting Cards. "And this is my lovely wife, who made it all possible," and we drank to Harry's lovely wife. And then we drank to Springbok. And then we drank to Feedurite. And then we were introduced to everyone at the party as the bright young men from England. And, a little giddy from bourbon and the sudden celebrity, we proposed a merger between Springbok and Feedurite, perhaps a whole new line of three-dimensional edible puzzles.

"Ralph, get over here. You gotta meet these boys. Ralph is our art director. These boys are brilliant. They just came over on Fulbrights. Talk to them, Ralph."

Ralph was a studious black man in his forties. It was his job, he told us, to choose the paintings which were then reproduced and cut up to form the puzzles. Essentially, he explained, there were four kinds of paintings—square, rectangular, round, and diamond-shaped. Oh, we said, we hadn't known about diamond-shaped.

Harry called for silence. "Tom and Ed have been working for almost a year on a film which they are now going to show us. Can we douse the lights."

Girls in summer dresses were snuggling up to men in lightweight suits. Glasses clinked. A thrill of anticipation ran through the room. We Fulbrighters nudged each other. We'd heard about these American office parties. The lights were dimmed. Late fiery evening sun filtered in through the Venetian blinds. The projector started to whir. It was over in less than a minute. An animated film of a Springbok Jigsaw Puzzle being put together very fast. It was circular.

After the applause, the party began to break up. Harry and his wife and Ralph and Anna took us out onto the balcony. Dusk was just beginning to creep in. Lights began to pop on in the forest of buildings around us. From here the city looked like magic, clear and bright, the buildings lined up in formation like soldiers, the tiny automobiles with their pinpricks of light nosing down the avenues, the last rays of the sun tinting the stone and glass of the city with a roseate glow.

"Down there, on that corner, in 1926," said Ralph, "the first traffic light in the world was erected."

"Over there is Brooklyn. Over there is another state—New Jersey," said Harry. "You see, it really is an island."

And we looked and we saw the pale ribbons of water and the fairy lights spring on to illuminate the bridges. And we felt the balmy air up here at 500 feet—or was that the number of the building?—waft by our faces and we looked at the New World spread out before us and it was good.

"Here's to you," we said. "We couldn't have asked for more."

Night fell and we went inside. Harry's wife, who had made it all possible, brought out an empty book, and wrote on the flyleaf, Guest Book, and each of us in turn wished Springbok well and signed our names. And Harry wouldn't let us leave without thrusting under each arm a Springbok Jigsaw Puzzle as a memento. Late that night, at the end of my first subway ride, at the northernmost end of the No. 1 line, at 242nd Street in the Bronx, I struggled up the hill to Fieldston with presents for the children—one rectangular, one square, one circular—they had run out of diamond-shaped.

On the weekend—Labor Day—Janet and I and the kids drove out to Montauk, picking up ducks and fruit and corn on the way. Fritz and Ellen welcomed me like visiting royalty. There was even a notice in the local paper announcing the arrival of Robin Marc David Hirsch, Fulbright scholar, from England.

Fritz was over seventy now, a wonderfully distinguished looking man, still very straight, but walking with just a trace of difficulty. He would take me out on the patio of the simple, spacious house they had built twenty-three years before, using my shoulder for support, and, pressing down on me with one hand, he would wave the other one in a wide arc taking in the hedgerow and the lawn sweeping down to the road and the unseen cliffs and the beach beyond and the huge expanse of the Atlantic which I had just crossed and the light dying on the horizon and he would say, "It's beautiful, no?" And I would nod, a little at a loss for words. And we would stare out together across the ocean, an old man and a young one, thinking our different thoughts. Was he too thinking of the Europe he had left—the turmoil, the excitement, the war, the terror? Had he found peace in this new land? I wondered.

Ellen had the vigor and the suppleness of a much younger woman and a certain aristocracy of spirit that allowed her to make mischief without ever losing her dignity. She would romp with the kids, stand on her head, zoom off in her Mustang, host a dinner party, without seeming to change gear. And then she would sit down with me and talk about the theater, about her days with Reinhardt, about some experiment she had seen in New York, about Berlin, about Brussels, about Paris. But every city was provincial compared to New York. And she would talk about the flight from Paris with her mother and her wounded son and the nursing convent at Chartres where she tended to the sick while Pierre gradually recovered his strength and the journey to Marseilles and the boat to America. And no, she would never set foot in Germany again, she would never fly a German plane or drive a German car or buy a German camera. Perhaps she could be so clear about all that because she was only half a Jew and she could see Germany, of which by an accident of birth she was never a citizen, with a cold unblinking eye which never wavered and never forgave.

And she talked of the gaiety of those early years in America, and the
sense of liberation, and the terrible moment when Fritz's younger brother
Rudy, a tormented and irrepressible man, an internationally renowned
biochemist, marked for a Nobel Prize, in the gazebo on the grounds of a
house they shared, put a gun to his head and ended it all—the women,
the fast cars, the acclaim, the burden of being a marked man—a Jew and
a genius.

So in both the Schoenheimer households I was family. I was like one of
the cousins who flew in periodically from Australia or Switzerland or
Israel or South Africa, except that I didn't fly out again. Over the years I
watched the children grow, become Bar Mitzvah and Bas Mitzvah, finish
high school and go on to college and romances and individual pursuits.
And I watched Fritz gradually relinquish the reins of his business empire
and Pierre take over, not without a struggle on both sides. And I saw
Pierre and Janet struggle with their marriage and when the children had
left the nest give up the house in Fieldston and go their separate ways.
And I watched as Fritz and Ellen moved into the heart of Manhattan to
take advantage of their beloved New York in the twilight of their lives.
And every year Fritz would lean a little more heavily on my shoulder until
in his eightieth year he could no longer walk. And I watched him die. And
I watched as Ellen, alone, indomitable, gradually drifted into senility,
losing her memory, forgetting names, forgetting places, forgetting faces,
forgetting me. And I watched her leave the magnificent apartment on
East 69th Street that she had shared with her beloved husband and the
peaceful house in Montauk that she had built with her beloved husband
and move silently and with resignation to an estate on Long Island where
with the most expensive attention she could walk the grounds and com-
mune with the spirits of those she no longer remembered.

At the end of Labor Day weekend Ellen left her guest book in my
room. I thumbed back through the years and came across my mother's
handwriting. Half a dozen years before, on her way back from Buenos
Aires, where she had visited her sister for the first time since the war, she
had, I remembered, passed through New York and Fritz and Ellen had
evidently taken her out to Montauk. "*Herrlich! Wunderschön!*" she had
written, "*Hier ist doch wirklich Paradies*" (Heavenly! Wonderful! This is
truly Paradise). And half a dozen years before that I found an entry from
my father, from the time he had bought me a cowboy outfit and visited
Jochem on the West Coast. It must have been Fritz who had driven him at
eighty miles an hour. He had written in English, "Garden and house and
beach excellent. Weather quite good. Host and hostess first-class. Could
have spent more time in New York. Herbert." I stayed up most of the
night composing an elaborate poem in which the first letters of each line

formed an acrostic spelling out FRITZ AND ELLEN SCHOENHEIMER. In its diction it owed quite a bit to Milton.

The next week I took a train, with my trunk, my luggage, and my trusty skis to the middle of Pennsylvania and then a bus for thirty miles to the exact geographical center where the state university whose postal address is University Park overwhelms a small satellite town called State College. The streets were full of huge bermuda-shorted, gum-chewing, crew-cut boys and girls. I fell into an immediate depression.

Almost overnight, however, in the fall of 1967, everybody's hair grew out, beards and mustaches sprouted, strange fumes rose from the slender cigarettes of shady characters sitting on the campus wall, complete strangers, some of them my students, would offer me substances the effects of which they couldn't describe and I was too chicken to try, Vietnam veterans who had seen things they couldn't describe would caution me against the dope smokers on the wall, all of whom were really narcotics agents. And the notion of free speech and student participation in university decisions and the university as an appropriate political forum seized the student body and buildings were occupied and nonnegotiable demands were issued and demonstrations were staged. And a tiny, strident black presence began to trickle through the milk-white population of central Pennsylvania.

And the following year Martin Luther King and Bobby Kennedy were killed. And the tension and the anger began to mount. And Johnson was brought down and Humphrey, scarred by his four years as Johnson's yes-man, was emasculated by the Yippies in Chicago, and Nixon squeezed in with a plan to end the war. And the bombing increased and in 1969 we marched on Washington, me and a Moroccan friend and a couple of girls and half a million others. And everywhere dope was in the air and music and sex and the smell of revolution.

However, while people's political and social positions were becoming clearer and clearer, the Purpose of Life, which I had so painfully articulated for the benefit of the Fulbright Commission, was becoming vaguer and vaguer. My Ph.D. was getting nowhere. I was supposed to be writing about the American avant-garde theater, and while it was happening all around me, the nearest formal approximation was the local community theater's production of *The Fantasticks*. After two and a half years, with Comps behind me and only a dissertation to write, it was time to move to New York.

I loaded my possessions into the battered VW I had acquired and set sail for the Big City, for the large house on Livingston Avenue where I thought I could string together a few hundred pages on the relationship between ritual and contemporary American theater and hang out my shingle.

But Life, let alone Academe, is rarely that simple. For one thing I had to support myself and my visa allowed me to teach English in Pennsylvania and that was it. So, slowly, slowly, I learned to insinuate myself, like so many other illegal immigrants, into the cracks of the enormous city. I sold toys, I did construction work, I had an interview with two elderly ladies eating blueberries who published pornography and paid a dollar a page, I wrote the occasional article, I appeared in the occasional play, I even directed an avant-garde musical, which netted me all of thirty-five dollars. And finally I scraped together enough money and courage to move out from under the comfortable wing of Pierre and Janet and plunge into the maelstrom of Manhattan.

There is something wildly invigorating about this time. I live for a year on the Lower East Side, broke, between Avenues B and C. My neighborhood looks like Hanoi after the bombing. Everyone in my building except me has been mugged. It is the height of the heroin wars and the contrast with Fieldston, where Pierre and Janet had housed me in splendor, could not be more startling. And yet I couldn't live in the lap of luxury forever, I couldn't live in New York without living in Manhattan, and I couldn't write about the theater without becoming involved in it.

In England I had clomped around on stage every night for a year, playing sixteen or twenty different roles, sometimes three or four in the same play, speaking the words of some of the great writers of the English and European stages—Shakespeare, Marlowe, Pinter, Osborne, Ibsen, Arbuzov, Feydeau, Beckett. In New York, in the experimental theater to which I was drawn, the emphasis was completely different. It was the actor, not the writer, who was important. Indeed much of the energy of the experimental theater was devoted to liberating the theatrical experience from the tyranny of the written word. By a series of accidents I became involved, as an actor, in one of those companies that sprang up in the wake of the Living Theatre and the Open Theater and the free-form theatrical experiments of the sixties. With the result that for the princely sum of twenty dollars a week, courtesy of the National Endowment for the Arts, I spent an entire year, not performing, but rehearsing. There were eight of us—a director, a writer, and six actors, one of them me. After a year of fighting and sweating and arguing and leaping and dancing and screaming and crying and laughing and crawling through the desert on our bellies we had a piece called *The Journey* which had something to do with Abraham and his two sons—Isaac and Ishmael—and the divergent traditions—Jewish and Arab—which sprang from his loins. The piece ran for a few weeks and made none of us rich or famous. I played Ishmael, but I knew no more about the Arab tradition—or the Jewish tradition, for that matter—at the end of the run than I had at the beginning of rehearsals. But I had grown and stretched in the course of that year in ways that my year at the Sheffield Playhouse could never have accomplished, and I found myself stitched, however tenuously, into the fabric of New York's avant-garde.

And so I met Naomi. Naomi was an actress in another Off Off Broadway company. She was starring in a play by one of the writers I was supposed to be writing my dissertation about. Her father was a rabbi in West Virginia, where Jews were not that thick on the ground, and both his daughters had escaped to New York and joined the theater. A terrible fate for a rabbi. Naomi and I fell into an easy friendship, eventually she moved in with me in that terrible neighborhood between B and C, but because we were both dark we blended in with the scenery and neither of us was touched. One night in a restaurant in the Village, talking about our parents and our respective childhoods and how we would bring up children, we found ourselves, by the end of the meal, the most comfortable thing in the world, engaged. In June of 1972 in Charleston, West Virginia, in front of four hundred strangers, her father married us.

Our honeymoon was spent scampering up the eastern seaboard, hounded by rainstorms. But our real honeymoon came shortly after we returned to New York, at the end of 1972, broke, with no real home and no work to speak of. My half-brother Isaac from *The Journey*—an Irish-American actor—tipped us off to a possible job which required a background in both pedagogy and performance. My checkered past paid off. We were hired by the National Humanities Series to tour small-town America with programs that we would devise together with the third member of our team, Jim Hollis, a young professor of literature from Indiana.

The three of us spent the month of January in Princeton developing seventeen programs under the general rubric which Jim had proposed—Language: The Human Connection. They ranged from the highly academic (Jim had a program on the opening sentence of the Gospel of John) to the frankly entertaining (Naomi and I had a program called "Going Through a Stage," which, according to the press release was supposed to tell small-town America everything it had ever wanted to know about the theater but was afraid to ask).

It was an extraordinarily intense and productive month. Naomi developed programs on Guatemala, where she had lived for a year as an exchange student, and on the words and paintings of van Gogh. One of my programs grew out of my still simmering dissertation—Ritual and Reality—in which I proposed to address the relationship between primitive rituals and present-day reality. Naomi and I together developed a program out of the extraordinary collection of children's poems recovered from the concentration camp of Terezin (or Theresienstadt).

My mother had an old friend, her closest living friend perhaps, Betty Joseph, who had survived Theresienstadt and now lived in Los Angeles. I had met her once in Holland ten years before, a quite remarkable woman, in her seventies then, she would be over eighty now, a woman with the most intense blue eyes, still smoked fiercely, dyed her hair, a deep throaty voice, radiantly alive, vibrant, a woman still—there was no other word for it—sexy. It astonished me that people who had survived such experiences could retain such vitality and reverence for life. In that respect she reminded me of my uncle. I thought about them both as I put the program together.

All of these programs were to be delivered in small towns, between five thousand and fifty thousand in population, scattered across America. We would carry everything we needed with us—lights, sound equipment, props, costumes, with arrangements for travel and accommodation made by advance parties from Princeton with the local Humanities Council in each town.

On the last day of January Naomi, Jim, and I, the language team, climbed into our white Ford LTD—the car they'd given us for a month in Princeton—and headed for Newark and a flight to Jamestown, New York. Finally, after five and a half years, I was going to see the country.

Allegheny Airlines Flight 793 to Jamestown, Bradford, and Pittsburgh. I had flown them once before to Pennsylvania, a grasshopper flight with stops every fifty miles and terrible turbulence and people throwing up left, right, and center, and the plane awash in a mixture of Coke and beef bouillon—courtesy of Allegheny Airlines. But this time an absolutely perfect flight. Coming in over Jamestown, it looks like Labrador with snowy wastelands stretching to the horizon. We make it—safe inside a tiny airport.

The Hertz girl doesn't know we need a station wagon. The Avis guy is sick, so Hertz has the whole market. We have to take two Chevy Impalas for our equipment. Seventeen dollars a day and seventeen cents a mile each. The Hertz girl tells us how to get to the Colony Motel. She's not a very good at directions, she says. She's right. We backtrack after several miles and find the Colony, a large white, colonnaded motel on route 17J. There is a message: the Reverend Christmas, co-chairman of the local Humanities Council, will pick us up at 5:30 for dinner. I wish he were a Catholic so we could call him Father Christmas, but he's a Lutheran. Out of our jeans, and into our glad rags—mustn't appear too raffish on the first day. Enter Father Christmas with Lynn Ann Eddy, the scheduling chairman. Father Christmas is thirty-one, with a giggle, and an almost ostentatious worldliness. Lynn Ann Eddy is young and fat and suffers from an excess of what Byron called "enthoosymoosy."

Dinner at the Town Club, a private dining club, in an elegant room. Jack Proudman, the facilities chairman, is waiting, drink in hand. In everyday life he is the affable personnel director of the local ball-bearings factory. He sports a white-on-white shirt, a daring tie and a fine blue blazer. Bloody Marys, a good steak, some preliminary discussion about scheduling, and Father Christmas picks up the check—it's deductible, he says. An odd almost nineteenth-century vignette: the manageress, a peroxided blonde from Munich with a hard face, in a tête-à-tête with Father Christmas, conferring about the tip, scooping up the money, the concerned clergyman and the town madam.

A reception at the Christmases for the entire council—thirty or so. We are followed in by the chief of police, who for the first time has a murder case on his hands—a fourteen-year-old girl who had run away from home and has just been found in a local lake. A thin middle-aged clergyman— not the hipster Christmas variety—and his shortsighted adoring wife, nursing for an eternity a single glass of nonalcoholic punch, cling to us because they're from West Virginia and so, they know from the press materials, is Naomi, and they have a friend who's the vicar of Purley in Surrey, which, you know, is not too far from London, he'd just called them from Miami after a month of Bible lectures in the South, just to say hello before going home, wasn't that nice. Did we know the South? Not yet, but it was coming up.

A. L. Hazard from the radio station sets up an interview with Jim for the following morning. He's known, inevitably, as Hap Hazard, a retiring man with spectacles and a quiet plaid suit. But he knows everything— and everyone. Tulla Hanley in Bradford, Pennsylvania, for example, our next port of call. Half Hungarian, half Egyptian, she used to be a belly dancer. Her mother, a fortune-teller, had told her she would marry a millionaire, so she refused all offers until one night at work Mr. Hanley, an octogenarian oil millionaire from Bradford, invited her to his table. Sixty years earlier, a young man at Yale, he had visited Europe and bought crateloads of paintings. They still lay in his house in boxes. He wanted finally to unpack them. Tulla consulted her mother and married him. Shortly thereafter he kicked the bucket, leaving her his millions, and, in the boxes, his Picassos, his Renoirs, his van Goghs. She hasn't forsaken her profession, however. She's writing a book called "The Love of Art and the Art of Love." She had opened a club for the disadvantaged kids of Bradford which she had decorated with paintings straight out of Mr. Hanley's boxes. It had just been closed down as a disorderly house. Apparently she would provide entertainment for the kids, with which the National Humanities Series could not hope to compete. And at the Hanley house, where she retained the best pieces, she had given tours of her art collection, discarding her clothes on the way. "This is a tour of my husband's art collection," she would say, "and I was his greatest work of art." She was under indictment now and might in fact be in jail.

The next morning Jim did his radio show and Naomi and I, at 8:20, did our first program, "Going Through a Stage," for eight hundred junior high school kids, shouting, yelling, screaming, talking—and no mikes. Baptism by fire.

There followed other programs—at Kiwanis Clubs, for welfare mothers, in banks, in churches, at people's homes, for medical groups, in libraries, in schools, in factories. In the morning, in the afternoon, at night. Sometimes the response was dull, sometimes perplexed, occasionally hostile, but most of the time it was overwhelming. People were thirsting for the kind of stimulation that these forays into unlikely territory provided. We were a tiny guerrilla force which took over a town for three days and wormed its way into the most guarded nooks and crannies. We became confessors, shoulders to cry on, instruments of hope, and catalysts for social change.

The second leg of the tour began in the South and we flew out of La Guardia to Jackson, Mississippi, where we met up with Jim again and drove to Yazoo City. In Yazoo, trouble was brewing. The local council had entreated Princeton to allow us to perform at the leading school in town, the Manchester Academy. The children of all the important people in Yazoo attended the Academy. If the Humanities Series was to have a real and significant impact on the town, we should do one program at the Academy. There was, however, a problem. The Academy was segregated. Oh, school segregation had of course been ended in the sixties, but private academies had sprung up in the South where rich whites could send their children in the sure knowledge that they would be safe from contamination. Princeton left the decision to us. Naomi and Jim were dead set against doing it. I was not so sure.

At the preliminary meeting with the local council that night the issue was the first thing on the agenda. Jim said he and Naomi categorically refused to appear before a segregated audience, but he couldn't speak for me. A young teacher from the Academy who was on the council said the structure of the town was such that performing at the Academy would begin to bring various elements of the community at least into talking range. I said that under certain circumstances I would be prepared to perform. She was delighted, but she had really hoped that Naomi and I would come and do our theater program for the students. Naomi, I said, wouldn't come, and as for me, there was only one program I would do—the program of poems from Terezin.

"Oh, but the kids were so looking forward to two real actors and a show."

"This'll be a show," I said. "They won't forget it."

In the end, Naomi agreed to do the program with me. We arrived at midmorning, ice-cold in the hot sun. At the entrance to the school there was a declaration of the rights of all students to an education of their choice. Our skin felt black. Word had evidently passed through the school. Teachers greeted us politely but at arm's length. Students gathered in the top-floor library, the top three grades, teenagers, flaxen-haired, blue-eyed, fair-skinned, serious. Everybody walked on eggshells. We set up our screen and projector and music stands. Nobody said a word.

When we were ready we stood by our stands and looked out silently at the sea of young, quiet, serious, pretty, taut faces. It was a moment not of awkwardness but, for all of us, of anticipation. Then the young teacher from the night before rose and addressed the students: "Robin and Naomi, as you know, have come to Yazoo with the National Humanities Series. We had hoped they would do their theater program for us, but they have chosen instead to present a program called "I Never Saw Another Butterfly." I want to thank them for coming and I hope we will all give them the attention they deserve." She sat down.

I looked again at the faces. "There is a reason that we have chosen to present 'I Never Saw Another Butterfly.' It's not because we don't enjoy doing theater. We enjoy it very much. But there are times when doing what you enjoy is not so important. And we felt today that there was something more important we could bring to you. It's a collection of poems by children, some your age, some younger, who lived in Europe thirty years or so ago, and most of whom died, some of them without ever reaching the age you are now. Today we are here in this lovely library with the sunlight streaming in through the windows. Thirty years ago in Europe these children saw the same sunlight. But they saw it from behind barbed wire. They were prisoners. They were prisoners not because they had done something wrong, but because of who they were. They were Jews. In 1933 in Germany Adolf Hitler had come to power. He instituted amongst other things a policy of discrimination against the Jews. These things don't begin suddenly, with concentration camps and killing centers and cattle cars crammed with human beings who are somehow not like you and gas chambers and wholesale extermination. They begin gradually, on a small scale, in large cities where a door may suddenly be closed or a window smashed or a business boycotted, and in small towns with lovely libraries and sunlight streaming through the windows, where some people, for whatever reason, cannot get in. They begin with the nicest people. In Germany, and then throughout Europe, in twelve short years, from 1933, when he came to power, to 1945, when the Second World War ended, and he committed suicide in a private bunker in Berlin, Hitler managed to rouse those perfectly normal people—the nicest people—to a pitch of hatred against the Jews. All over Europe—or the parts of Europe that Germany invaded—Jews were rounded up, herded into cattle cars, shunted through the night to concentration camps where they were killed. Altogether 6,000,000 Jews were exterminated—more than half the Jewish population of Europe. It is difficult, if not impossible, to grasp a figure like that—it's too big, it's too impersonal. But it is important, if the world is to survive, if we as human beings are to survive with any dignity, to remember what we as human beings are capable of doing. These kinds of things do not begin suddenly, on a large scale, overnight; they begin gradually, with each one of us who in our hearts allow the seed of discrimination, however tiny, however imperceptible, to grow. They begin with the individual. And of course they end with the individual—not that big, impersonal figure of 6,000,000 but 6,000,000 individuals, men, women, children, like each one of us here in this room, with the sunlight streaming in through the windows.

"And so, in the program you are about to see, we have tried to come to terms with the nature of this almost unimaginable event—the Holocaust— from the perspective of the individual. From one concentration camp, the concentration camp at Terezin in Czechoslovakia, there survives a body of poetry, paintings, and drawings, the work of children carried out, not in sunlit rooms like these, but in clandestine classes, behind barbed wire. Terezin was not typical. It was small. It was set up as an old-age ghetto. It was maintained as a model camp. It was opened up to international inspection and was in fact inspected by the International Red Cross. But in reality it served as a halfway house on the road to a much larger and more terrible camp called Auschwitz. Of the 140,000 Jews who passed through Terezin in the three years of its existence, 17,000 survived when it was liberated by the Russians in 1945. I know one of them, a friend of my mother's. She came to America. She lives in Los Angeles. Of the 15,000 children who passed through Terezin, 100 survived. We have chosen a number of poems and paintings, which were hidden, and smuggled out or retrieved after the liberation. We offer them in memory of these children in particular, in memory of all the inmates of Terezin in general, in memory of the 6,000,000 who stand behind them, and in memory of all the victims of racial discrimination, oppression, and genocide whose fate reverberates through human history. The program takes its title from a line in one of the poems, 'I Never Saw Another Butterfly.' "

On the screen appeared the gorgeous, bright, multicolored painting of a butterfly by Eva Bulova. And Naomi began:

The Butterfly

The last, the very last,
So richly, brightly, dazzlingly yellow.
Perhaps if the sun's tears would sing
against a white stone . . .

At the end of the poem she named the author: "Pavel Friedmann, born January 7, 1921, in Prague, deported to Terezin April 26, 1942, died at Auschwitz September 29, 1944, age twenty-three."

With Eva Bulova's picture still on the screen I described Terezin: "Terezin, or Theresienstadt as we call it now—its German name—is a little town about sixty kilometers from Prague in Czechoslovakia. It was founded about two hundred years ago by the Emperor Joseph II of Austria, who named it after his mother, Maria Theresa. It is a fortress with twelve ramparts which enclose the town in the shape of a star. It sits in the middle of the countryside."

And then, intercut with poems and backed by the vibrant life-affirming paintings of these extraordinary doomed children, we began the litany of Hitler's rise to power and its effect on the town: the invasion of Czechoslovakia, the edict setting up in Czechoslovakia a Headquarters for the Deportation of the Jews, the census of Jewish inhabitants, the exclusion of Jewish children from state elementary schools, the evacuation of Terezin, the establishment of Theresienstadt as "an old-age ghetto," the euphemistic order called "Transfers of Residence to Theresienstadt," the deportations.

And then a poem.

And the construction of a concentration camp at Oświęcim in Upper Silesia—known to us also by its German name: Auschwitz.

And then a poem.

And the role of Himmler.

And Himmler's order to Rudolf Hoess, the commandant at Auschwitz, for, quote, the Final Solution to the Jewish problem.

And the details of Hoess's compliance: the installation of combination units, each containing an anteroom, a gas chamber, and an oven for body disposal: the underground *Leichenkeller* or corpse cellars which had elevators for bringing up bodies and could accommodate two thousand people at a time; the surface *Badeanstalten* or bath houses, which were slightly smaller. Five crematoria in all.

And then a poem.

And Hoess's decision after visiting the concentration camp at Treblinka that carbon monoxide was not very, in his word, "efficient" for mass killing.

And the introduction of quick-working hydrogen cyanide or prussic acid, known by its commercial name: Zyklon B.

And the history of Zyklon B—its development by private manufacturers, originally for the extermination of vermin; its use for the large-scale fumigation of buildings, barracks, and ships, for the disinfection of clothes in special gas chambers, and for the delousing of human beings, who wore gas masks for this purpose.

And Himmler's repeated description of the Jews as parasites who must be exterminated like vermin.

And then a poem.

And then Himmler's address to his top commanders in October 1943:

> Most of you know what it means when a hundred corpses lie there, or when five hundred corpses lie there, or when a thousand corpses lie there. To have gone through this and— apart from a few exceptions caused by human weakness—to have remained decent, that has made us great.

Finally against the glorious purple, red, and yellow sunset of Nelly Silvinova—born December 21, 1931, in Prague, deported to Terezin September 10, 1942, died at Auschwitz October 4, 1944, age twelve, Naomi concluded:

Birdsong

He doesn't know the world at all
Who stays in his nest and doesn't go out.
He doesn't know what birds know best

Nor what I want to sing about,
That the world is full of loveliness.

When dewdrops sparkle in the grass
And earth's aflood with morning light,
A blackbird sings upon a bush
To greet the dawning after night.
Then I know how fine it is to live.

Hey, try to open up your heart
To beauty; go to the woods someday
And weave a wreath of memory there.
Then if the tears obscure your way
You'll know how wonderful it is
    To be alive

"We have no information about who wrote this poem."

The sunset on the screen vanished and we looked out in silence at these young faces dappled by the Mississippi sun. We looked at them and they at us for a long time and then slowly, in silence, almost as if in a dream, we dismantled our screen, unplugged our projector, gathered our scripts from the music stands, and with a last look—a look not of awkwardness but of recognition—walked to the handsome staircase and left the room. Nobody said a word.

In the afternoon Naomi was due to give her Guatemala program at the house of a black couple and I was taken by car to a small town thirty miles from Yazoo to talk about Ritual and Reality. On the way my driver, Martha, the local librarian, talked to me about the racial divisions in the community. Yazoo had felt the impact of the civil rights marches of the '60s—indeed all of Mississippi had been a primary target. Genuine progress had been made, though in Yazoo itself there was more lip service to the programs set in motion by the Johnson administration than any sea change in the attitude of the majority of the white population.

But how could places like Manchester Academy exist, I asked.

Well, there were always ways to circumvent the law, she said. But what was remarkable, and ironic, and peculiarly gratifying was that the very nature of bureaucratic change, its maddening slowness, was now working in favor of integration. Now, just when the rightward drift of the second Nixon administration, and in particular of the Nixon Supreme Court, was seeking to reverse, or at the very least not enforce, many of the decisions of the Warren Court, all the Johnson-era legislation was at last beginning to filter down to the local level and it would doubtless take another ten years for that gigantic lumbering vessel to be turned round again. And by that time Yazoo City, like the rest of Mississippi, would have already accommodated its black citizens.

Despite the Manchester Academies, I asked.

Well, there were bound to be some remaining strongholds, but on the whole, yes.

Oil City was an entirely black community of some three hundred souls, a shantytown, without water, without electricity, without paved roads, a collection of fifty or sixty corrugated-iron shacks. We pulled up outside a simple whitewashed wooden structure, the one wooden building, the church. "We are supposed to meet Reverend Paris," Martha said.

We got out of the car. The heat shimmered. The doors made a startling sound, closing like bullets in the thin air. Gingerly, we climbed the steps to the front door of the church and knocked. Our knocks echoed hollowly but no one answered. I tried the door but it was locked.

"I don't know," said Martha, "maybe he's at his house." We turned around. A tall elderly black man was striding towards us. "We are looking for the Reverend Paris," Martha said.

"Well, ma'am, you have found him."

"We are from Yazoo City. This is Robin Hirsch from the National Humanities Series."

"You do us a great honor, sir," said the Reverend Paris with a gentle sweep of his arm and the slightest indication of a bow. "On behalf of my congregation I welcome you."

"Well, I'll leave the two of you together, then," said Martha. "I'll be back to pick up Mr. Hirsch in an hour and a half or two hours."

"As you say, ma'am."

Martha made for the car door, but the Reverend Paris reached out his long arm and opened it for her, again with that slight inclination of the body. "You drive carefully, now, ma'am." The door closed, the huge machine started up, she reversed, turned, honked the horn, and in a cloud of dust disappeared.

What on earth was I going to tell this black congregation?

"Well, sir, I must gather up my flock. Will you accompany me, or will you wait?"

"Oh, I'd like very much to come with you, if that's alright."

"You are most heartily welcome, sir."

We set off down the road. The Reverend Paris was in his sixties. In his youth he had been an athlete, a hurdler. He and Jesse Owens had been friends, and rivals. "That was one way out for a black boy in those days.

But I didn't have what Jesse had. Jesse had something special. He was touched by grace. And he went over there . . . ," he gestured in the general direction of Europe, "And he showed them." An extraordinary mixture of tenderness, affection, pride, and righteousness crept into his voice. "Jesse, he showed that Mr. Hitler, now, didn't he?"

I nodded.

"He showed that Mr. Hitler a thing or two."

In the heat and dust, the Reverend Paris stopped at huts and called out names and from some of the huts would come a voice, always a woman's voice, always melodious, and it would sing out, "Oh, no, Mr. Paris, I can't come out today," or "I got things to do," or "My baby's sick," and from some of them would issue forth a great big black mama herself, dressed in her church finery and I would be introduced to her as having come all the way from New York to talk to them and she would welcome me and she would touch the Reverend Paris and she would link arms with her sisters and we would trudge on together to the next house.

In twenty minutes or so we were back at the church, the Reverend Paris and me and seven or eight immense black women in hats and cotton dresses, some with fans, some with parasols. The preacher unlocked his church and his congregants sailed in, me in tow. It was cool and, by comparison with the outside, dark, although after a few moments my eyes adjusted and the cool light from the one window picked out the women sitting in the front two pews. The Reverend Paris conducted me to a seat, the only seat, on the dais that served as both altar and pulpit, bade me sit and then went over to the organ, put his foot to the pump and struck a chord. Together, he and the women began a hymn. The sound built and swelled, the women rocked and swayed, all these voices one voice, one enormous voice, filling this small white wooden building, shaking it, rattling the window pane. One hymn followed another, tears streamed down their faces as they sang and sang and the sun caressed them.

There was nothing I could possibly tell these people.

After five or six hymns, the Reverend Paris turned to his congregation and still swaying gently they came to rest. "Mr. Hirsch here has come all the way from New York to talk to us today. He's here though the good offices of the National Humanities Series and the local Humanities Council in Yazoo City. And he is going to talk to us about Ritual and Reality. And he's going to talk about it from a religious perspective."

Oh, my God, I had forgotten that this program offered the local audience the choice of perspective—social, political, dramatic, or religious. It was essentially the same material, the fruits of my dissertation, with a slightly different coloring for each point of view. It took as its starting point two primitive ritual forms—the ritual of fertility or sexual celebration and the ritual of sacrifice or tribal execution—and developed a kind of parable out of their confluence, a parable of the gradual submergence of the individual to the state, of passion to reason, of the country to the city, in short of the ritual of sexual celebration—of connectedness to the earth, the land—to the ritual of sacrifice—of ties to the political system and the loss of a tangible god.

"I am here as a guest in the House of God," I began.

"Amen! Amen!" they responded.

And I, this emissary from New York, this Jew, this foreigner, stammered on about the roots of religion, about our ties to the land, about the importance of good harvests, about the principle of fertility, about the development of god-figures, about ritual dances, about communal meals, about the shedding of kindred blood, about the participation of the whole community in the act of ritual slaughter, about the increasingly spiritual conception of the deity, about the blood which was poured out on the ground and became an offering to the gods who imbibed it from below, about the sacred seats of life—the organs—which were consigned to the flames and which became an offering to the gods who inhaled the fumes from the air, and about a symbolic moment where the ritual associated with sacrifice, with execution, with moderation and the political system, with the city, absorbed the ritual associated with fertility, with sexual celebration, with chaos and ecstasy, with the countryside, and that the world in which we lived today reflected that loss, that surrender.

I tried to make it short. The women would throw in the occasional "Amen" if ever I mentioned the name of God, but after half an hour the "Amens" which had become fainter had vanished altogether and my entire audience, with the exception of the Reverend Paris, was asleep. I finished, the Reverend Paris struck the organ gently and his congregation came slowly back to life. "I want to thank Mr. Hirsch for coming all the way from New York to tell us about Ritual and Reality. Nothing Mr. Hirsch has told us here today—and he has told us a great deal—in any way contradicts what is said in the Good Book."

"Amen!" said the sisters.

"And now let us raise our voices again and praise the Lord."

And raise their beautiful voices they did. And in the middle of a hymn the door behind them opened slowly and the light streamed in and standing in the light was Martha.

"Well, how did it go?" she asked me as we drove back.

"How did it go? It was a disaster, what do you think? If a Stokely

Carmichael or an Eldridge Cleaver or a Rap Brown came to Oil City to rouse these people to revolution they would send him away singing. Their faith is the only thing they have. If you try to take that away from them they have nothing. I don't mind talking about this stuff to Kiwanis Clubs or little white church groups whom no one in a million years is going to rouse to revolution, but these people, it's an insult."

"Well, you did the best you could. It's important to reach out to the black community. And I'm glad we did it."

"What did we do? We didn't bring food, we didn't bring clothing, we didn't bring electricity. I'm ashamed of what I tried to tell these people."

When I got back to the motel, Naomi was brimming with enthusiasm. Her program on Guatemala had gone by the boards. The home in which she had been invited to speak was a black home, the home of a Jamaican doctor and his wife who owned a liquor store. It was the first time that blacks and whites had met openly together in someone's home. Jewelle Wesley had taken the bull by the horns and invited all kinds of people. The only social visiting up till today had been furtively, often at night, between the Wesleys and the young Episcopalian minister and his wife. Today was an important day in the history of Yazoo City, and the relationship between the blacks and whites at Mrs. Wesley's house had entirely eclipsed the relationship between Mayan and Spaniard in Guatemala and contemporary attempts at fusion.

The following night we did our big show, all three of us, with several hundred people, black and white, in the audience. Many we recognized from our separate forays into the community. Some had become, in this short time, friends; some would never become friends if we spent the rest of our lives in Mississippi.

After the discussion session there was a party. It was a party in a big mansion. The air smelled of honeysuckle, uniformed servants greeted us when we arrived. It was the home of the local senator. In his most gracious manner he welcomed us and thanked us for having brought so much to his home town. There were drinks and an abundance of food and hundreds of people, charming and gracious and hospitable. But with the exception of those in uniform, they were all white. We had a drink, we thanked the members of the local committee, we gathered the Episcopalian minister and his wife and drove to the Wesley house. For many hours, late into the night, we sat and drank and laughed and cursed and wondered what the future would bring to a city, a society so desperately afraid of change.

*   *   *

Yazoo City was the beginning of our second tour and the next morning we packed our bags, our three hundred pounds of equipment, and our raw and complex feelings and headed for El Dorado, Arkansas. From Arkansas to Tennessee, from Tennessee to Missouri, from Missouri to Kansas, and from Kansas to Oklahoma. In each community some of the feelings which lay beneath the surface of everyday life, beneath the identical townships with their Exxon signs, their ribbon of road, their donut shops and hamburger joints, their shopping malls, their banks, their Main Streets, their car dealerships, their churches, their schools, their billboards, their lawns, their houses, their bus stations, their TV antennae, from beneath the veneer of respectability and politeness and homogeneity would bubble forth an amalgam of deep and complicated and raw and delicate and frightening feelings, quiescent, unspoken until the hurried passage of these three guerrillas in their rented car. And beyond the Kiwanis Clubs and the Homemakers Units there would be blacks and Indians and Italians and Jews and prisoners and welfare mothers and homosexuals and libertines and covert scholars. And in the two and a half days that we were there we would be plugged into all kinds of circuits and somehow, inevitably, all kinds of wires would get crossed, all kinds of connections that did not normally get made would get made, and all kinds of sparks would fly. Sometimes a fire would start, a small one in someone's heart or a large one in an entire community. People would confess secrets they had never confessed, feelings they had never identified, longings they had all but forgotten. But the ones in whom the fires burned strongest, the ones in whom the complex well of unanticipated feelings was most deeply stirred, the ones for whom the whole rapid process became a slow and genuine revelation were the three of us.

In Ponca City, Oklahoma, the third richest community per capita in the United States, a town with a substantial minority of Indians, beckoned from the reservations with the promise of jobs and money and now poor, given to crime and drink, a silent presence on the fringe of plenty, in Ponca City we got a break. Jim flew home to his wife and children in Indiana. Naomi and I took a plane to Los Angeles.

Janet's brother Paul, who had had the terrible misfortune to be conscripted during the height of the Vietnam War but the extraordinary good fortune to have been sent to Europe, had taken up photography as part of his army career and after his safe return had moved out West and set himself up as a photographer in L.A. He booked us a room in a hotel in Hollywood.

"Paul, we're going to be there for three nights—and then we'll spend a week in San Francisco. There's someone else I'm trying to get in touch with but I haven't been able to get a reply. Could you try him for me? He's my mother's first husband. He lives in Beverly Hills. If you get hold of him tell him I'm going to be there for three days with my wife, and that I hope to see him."

In our hotel, a seedy modest-priced affair, we were shown to our room. On the bed was a huge bouquet of flowers with a note: "My dear Naomi, welcome to Los Angeles. Jochem Sachs."

"My goodness, this is unexpected. He really is a chevalier."

I nodded. Jochem was seventy-three now, as old as the century. A lot of things had changed, a lot of water under a lot of bridges. And here he was in this American city, this fragmented, paved-over, dehumanized monument to the automobile, hardly the Berlin of his youth, and somehow he hadn't changed. He was still sending women flowers.

The phone rang.

"Hello."

"Robin, my boy, welcome to Los Angeles."

"Jochem, thank you. How are you? And thank you for the flowers."

"Oh, the flowers, they are not for you, so do not thank me. How long will you stay?"

"Just three days."

"Well, we must make the most of it. Tonight, are you free?"

"Yes, we had planned on seeing you."

"Good, then you will come and I will cook you dinner. I will pick you up at seven, is that good?"

"I think that will be fine."

"Good, now get off the phone and let me speak to your wife."

"Naomi," I said, handing her the phone, "it's your chevalier."

"Oh, Mr. Sachs, the flowers are gorgeous, thank you. Oh, alright—Jochem." They chatted intimately for a good many minutes and finally Naomi said, "Jochem, we'll see you at seven. I'm dying to meet you." She hung up. "He's a charmer, your Mr. Sachs, isn't he?"

"Dying to meet him, are we? That's pretty quick work."

"Do I detect a note of jealousy?"

"Well, you know, he has quite a reputation."

"Ah yes, Marlene Dietrich, your mother, the Countess whatever her name is, and now me—you better watch out."

At seven a battered old Plymouth pulled up outside the hotel. It was drizzling. The driver's door opened and a man in a hat and raincoat got out. He turned back, reached in and pulled out an umbrella. It was clearly Jochem and the umbrella was clearly not for him but in order to escort us down to the car. We came down the steps just as he was crossing the driveway.

"Jochem," I said.

"*Ach, mein Sohn*," he threw his arms around me. "How good to see you." Then he released me, unfolded the umbrella, and turned to Naomi. "And this is Naomi. You must forgive me if I embrace your husband, but we are old friends. Now," and there on the steps of the Hollywood Hideaway Motel and Coffee Shop, under an umbrella in the rain, he raised my wife's hand to his lips and with ever so slight an inclination of the body bent down and kissed it. "*Enchanté*," he said. And then he turned to me: "*Bildhübsch*, Robin. *Bildhübsch*."

We climbed into the car. "Well, my dears, it is wonderful to have you here. Tonight nothing but talk—and food, although I must warn you I am hardly a great cook. And now we must pray that this old machine will start." He turned the key in the ignition. The engine coughed and coughed but didn't catch. "It is the rain." He tried again. "Or it isn't the rain. Things aren't what they used to be. This car, it's not so old. But you can't rely on it anymore." He tried once more and this time the engine sprang to life. "You see, a little patience, a little affection," and he caressed the dashboard. "Now, to my palace."

We drove for perhaps twenty minutes along nondescript roads, past undifferentiated housing tracts, with half-hearted attempts at shrubbery and strings of identical shopping malls, and endless cars. "Ah, the land of the automobile," said Jochem. "In Los Angeles, if you do not have a car, you are not a person. Now, tell me, you have been on a great adventure, you have traveled across this huge country, this continent, tell me is it all like this now?"

"Well, Jochem, not exactly."

"No, I know. I am pulling your leg a little. I traveled the country too, for years and years, selling jewelry to people who knew nothing about beautiful stones, selling art reproductions to people who knew nothing about art. But now I am here and this is where I will end my days and this old car takes me on my errands—it has been through the wars, you know. But it is sufficient, I have no great journeys to undertake. So I must hear about yours." We turned off onto a small side street. "This is Beverly Hills, although perhaps not the Beverly Hills you imagine." We pulled up in front of a simple whitewashed apartment building. "Now, I'm afraid we will have to make a little climb."

We got out of the car, climbed the simple cement stairs to the second floor, and Jochem fumbled for his key. "The light has gone out again in the hallway. It's too bad." Presently he found the key, turned the lock, and threw open the door. "Welcome to my palace."

The room was warm and inviting and relatively spacious. It had, in this modern Los Angeles suburb, an uncannily European feel. There was a faded but evidently once-rich Persian carpet, a huge sofa and overstuffed armchairs, an old mahogany dining-table, piled with books and magazines. The piles had obviously been consolidated to make room for three dinner settings and a vase with flowers. And everywhere there were paintings, on the walls, in frames and bare canvases, on chairs, on the coffee table, even on the floor.

"Ah, the paintings," Jochem said, "for the last few years, for what reason I do not know, suddenly out of me there come these paintings. I never painted, but now I am in love with painting. I am up every day at 5:30, I go out on my little *Balkon*, and I paint. Oil paint, imagine. Like Rembrandt. I who know nothing, I have to paint in oil. *Meshugge*, no?" He took our coats and hung them in the closet.

"Now, we go to the kitchen."

Going to the kitchen was not exactly an expedition since the kitchen was a little alcove with a tiny bar separating it from the living area. He reached into a cupboard above the sink and produced three wine glasses, long, elegant, with a slight greenish hue, an exact replica of the good glasses which were never used, in the glass case in my parents' living room. Then he opened the refrigerator and pulled out a bottle of champagne.

"Now, my dear children, we make a toast. But first, Robin, you have to open this bottle. I was never good at opening champagne. Only at drinking it. Very good," he said as the cork burst forth and the foaming liquid began to mount the sides of the glass. "Now, my dears," he raised the glass, "we have to drink to you and to your future. My dear Naomi, we have only just met, but I already have a very good feeling about you. You are a warm and sensitive person and the entry into this marriage, into this family, I know has not been an easy one. But you are a strong person also and you will fight to make a go of it and you will make a home and a future and since you have chosen to make it with this *Lausejunge* here, for better or worse so be it. And if it's for worse don't you hesitate a minute, you throw him over and you come right out here to Beverly Hills and I show you how to paint. And you, with your beard and your hair and your jeans and your boots, how did you get so lucky? Is this the polite young man I met in Hamburg. Is this the little boy in the short trousers whose picture I have in my photo album?" And then he slapped me gently across the face. "No, of course it isn't. It's a grown man with a mind of his own, with feelings and a history. And a beautiful wife. Now we drink to the future, to both of you, to youth and happiness and long life and to the long journey you both have ahead of you." And we clinked glasses around the little formica bar and drank to the future.

The champagne went to our heads. The weeks on the road, the accumulated jumble of impressions, of other people's lives, began to recede, and in the warmth of the little flat the three of us drew closer. Jochem removed his jacket and put on an apron. "Now I make dinner. First, a little *Vorspeise*, it's not much, but one must have something to begin, to whet the appetite." And he pulled out from the refrigerator a plate with a little paté and smoked fish on it. "A mishmash, no? The meat is French, the fish is Jewish. Not a bad combination, huh? Now you eat and I cook. Dinner tonight will be Schnitzel à la Holstein. Unfortunately, Schnitzel à la Holstein is my only dish. However, that is one more than your beautiful mother could do when I married her."

"That's funny. My mother is a wonderful cook now."

"That is a result of your father. Your mother, when I married her, was a bohemian. She was a ravishing beauty. All Berlin was in love with her. But she couldn't cook. She scarcely knew what dinner was. We could have six people over for dinner and she would be at the opera. There we would be, waiting for dinner and at ten o'clock she would rush in and say, 'Oh, Jochem, I completely forgot, but they were giving *Rosenkavalier* and how could I miss it and anyhow here are some chocolates and some flowers.' And we would open some tins for our guests and eat sauerkraut and chocolates. But of course always flowers and always champagne." He turned to the stove. "Now I cook and you talk. Tell me about your great adventure."

And while the schnitzels sizzled and he broke the eggs, we talked about America and the great variety of the country that we had been exposed to, the whites, the blacks, the rich, the poor, the huge disparities, the eagerness to learn, the sometimes appalling ignorance.

"About history?"

"Yes, about history. The program that we do about Theresienstadt— some people don't even know who Hitler was."

"You do a program about Theresienstadt?"

I nodded.

"Betty was in Theresienstadt."

"Yes, I know. I thought about her a lot."

"She played the violin in the camp orchestra."

"I didn't know that."

"It kept her alive."

"She must be eighty now."

"No, no, Robin, we don't talk about that. She lives around the corner.

In Burbank. But she's always off somewhere. She's in Peru now. She'll be heartbroken to have missed you."

The schnitzels were ready.

"Come, we go to the table and eat like proper people."

We took our plates over to the dining table.

"Come, Naomi, you sit here on my right so the candle shines on your beautiful face. And, Robin, you sit here in this chair. It is a special chair. It is from Thomas Mann."

"Thomas Mann?"

"Yes, he lived here in Los Angeles. He, Heinrich also. We were quite a colony. Feuchtwanger. Peter Lorre, the actor. Fritz Lang. Paul Dessau. Hans Eissler. And of course Brecht. But Brecht was never happy here. His wife, the great Weigel, would make *Apfelstrudel* and they would have people in their house all the time, sitting on those hard chairs. But they never liked it. And then what they did to him with that dreadful McCarthy, those hearings. But he never really learned the language. So he didn't understand their questions. Or he pretended. And they didn't understand his answers."

"You know, I saw Helene Weigel in Berlin, the year I first met you."

"On the stage?"

"No. In a cemetery. All alone. She must have been visiting Brecht's grave."

"Of course. They went back. He was a hero. They gave him a theater. He made a big success. And then he died."

We cleared away the plates. Naomi and I did the dishes. Jochem sat on the sofa and began to peel an apple. "Come, you finish with those dishes now and have some fruit. It is good for the digestion."

"Jochem, why did you and my mother break up?"

He smiled ruefully and shook his head. "Too silly. An actress. Some little actress. An infatuation. I was always infatuated with women. I don't even remember her name. Some little actress in Berlin. 'I must have a divorce,' I said and this time your mother had had enough. We cried all the way to the Registry Office and then we lived together for a year after the divorce." He began to cut the apple into slices. "Too silly. Your mother was the most beautiful woman in the world. I have known all kinds of women but your mother was the one true love of my life. Here, have some apple. It's good for you. Naomi, did you ever see pictures of your mother-in-law as a young woman?"

Naomi shook her head.

"Robin, did you?"

"I have seen one or two."

"Here, I will show you." And he went over to the sideboard and rummaged around and came back with three or four old photograph albums. "You are interested?"

"Yes, of course."

He picked up the most tattered of the albums and began to leaf through it. "This is me as a boy. My parents. My brother and me. My first girlfriend. Ah, here is the first picture your mother gave me. Here is the famous Nefertiti picture. Tell me, have you ever seen anything so beautiful? Here we are on the Kurfürstendamm. And here we are in the mountains, on a ski holiday—she was never a great skier. Oh, this is interesting—here we are in New York, in a house on Fifth Avenue."

"You were in New York with my mother?"

"You didn't know we lived in America?"

"You lived in America?"

"For a year and a half after our marriage."

"I hadn't the faintest idea."

"Don't look so shocked."

"Well, I'm amazed. She hasn't been exactly reticent. I mean, I knew about you. All that was quite open. But here she has her only son living in America for six years and she had lived here forty years ago . . ."

"More, more, I'm afraid. You know, my children, you are not the only ones to have trouble with families. Your mother's family was dead set against our marriage. They were extremely respectable, with two ravishing daughters—Herta the older one was not as beautiful as Käthe, but she was blond so everyone fell at her feet—she lives now in Buenos Aires, doesn't she? Well, anyhow, the family thoroughly disapproved of me. I was an unknown quantity, my friends were artists and bohemians. And her father absolutely forbade the marriage. But she was in love too. So when she was twenty-one and her father was away on a business trip we married. And then we jumped on a boat in Hamburg and sailed to America. I had a brother here with a big house on Long Island."

"And what did you do here?"

"I worked for my brother. He was in banking."

"And my mother?"

"She worked also."

"And why did you leave?"

"Well, we were homesick. It was a young country. No culture. Long Island was like a desert—no *Rosenkavalier*. And even New York . . . And Käthe missed her family. So we got on a boat and went back."

"And then you fell in love with an actress."

"And then I became infatuated, but it was nothing. A foolishness. Not," he turned to Naomi, "that all actresses are a foolishness."

Naomi smiled. "I think you are very honest, Jochem."

"Honest? What's there to be honest? I'm seventy-three years old. I've lived through two world wars. I've had money, I've been broke. I've known beautiful women and talented artists and scoundrels and some were the same thing. My best friend was a lifelong homosexual. Nothing shocks me. So what's to be honest? To be decent, to enjoy life, to have friends, to have a little panache, that's what's important."

"Well, then," she said, "you have panache."

He inclined his head in a slight bow. "I thank you, madame. Coming from you that is indeed a compliment."

"Where in New York did you live?"

"I don't remember. It was so long ago. But why she didn't tell you . . ."

"Well, it's been a wonderful evening," Naomi broke in, "and you cook a wonderful schnitzel, even if it is the only dish in your repertoire. But you have to be up at five in the morning to paint and we have a long day behind us and perhaps we should think about going."

"I will take you back to your hotel but not without a little brandy to round out the evening. And while I go to get the brandy you look in this book," he pushed one of the albums towards her, "somewhere in the middle."

He stood up and retired behind the bar. We opened the book. A host of unfamiliar faces. "Jochem, where are we supposed to be looking?"

"Somewhere in the middle. There's a London section."

There was indeed a section entitled London.

"They may not be in order and they may be loose. But they should be there. You know, I lived in London for a bit during the war. Before you were born. Your father was in fact quite decent to me. I also had a cousin there, whose wife I was in love with. But that's another story. He died after the war and I almost married her. But after Käthe, I don't know, I just couldn't marry again."

He arrived with three glasses and a bottle of brandy. "Here, just a drop for each of us. A nightcap." He poured a little into each glass. "*L'chaim!* You know what *l'chaim* means, Naomi? Of course you do, your father is a rabbi. Are you religious? No? Well, it doesn't matter, religion is not so important. It's what's in the heart that's important."

We clinked glasses and drank.

"There! There you are." Jochem pointed to the album. "You see, your husband when he was young and beautiful."

And there indeed were pictures of me in my pram, with my sister on a stone sculpture outside Grove End Gardens after the war, in my Arnold House uniform, at my Bar Mitzvah in my St. Paul's school uniform, at Oxford in my gown and white bow tie, pictures that I remembered from my parents' home, that I had seen at my uncle's flat in Amsterdam, that doubtless were stacked away somewhere at the Schoenheimers' in New York, at my aunt's in Buenos Aires, at Betty Joseph's in Burbank, at the homes of countless friends and relatives of my parents, known and unknown to me, the survivors, in Israel, in France, in Australia, in Florida, in South Africa, in Brazil, in Scandinavia, fragments of a life scattered about the globe, a signal to the farthest reaches of the universe that even after the explosion life continues.

"Wasn't he a beautiful boy?" said Jochem.

"He still is," said Naomi.

"He still is," said Jochem. "My *Lausejunge.*" And he reached over and patted me on the leg.

"What does that mean?" Naomi asked.

"Oh, you must forgive me. We *Jäckes* mix everything up. How would you translate it, Robin?"

"It means scoundrel," I said.

Jochem insisted on driving us back to the hotel. This time the car started. "You see, she obeys." Before we got out Jochem made us promise to spend our last night together. "I am so happy to have met you, Naomi. And don't you forget, the first sign of trouble and you come straight back to Beverly Hills." He kissed her on the cheek and then he turned round to me in the back seat: "Remember, there is nothing on this earth like a good woman. You are a very lucky boy." Then he took my cheek between his thumb and forefinger and squeezed it. Then he said: "Now go with God, but go."

The next day we spent with Paul and his girlfriend, Kress, an actress. We had lunch in Venice, we drove in their van to Santa Monica, we swam in the Pacific, and at night we all cooked dinner together at their flat.

"I want to meet this Jochem," Paul said. "Why don't we all have dinner tomorrow night. In fact, why don't you bring him down to the studio first and I can take a few pictures. I'd like you to see the studio while you're here."

So the next night, our last night in Los Angeles, we picked up Jochem in a taxi and drove down to Paul's studio. It was a huge high-ceilinged affair in a dilapidated building. The neighborhood was deserted. Kress opened the door. "Paul's in the darkroom. Come in. Come in."

"Kress Mersky. This is Jochem Sachs."

"*Enchanté.*"

"Nice to meet you, Mr. Sachs."

"No, no. Jochem. Please."

"Jochem." And she gave him an elaborate curtsey.

Jochem raised her hand to his lips. "I can see I am going to have a good time tonight."

Kress took our coats and put them on an old Victorian sofa. "Would you like coffee? Or a drink?" We each took a glass of wine. "Paul, they're here. Come on out."

"Coming. Coming."

We stepped into the huge room.

"What a wonderful place," Jochem said, gazing up at the ceiling and turning around like a child. "What space."

A door opened and Paul's huge frame appeared, two sheets dripping with chemicals in his hands: "God, it's dark in there. I've just got to hang these up. It's for a catalogue. A deadline. It pays the rent." He bounded over to a desk and hung them to a line with clothes-pegs. Then he rinsed his hands at a sink and lumbered back to join us. "So, this is Jochem. I'm really pleased to meet you. I'm Paul."

"You have a wonderful place here. Such space."

"Yes. It is big, isn't it? Come with me."

And this young bearded giant, in his workboots and jeans and work-shirt, put his arm comfortably around the delicate frame of my mother's elegant former husband and led him gently into the center of the room. "This is where I take my pictures. You see. We pull down this paper here," and he walked to the wall and pulled down a huge roll of photographic paper. "The subject sits right here on a stool," and Paul's arm reached out and produced a stool. "And then we switch on these lights," and he walked to three tripods stationed on the perimeter of the space, switching on lights as he went, white umbrellas hovering above them, and suddenly Jochem was caught in brilliant, dazzling light, a drink in his hand, his eyes sparkling, his striped shirt gleaming against the blue of his blazer, and the black of his velvet bow tie.

"Jochem, why don't you sit on the stool?" Click, click.

"You want to take a picture of me?" Jochem smiled. "How wonderful!"

"These are just Polaroids, to see if the light's right." Click. Click. Paul pulled the pictures out of the camera. "Robin and Naomi should have a decent picture of you. I bet you don't have a decent picture of yourself. Very few people do. These look just about right. What do you think, Robin?"

"It's amazing how these things develop right in front of your eyes."

"It is, isn't it? Well, what do you think?"

"It looks fine to me."

"Well, give them to Jochem."

"I want to keep one," said Naomi, "so we have something to take with us." Jochem studied the pictures.

"You have a wonderful face, Jochem. Maybe I should do a series."

"Whatever you say, my boy. You're an artist. I trust you."

"We'll take some now and then maybe next week when they're gone and that catalogue job is done we can have another session."

"Fine, fine. So long as we have fun."

Click. Click.

"Jochem, where are you living?"

"I have a small flat in Beverly Hills." Click.

"It's not much but it's home." Click, click. "Home, you know, is not a place, it's not a building, it's not a collection of bricks. It's what you carry with you. Your memories, your friends." Click, click. "We all had to pack up and move too often." Click. "Now I have a little studio, I have my painting, I have my friends, those who are left, and I am happy." Click. "Three years ago, when I was seventy, they gave me a big party in a big hotel in Beverly Hills." Click. "Seventy friends they collected together, one for every year of my life." Click. "It was beautiful. I cried." Click. "There were friends from all walks of life, some young, some old." Click. "Betty was there." Click. "Some of my closest friends are gone." Click. "But I am used to that. And I make new friends. You, for example." Click. "You, the photographer." Click. "And your enchanting lady." Click. "And friends are what sustain you. Friends are what keep you alive." Click. "Do you know what I do now, what I do for a living?" Click. "I have a friend who's a dentist. He knows I love to paint. So I make deliveries for him during the week after the early light has gone." Click. "In my old Plymouth." Click. "Dentures, bridges, plates." Click. "And I am happy. I don't need much to live. I have my paints." Click. "I have my friends." Click. "And I have my memories."

"Damn," said Paul. "I just have one picture left. Come on, the two of you. Get up there with Jochem. That's right. Jochem, give me your glass. Now, Robin, you put your arm round his shoulder. And Jochem, you put your arm round Naomi. O.K. Good. Are you happy to be here?" Click. "Good. Some of these are going to be great. Aren't you guys hungry? Let's get out of here." He laughed and switched out the lights. We gathered our belongings and stepped out into the night.

"This is on us," I said. "But you'll have to tell us where to go."

"There's this great place downtown where you eat family style and they just serve you a huge amount of food and drink, no special orders."

"There's a downtown in this place?"

"Of course there is."

"Sounds fine to me."

The five of us piled into Paul's van and sped off in the direction of downtown.

"This is fun," said Jochem. "I've never been in one of these."

"Well, hold tight, we take corners on two wheels."

At the restaurant there seemed to be hundreds of people at large tables. We found a table for the five of us and an elderly waiter plied us with huge platters of food and a good many glasses of wine. A great feeling of good fellowship spread round the table. Jochem regaled us with stories about Berlin, about the war, about London, about his travels through America, and at midnight, full and more than a little tipsy, we clambered aboard the van again.

The lights of downtown lit up the night, one clip joint after another, one porno house after another, one topless bar after another. "Topless." "Topless." "Topless." "Topless." In neon lights, in flashing lights, in little light bulbs.

"You know, while we're in Los Angeles, maybe we should see what all this topless business is about."

"It's very matter-of-fact, you know. They just walk around with their tits hanging out."

"Paul."

"Well, it's true. But maybe while you're here you should. Naomi?"

"Sure. Why not?"

"Jochem, would you like to join us?"

"I have no objection."

Close to where Jochem lived we pulled up at a little corner bar. The *p* in the Topless sign was missing.

"There's no *p* in that sign. See, when it flashes, there's no *p*. Maybe it's Toeless. Maybe this is a bar for amputees."

"Oh, shut up, Robin."

The room was tiny and dark with a few disconsolate patrons, all elderly men, scattered forlornly at a dozen small circular tables. Behind the tiny bar, in the gloom, a young woman patroled. It was hard to see, but it seemed possible that she might indeed be naked from the waist up. From the waist down, too, for that matter. At the other end of the room from the bar—an adequate dancer could have made it in a single leap—was a tiny platform with two drapes and beside it a jukebox. From the jukebox came the Beach Boys singing "Surfin' U.S.A." and on the platform illuminated in red and blue light was another young woman in high heels and fishnet stockings and a bikini, who was trying to do three things at once—dance, smoke a cigarette, and unhook her brassiere. Her heart was quite evidently not in it.

"Come," said Jochem, "we sit down." He led us unabashedly to the front two tables, which we joined together. "Now, we have a good view."

"What would you like to drink?" A third young woman had materialized behind us.

"Er, I'll have a cognac."

"There's a two-drink minimum, honey."

"Er, I'll have two cognacs."

Everybody ordered, she sashayed back to the bar, the Beach Boys finished their song, and the young woman on the stage retrieved her discarded clothing, stubbed out her cigarette, stepped down onto the floor, and replaced the girl behind the bar. The girl behind the bar became our waitress and our erstwhile waitress ambled over to the jukebox, dropped in a coin, made three selections and climbed up on the platform. Jochem gazed up at her attentively. A long slow sensuous introduction from the jukebox and the girl on stage turned her back to us and began to move almost imperceptibly in time to the music. The unaccompanied voices of the London Bach Choir started quietly. Jochem looked at me mystified. Then a guitar and horns and Mick Jagger's voice croaking out, "You Can't Always Get What You Want." A small smile appeared on Jochem's lips and the girl on stage began to move. The song built and the girl picked up momentum, shaking her hips, shaking her torso, and turning around. "She has something," Jochem whispered to me. She stood over us, oblivious, shaking off into her own private world.

Something brushed against my left cheek.

I turned.

"You the brandy?"

"Er, yes," I said to the waitress's right breast.

"Here you are. It's a double."

"Thank you."

She put it down in front of me. I moved my face out of the way. So that was what Paul meant by matter-of-fact.

The Stones and the London Bach Choir and the girl on stage were building to a climax, Jochem's gaze was transfixed and with one hand he was quietly snapping his fingers in time to the music. When they finished he burst into applause. Some of the other patrons stared as though their peace was being disturbed but Jochem continued to applaud. From the girl on stage there was the tiniest flicker of acknowledgment. And then the next number boomed out. By the end of her last number, a rousing Jerry Lee Lewis rocker with a thumping piano, she was dancing almost entirely for Jochem. When she finished, gathered her clothing, and stepped down, Jochem accorded her a little bow. She covered her breasts with her arm and gave him a quick smile, as she hurried to the bar.

The waitress with whose breast I had just made acquaintance replaced her on the stage and the surly dancer we had seen when we came in became the waitress. Quite an ecological system they had here. What kept it going, I wondered? Was one of the disconsolate patrons really the boss? Was there a huge meaty-muscled man lurking in the shadows? How did they deal with trouble? Was this some sort of private club and had we stumbled in by accident? Or had these three girls invented a kind of applied socialism where everybody did everything and split the profits down the middle?

The present dancer was a black girl of quite striking proportions. She had quite clearly figured out that Jochem was the only person in the room who gave a fig for her art and she launched into her act with gusto. James Brown, Aretha Franklin, Jimi Hendrix. Jochem appraised her with a connoisseur's eye, with every now and then a smile, a look, a gesture. By the end other people in the room were applauding and Jochem was on his feet shouting, "Bravo! Bravo!" My last memory is of the surly dancer blowing us a kiss from the stage and the black girl in animated conversation with Jochem.

The next day we left for San Francisco and a week later we flew to Pierre, South Dakota, joined up with Jim and our equipment, and drove to Fort Thompson and the Stephan Indian Mission. We were plunged back into the maelstrom of American life. Things were getting hotter and hotter for Nixon in the White House. Wounded Knee had brought the political conflagration right to the doorstep and here on the reservation hard-nosed nuns with men's names were bringing Christ to their beautiful, silent charges, dispensing chewing gum while the State stood at the gates and sold their parents liquor.

Of all the communities we spent time with in these few months, our days with the Crow Creek Sioux were the most dispiriting. An entire culture deracinated. A silence in the air like wet clouds. And nuns feeding them Christ and chewing gum. We accomplished nothing. We packed our bags, as close to despair as we had come, and trudged on.

North Dakota, Montana, Wyoming, Nebraska, Colorado. And then a break. And then a long swing through Ohio where on television, in the heart of John Birch country, Nixon bade farewell to Haldeman, Ehrlichman, and Dean. And then a final swing through the South—Louisiana, Mississippi again, and South Carolina. And finally, after five months on the road through America, back home to New York.

At home there was a letter from Paul. Three days after we had left L.A., Jochem had collapsed. Paul had discovered only by chance. He'd called him to set up another photo session but could never reach him. Finally he sent him some proofs. A woman called to tell him Jochem was in the hospital. He hadn't known how to reach us on the road.

I called California: "Paul, it's Robin."

"Oh, Robin. Bad news."

"He's dead, huh?"

"Yes, more than two weeks ago. He was in a coma. Pleurisy, pneumonia, emphysema. All sorts of complications. But you remember that picture, the last one I took, of the three of you. It came out beautifully. I blew it up and took it to him. I put it at the foot of his bed. And he opened his eyes. He looked at me. And I don't think he knew who I was. And then he looked at the picture. And he smiled. That picture was with him when he died."

Naomi dug out the little Polaroid picture of Jochem and stuck it on the mirror in the bedroom. The following summer Paul and Kress came East in their van. They stayed up in Riverdale with Pierre and Janet. And one night they came to dinner.

"I have something for you," said Paul and he unwrapped a huge photograph. It really was a wonderful picture. We propped it up on the dining table. I had my arm on Jochem's shoulder and he had his arm around Naomi. He was wearing his blazer, his striped shirt, his velvet bow tie, with a white handkerchief just making an appearance from his breast pocket. Naomi was wearing her Guatemalan smock. I had long hair, a beard, a denim shirt, an old vest. We were all smiling, laughing even. But there was something special about Jochem's smile. It was the smile of a man who was exactly where he wanted to be at the moment the picture was taken.

I still have that picture. Occasionally I take it out and look at it. It is from a different era. I no longer have a beard. Naomi is no longer my wife. And the man who danced with Marlene Dietrich is dead.

Part III

Towards Home

(1972—1982)

Dubrovnik

"Robin, I want you to meet the Krasnapolskys," Annie said in her gravelly voice, and she took me by the arm and maneuvered me through the crowded room. It was Christmas Eve and every Christmas Eve Annie held open house in her apartment, up on the thirty-third floor of Kipps Bay, looking down on the East Side of Manhattan, city lights pricking the crystalline air—car lights, street lights, Christmas lights, floodlights picking the tops of skyscrapers out of the night sky, the lights of boats bobbing on the black ribbon of the East River, and the fairy lights on the bridges dancing over the water into Brooklyn.

I'd met Annie my first Christmas in New York. Her daughter Julia and I had been at Oxford together, though I had scarcely known her, but we had a mutual friend, Liz, who was over in America on the same sort of scheme as I, and our first Christmas we had met in New York, she from Kansas, I from Pennsylvania, and she had taken me to Annie's. I'd met Julia, I'd met Annie, and Annie's on Christmas Eve had become an annual event for me long after Liz had returned to England.

Annie's husband, Julia's father, had been an important figure in the early days of the U.N. He'd been very close with Hammarskjöld. They had worked together, they had traveled the world together, and on that fatal day in 1961 when the plane went down they had died together.

It was maybe in memory of that day that Annie always wore black. She was a designer, like my aunt, but I never saw her in any color but black. A long elegant black gown on these occasions, with a long black scarf around her neck, a craggy face like, of all people, Auden's, steel-gray hair, cut like a girl's, no makeup, but on her eyes, incongruously, the most enormous false eyelashes, huge, upswept, like fans.

"Come on, my dear," she said, "fight your way through," and, clenching her long black cigarette-holder between her teeth, "Out of my way, m'dears, we're coming through."

"Michael and Fara Krasnapolsky. Robin Hirsch."

The Krasnapolskys were small, elderly, and very Russian.

"How do you do?" the man stuck out his hand. "Krasnapolsky."

"Oh," I said, shaking it, "like the Grand Hotel."

"Oh, you know the Grand Hotel?" said the woman.

"I have an uncle in Amsterdam. I don't stay there. I know it from the outside, not the inside."

"Well, it's not so grand any more. Anyhow, they spell it with an *i*, we with a *y*."

"Alright, Fara, that is enough. He is not interested in our spelling."

"Why not? He is a young man. He is bright. He is interested."

"You are friend of Julia's?" Michael asked.

"No, as a matter of fact, I hardly know her. We were at Oxford together but our paths didn't really cross. We had a mutual friend, Liz."

"Oh, Liz. Beautiful girl. She was here sometimes. Very bright."

"Yes," I said. "She introduced me to Annie."

"So you are friend of Annie's."

"Well, I suppose you could say that."

"Wonderful woman. Very wonderful woman."

"Oh, Michael," Fara looked at me. "Dere he goes again."

Michael, Fara, and I were the only Jews at this celebration of the Savior's birth and, amidst the angels and the glitter, we huddled together like refugees. Theirs was a relationship in which the grit of mutual irritation struggled to produce a pearl. Michael, balding, owlish behind his glasses, intensely serious, had played the bass for years under Toscanini. Fara, slight, light, elegant, high-cheekboned, almond-eyed, had been a ballerina. Later I found out that Michael had, to Fara's profound disgust, discovered Christian Science, and occasionally in their home on the Upper West Side, after a concert, he would take me into the back room and talk to me about higher values. "Ech," Fara would say, "for a Jew, all those people dead, it's disgusting."

The Krasnapolskys adopted me. Later, when I moved to New York and became involved in the experimental theater, they would religiously trudge down to obscure lofts on the Lower East Side, Michael in his somber suit, Fara in her fur hats and earrings, and with earnestness and mystification try to figure out what I was doing.

They took a genuine interest in my life and aspirations, and one summer as they prepared for a trip to Europe they expressed the wish to meet my family while they were in London. At this time I was living on East 6th Street, between Avenue B and Avenue C, in the heart of heroin country. My neighborhood looked like Hanoi after the bombing. I had friends and acquaintances in all walks of life, some of them less salubrious than others. My parents had the fixed idea that my entire circle consisted of layabouts, pimps, prostitutes, drug dealers, dancers, arsonists, boxers, and ex-cons. I thought the arrival of the Krasnapolskys, as my friends, might perhaps adjust the picture a little in my favor.

One can never anticipate the reactions of one's family. To their credit, the Krasnapolskys succeeded in accomplishing something no one had really managed to do before. They had the same unifying effect on my family that the State of Israel exerted on its Arab neighbors. For the duration of their visit all family differences were forgotten and my sister and my parents formed an alliance in the face of the Russian invasion.

"How could you send us those people?"

"They never stop talking."

"He is so boring."

"She is so loud."

"They are so demanding."

My sister apparently took them to Victoria Station and my family did a dance of liberation before returning to their quotidian internecine disputes.

While my family was entertaining the Krasnapolskys, I met Naomi. In the autumn she moved in with me, and one winter night at dinner, discussing our respective childhoods, discussing childhood in general, discussing bringing up children, suddenly at one particular moment in a quiet restaurant, without having to say it out loud, we realized we had become engaged. Elated, we rushed up to the apartment of our landlord, Alan, who opened a bottle of champagne and toasted us. And then euphorically back through the West Village to the East Village, to the burnt-out block on which we lived to call her parents.

Naomi's father was a rabbi. He was descended from thirteen generations of Orthodox rabbis. He had arrived in America at the age of two, had grown up in Chicago, had come under the influence of liberal thinkers, and had become a Reform rabbi. For this departure God had punished him by giving him two daughters, both of whom became actresses. And a congregation in Charleston, West Virginia, where Jews were not that thick on the ground.

"Mother, it's Naomi."

"Well, Naomi, how kinda you t'call." The voice at the other end of the phone had an unmistakable southern drawl. It was faintly unsettling. A rebbitzin out of Tennessee Williams.

"Mother, I have some wonderful news."

"Well, honey, if it's that wonderful, maybe I should fetch the Rabbi."

"Yes, Mother."

"Jo, honey, pick up the phone, it's Naomi."

"Hello, dear."

"Hello, Dad. Mother, Dad. I have some wonderful news. I'm going to get married."

"Darlin', that's jus' wonderful."

"I'm happy for you, my dear."

"His name is Robin and he's on the phone too."

"Hello."

"Hello."

"Hello."

"What's his name again, honey?"

"Robin."

"Well, Robin, welcome to our family."

"Thank you very much."

"What kind of a name is that, anyhow?"

"It's alright, mother, he's Jewish."

"I'm English Jewish."

"Oh, isn't that a darlin' accent. When y'all comin' down here?"

"Soon, I hope."

And so it went.

The next morning we called London. My father picked up the phone.

"Hullo?"

"Hello, Daddy."

"Hullo?"

"Hello, Daddy, it's Robin."

"Who?"

"Robin."

"Who?"

"Your son, Robin."

"Ach, RRRawbeen."

"Is Mummy there?"

"Käthe," he yelled, "*dein Sohn ist am Apparat.*"

My mother picked up the other phone. "Ach, Robin, you haven't written for so long."

"I'm sorry, Mummy."

"Daddy is still waiting for an answer to his letter."

"I'm sorry, Daddy."

"*Nichts neues*" (Nothing new).

"Listen, I'm calling because I have some important news."

"You have to telephone, writing is too complicated?"

"Herbert."

"A Fulbright scholar who can't write."

"Daddy, please, I'm trying to tell you something. I'm getting married."

My mother could be heard across the Atlantic jumping up and down. "Ach, my darling, that is wonderful. I am so happy."

"*Ruhig*," my father hissed, "*was sagst du*" (Quiet. What are you saying)?

"I'm getting married. Her name is Naomi. She's on the phone."

"Hello, Mr. and Mrs. Hirsch. I'm so pleased to meet you. Robin is a wonderful person. I'm so lucky to have found him."

"Who?"

"Ach, Herbert. Naomi, this is *doch* a terrible way to meet, over the telephone, but we are so happy. I'm sure you must be a wonderful person to put up with him."

"Oh, no, Mrs. Hirsch, he's not so bad."

"How did you meet?"

"Käthe, this costs money. Let them write."

"Daddy, I'm paying for this call."

"You can still write."

"We will, Mr. Hirsch, very soon."

"*Ach so*, a girl after my own heart."

The next month we flew down to Charleston, a small airplane coming into a dangerous airport, flying low over the mountains in a snowstorm and dropping suddenly to land. Rabbi Jo picked us up in the Buick.

"Hello, Dad," Naomi reached up to kiss him.

"Hello, my dear. Mother's waiting at home. Here," he took her bag.

"How do you do, Rabbi?"

He gave me an uneasy look. "How do you do, son?" He put down Naomi's bag and reached out his hand. I put down my bag and took it. "Welcome to Charleston, son."

"It's a pleasure to be here."

We drove through Charleston, past factories, past the capitol ("an exact replica of Washington's"), past poorer districts, to a comfortable house on a hilly street.

"Julie sends her love."

"Oh," the rabbi said coldly, "how is she?"

"Dad, you know how she is. She misses you terribly."

There was silence. We drew up at the house. A small plump pretty woman tiptoed incongruously out to the driveway. "Hi, y'all. Y'all made it safe, well, that's good," she reached up and kissed her daughter, "My, what have you done to yo' hair, and you must be Robin, why, thank you, they're so pretty, all the way from New York, you shouldn't have, ain't he jus' the cutest thing, darlin' I'm so happy, don't stand out here in the cold, come in, come in."

We were shown demurely to separate rooms, we washed and changed, and Naomi joined her mother in the kitchen. The rabbi offered me a glass of sherry in the living room.

"*L'chaim,*" I said.

"*L'chaim.*"

We drank in silence.

"Er, how big is the congregation here?"

"There are about three hundred Jewish families in Charleston, a Conservative temple with about one hundred and fifty families and Temple Israel—my congregation—with about two hundred and fifty."

"I thought there were only . . ."

"Some are members of both."

"Oh."

"They have fewer members, they meet in a converted school hall, the rabbi is an old Yid—you know, beard, accent, from the old country—there is no cantor, everything's in Hebrew, but for some reason they are better attended."

"Are we going to services tonight?"

"Oh, there's no need to do that."

"No, I would like to."

"Well, if you and Naomi insist."

"I would like to, and I'm sure Naomi would, too."

"She's changed, then."

"I'm sure she would."

"It's a brand-new temple, the congregation is affluent. There are tapestries and quite beautiful stained-glass windows. There is an elaborate Ark. But not enough people come on a Friday night to use the main sanctuary. We use the little chapel. And on Saturday morning we have no service, unless there's a Bar Mitzvah. There are classes on Sunday. And basketball. We have services on Friday night. They have services on Saturday morning. They are always full."

"Dinner's ready."

We brought our sherry glasses to the table. In the center of the table was a kiddush cup, two silver candlesticks, and a loaf of challah covered with an embroidered silk cloth.

"Well," said Naomi's mother, "I guess I better say the blessing," and in her incongruous Tennessee Williams she recited the traditional Sabbath blessing over the candles, "Blessed be Thou, O Lord Our God, King of the Universe, who commandest us to light the Sabbath candles."

"*Omein*," I said.

"Amen," said Naomi's father.

Naomi said nothing.

Jo lifted the cloth from the bread and said, "Blessed be Thou, O Lord Our God, King of the Universe, who bringest forth food from the earth." He cut the bread and gave us each a slice. Then he opened the Beaujolais.

"Unusual wine," I said.

"It doesn't have to be awful," he said. "Blessed be Thou, O Lord Our God, King of the Universe, who bringest forth fruit from the vine." He poured a little into the silver cup and drank. "Not bad." Then he filled our glasses. "Well, to you," he said. And we drank.

We drove to services in the Buick. "More cars than usual," the rabbi said as we approached.

"Well, honey, they all know about Naomi and they're dyin' to meet her English beau."

"The wires have been clacketing all week, sister."

"Well, the sisterhood is giving a little kiddush this evening. I can't help it if all those women want to meet him."

"Oh well, there goes the telephone allowance for this month."

An old black man greeted us as we entered the building. "Evening, Rabbi."

"Hello, Jimmy."

"Mrs. Rosenblum."

"Jimmy, is everything set up for the kiddush."

"Yes, ma'am. Why, Miss Naomi, haven't seen you in a hundred years."

"Hello, Jimmy, I want you to meet my fiancé."

"It's a real pleasure. You're marrying a fine young lady."

"Thank you."

"And if I may say so, welcome to the South."

"Thank you."

"Jimmy, I need my gown."

Naomi's father and the caretaker disappeared into the rabbi's study. Her mother took us into the chapel and immediately we were surrounded by well-wishers in well-cut suits and elegant dresses.

"Say hello to the Abramowitzes."

"How do you do?"

"Congratulations."

"Thank you very much."

"The Weinsteins."

"How do you do?"

"Congratulations."

"Thank you very much."

"The Pincuses."

"How do you do?"

"Congratulations."

"Thank you very much."

"The Carters." The Carters?

"Congratulations."

"How do you do? Thank you very much."

An elderly woman played a chord on the harmonium.

"Well, I guess we better sit down." Naomi's mother, waving and smiling, led us to seats in the front row.

The service was short, dry, and in English. Nobody wore a yarmulke. The rabbi spoke briefly on the importance of faith in a shrinking world. His parishioners nodded, smiled, whispered, adjusted their ties, their makeup, their hair, consulted their watches, nodded, stifled a yawn, nodded, played with their jewelry, looked at the dais, and flexed their feet. After a final hymn, Naomi's mother led us into a reception area where the rabbi made kiddush and there were more congratulations. The rabbi removed his gown. We said good-bye to Jimmy, got into the Buick, and drove back.

"Joseph is real busy with weddings and Bar Mitzvahs. The first date would be June 4th."

"Now, Mother, we want something small and intimate. Robin doesn't know any of these people."

"Naomi, this is your father's congregation. There are four hundred people here who want to see their rabbi's daughter married in their temple. Not like your sister."

"Mother, keep Julie out of this."

"Your father could lose his job, do you know that?"

"Come on, Mother."

"Your father serves at the pleasure of his board. And their rabbi's eldest daughter taking up with some Italian, *marrying* some Italian, God forbid, they could remove him for that."

"Father, it's not true, is it—tell her it's not true."

Her father looked at her coldly, his lips pressed tightly together. Then he rose to his feet and left the room.

"Now, Naomi, you see what you've done. Your father is mighty upset.

Robin, I'm awful sorry you have to be exposed to all this. Naomi's sister, Julie, whom we love dearly, has been a terrible trial to her poor father."

"I know Julie."

"Oh, do you, how is the sweet thing?"

"I know Tony too and he seems to care for her deeply."

"Mother, she misses you and Father dreadfully. Yes, she does want to get married. And she wants Dad to marry her."

"Well, honey child, you know that ain't possible."

"Marry her? *Marry her?*" Jo reappeared in the doorway with a sandwich in his hand. "The impudence. Marry her? Marry my daughter to that Italian lowlife? What does she expect? The temple? A brilliant idea. They'd really love it. The rabbi of Charleston gives away his beautiful firstborn daughter before the Ark, underneath the *chuppah* to some swarthy Iti, yes, you heard me, some Iti, some guinea, some dirty little anti-Semite with a giant dong and a foreskin to match, under the *chuppah* to sanctify their filthy union. She's dead in this house, dead, do you hear me?" He was almost weeping. The sandwich was a pulp in his hand.

"Jo, Joseph, honey, it's alright." Naomi's mother followed her husband into the kitchen.

Naomi and I sat on the sofa, numb.

"Darling, I'm sorry."

"My God, he really loves her."

The incident was never mentioned again. Over the course of the weekend it was agreed that there would be a private ceremony at home in front of close relatives and friends and then a reception for the entire congregation and other well-wishers from the community at the temple. On Sunday we called London.

"How is June 4th?"

"*Ach, ja,*" said my father, "if I don't just have a funeral that day."

One month later we spent thirty hours at Kennedy Airport after our charter flight operator had absconded with our money. Eventually we argued our way onto a Japan Airlines flight to London and, with the ministrations of hot towels and kimono-clad hostesses, prepared ourselves for Naomi's introduction to my family.

We stayed with my parents, Naomi in Barbie's old room, me in mine. My mother embraced us. My father bombarded me with his usual questions—how much is breakfast in a restaurant, how much are eggs, why do you eat out, where do you live *exactly,* *why* do you live there, why did you leave Riverdale, how often do you see Fritz and Ellen, why haven't they replied to my letter, what, where, why, why, why . . .

After three days Naomi took me aside. "Robin, I can't stand it any more; your father hasn't addressed a word to me in three days. It's as if I don't exist."

Like so many times in my childhood I knocked on the door of my father's study.

"*Ja.*"

The familiar cloud of cigarette smoke swirled at the desk. The aroma clung to the walls. "*Ach, du.*"

"Daddy, I need to talk to you."

"Not now, I'm busy."

"I don't care how busy you are."

"Don't raise your voice at me."

"As if you never raise your voice."

"How dare you! *Raus! Raus!*"

"No, I'm not leaving. I'm not here for long. I've come over from America with my fiancée. I'm going to get married. I want to know why you have ignored her."

"Oh, have I been ignoring her?"

"You haven't said a word to her in three days."

"Well, maybe there's a reason."

"What is it?"

"I don't like the way she looks."

"You don't like the way she looks?"

"You heard correct."

"And what may I ask don't you like."

"Don't use that tone with me."

"I want to know. What don't you like?"

"Her dress. Also her nose. It's not like the picture. Here," he started to pull out Naomi's acting pictures we had sent from America. "In the picture, her nose . . ."

"That's enough. I won't listen to this."

"You ask a question and then you can't listen to the answer."

"Answer, that's not an answer. That's a Hitler answer."

"I warn you. Be careful."

"If this is all you have to say about my future wife, that's it, we're leaving."

"Leave, leave. Go to your sister. She shouts even better than you."

"I don't shout. You shout. You never stop shouting."

"She put you up to this, your *Amerikanerin*. You don't have the strength to do this yourself. *Verdammte* witch. Go on. Let her take you away. Crawl after her like a good little boy. Crawl to your sister's. You can all shout together. Shout at me. Now," he had suddenly grown ice-cold, "out of my sight."

I was still standing. He was still sitting. He turned back to the desk. I started to tremble. Naomi's picture and our letters disappeared into a folder, the folder disappeared beneath a mountain of other papers, a thousand possibilities raced through my head. I stood immobilized for an instant, then I rushed to the door.

"Close the door properly behind you. I don't like it open." He didn't look round.

I slammed the door shut with all my strength and the dam burst.

We moved to my sister's.

Everybody wept.

My uncle arrived from Amsterdam and received us in his hotel room.

"You have to understand my brother. He means well. He is a little *meshugge*. He is difficult. But he is a rock. If anybody needs anything, he is there. All those questions, all those papers, all those details. He doesn't make it easy. He doesn't show affection. But, believe me, he has it."

"Georg, this time he has gone too far."

"He is still your father."

"I am still his son. Naomi is still going to be his daughter-in-law."

"For you, my dear Naomi, I am grieved. To come here, all this way, for this to happen, it is a shame. But you must not be so defiant. You must win him over."

"I have no wish to win him over. I am here because I love Robin. These are old wounds. I cannot heal them."

"Georg, it's like my mother. When we were children and my father stormed down the corridor and hit us."

"He hit you?"

"Of course he hit us, Georg, you know that."

"*Nein, nein, nein.*"

"When we were locked in our room, crying, hurt, and angry, my mother would come down the corridor and beg us from the other side of the door to apologize. Somehow, it had been our fault, we had provoked it, we had to make it better. Well, it didn't make it better then and it won't make it better now."

"Robin is right."

"You are both very stubborn. But I can't say you are wrong."

*   *   *

My mother took us shopping. "I want to buy you something."

In Debenham and Freebody's, in the linen department, a voice said, "Robin?"

I turned round.

"Liz. My God, Liz, I haven't seen you since Annie's. Darling, this is an old friend of mine from Oxford. Liz, Naomi. She's how I know Annie, and the Krasnapolskys. This is my mother. Mummy, you remember those Russians I sent you?"

"*Ach, Gott, ja.* You are not related, I hope?"

"No, no," Liz smiled wanly. "So you still see them?"

"Occasionally."

"And you still live in America?"

"Yes, in New York, now. Naomi and I are getting married."

"Oh, how wonderful. Congratulations."

"And you?"

"I'm married. My husband's a diplomat. I met him in Kansas. We live in Nigeria." She smiled sadly. "Every so often I come home to shop, to see people. We have a nanny. She looks after the children. It was so nice seeing you again. I must go now. Good-bye." She hesitated for an instant, then she plunged into the crowd of shoppers, headed for Oxford Street and Africa.

"What a nice girl," said my mother.

"Yes, but she used to be so . . ."

My mother bought us a mohair blanket.

"I don't know what's got into Daddy," she said over lunch. "It's terrible."

There were a couple of attempts at reconciliation. The last was on the eve of our departure. My parents took us all out for dinner—my sister, her husband, Naomi, and me—my uncle had returned to Holland. Naomi wore a striking gown. My father was at his most charming. He tipped the maitre d', he ordered wine, his behavior bordered on the flirtatious.

The next morning, in silence, they drove us to Victoria Station. At the barrier, while Naomi and my mother kissed good-bye, my father took me aside.

"Here is money for your flight. I shall not come to your wedding. Your mother may come if she wishes."

"I'm sorry it always ends like this. I don't want the bloody money."

"Take it."

"No."

"You need it."

"I don't care."

My father looked at me coldly. "Do as you wish." He turned on his heel and went to the car.

My mother kissed me. "He'll come. He'll come. We'll work on him."

"Don't. I don't want him. That's just what he wants—to be begged."

"Ach, why does it always have to end like this?"

"Good-bye, Mummy. Take care. See you in June."

In May in New York Julie and Tony got married. They had a private ceremony in a tiny apartment in Greenwich Village. It was the home of Ralph Meredith, an old man, whom Tony had known for many years. He had in his youth been an ordained minister. He had traveled widely in the Far East as a missionary. He had known Gandhi. When he returned to the States he had given up religion for social activism. He had campaigned on behalf of the poor, he had run for vice-president with Norman Thomas. He had been active in the civil rights movement. He had been a friend of Martin Luther King. A year before he had suffered a stroke. So now he sat propped in a chair, half paralyzed, a red fez on his head and various holy symbols from his travels placed about him, from China, from Japan, from India, from Egypt, from the Holy Land, and in the presence of these symbols, in a faint, barely audible voice, he invited Tony and Julie to join together, to intertwine their lives, their backgrounds, their different faiths, and to gain strength from those differences.

Julie's father had finally relented and her parents had come up the previous day. That night Naomi and I had taken them all out for dinner. Now, in the dim light of this apartment, the old man extended a shaking hand to Jo and asked him to add a blessing to his daughter's marriage. Very quietly Jo recited in Hebrew the ancient Jewish blessing, "*Yivoreche-chu adonai v'yishmorechu* . . . May the Lord bless you and keep you, may He cause His countenance to shine upon you and be gracious unto you, and may He give you peace . . ." Julie wept. Naomi held her arm.

At the end of the month Naomi and I packed up our belongings, put them in storage with a friend, and drove to West Virginia. I had a room at the Holiday Inn. Naomi stayed with her parents. There followed a week of parties in which, for lunch and dinner every day, we were invited to a series of increasingly lavish events given by people I had never met and would never see again. The Goulds. How do you do? Congratulations. Thank you very much. The Katzes. How do you do? Congratulations.

Thank you very much. The Winthrops. How do you do? Congratulations. Thank you very much. The Abramowitzes. Oh, I remember you. Congratulations. Thank you very much.

My mother and Georg landed in Washington and arrived in Charleston on Tuesday. They also stayed at the Holiday Inn. As the week progressed, my mother became a figure of considerable attention in Charleston. Alone in a foreign country, with her only son about to get married, she rose to the occasion with dignity, warmth, and humor. And in the splendid rich homes of the Jews of Charleston, she lent a touch of European sophistication.

My uncle, loosed from the depressing climate of Amsterdam and for a moment free of the shadow of his wife's death, launched himself into the festivities with an élan and a gregariousness I had never seen before. At night on the pianos in the splendid rich homes of the Jews of Charleston he would bang out waltzes and mazurkas and operetta tunes. And he would drink a little too much and he would get tipsy.

And one of Naomi's friends, a shy gentle creature in her twenties for whom most men seemed too coarse, fell irresistibly in love with Georg, and on a night scented with dogwood and magnolia and honeysuckle, in the spacious gardens of one of the splendid rich homes of the Jews of Charleston one could see them strolling, deep in conversation, the young quiet studious girl from New York and the elderly bald-headed elegantly-suited concentration-camp survivor from a time and a continent she had until this moment only read about. And as the cars of this ever-growing caravan started to rev up in the driveway and guests and hosts made their adieus, one might have seen them too beneath a huge oak on the front lawn ever so formally kiss good-bye.

The out-of-town guests kept arriving, and on Friday the Schoenheimers flew in. Fritz, who had known my father, and to a lesser extent Georg, since the early rowing days in Berlin before the First World War, embraced my mother.

"*Also, er ist doch nicht mitgekommen*" (So he didn't come after all).

"*Nein.*"

"*Nicht zu glauben*" (Unbelievable).

In the spring Fritz and Ellen had met my parents in Tenerife, and on the beach in the Canary Islands, after so many years of war and struggle and dispersion and rebuilding, Fritz had given my father a scolding, as perhaps only he, of all people still living on earth, had the unassailable authority to do. It hadn't worked.

My mother arrived at the pool in the afternoon with a postcard. *"Er ist in Jugoslavien."*

"Was?"

"Jugoslavien. He writes from Dubrovnik."

"Er muss sich von der Anstrengung der Wedding *erholen"* (He has to recover from the strain of the wedding).

My mother laughed. Fritz took the card and read it.

"How's the weather?" I asked.

Ellen smiled ruefully and winked at me.

Naomi's mother had reconsidered while we were away and, to our astonishment, we were now to be married in the temple. There was nothing to be done. This was an important event in the community. It was incumbent upon Naomi's father. And, anyhow, the invitations could hardly be retracted.

On Sunday morning, in a last paroxysm of southern hospitality, somebody managed to get one last party in. At the Holiday Inn, at lunchtime, I changed into my dinner suit, the suit my father had insisted on buying when I went up to Oxford, made to measure over my strenuous objections, at John Collier's in London, a chain of outfitters for the middle classes. My hair was very long, and in one tiny gesture of rebellion, underneath the jacket I put on a hideous flowered and ruffled pink shirt, a last vestige of my hippie days. Tony picked us up at the hotel and took us to the temple.

"How is everything at the house?"

"It's crazy, what do you expect? Everybody's shouting at everybody else. Naomi's mother is dying. Her father refuses to perform the ceremony. Julie doesn't like her dress. Naomi is in tears. You know, I've no idea why you want to do this. It was much easier for us. They did us a real service. My advice to you is, don't do it."

"Oh, Anthony, thank goodness for you," said my mother.

"Oh, no, Mrs. Hirsch, I'm only the chauffeur. They only brought me down to drive the car. And you know what, my license expired a year ago."

"For a chauffeur, you have a lot of chutzpah," I said.

"What's that—I thought that's what you said when you trod on the glass."

"No, that's *meshugge.*"

Georg and my mother both laughed.

"*Meshugge*, I'll remember that. As soon as you step on the glass . . ."

Underneath the *chuppah*, in front of four hundred strangers, we waited, my mother, my uncle, Alan, our landlord, who was my best man, and I. Eventually Naomi's mother appeared, supported by Julie. Julie made a flamboyant entrance, in a shimmering green gown, the sort of entrance Callas would have made if she'd had an ailing mother to support. Naomi's mother was white. She looked as though at any moment she would expire. When they reached the steps Alan and I bent down to help her up.

"I can't go through with this. I can't."

"It's alright, Mother, it'll be over soon."

"Where's Jo?"

"He's right behind us. As soon as we turn round."

"Oh, my God, I can't face all those people."

We managed to turn her round. The organist plunged into "Here Comes the Bride," and at the entrance Naomi appeared in a pink gown on the arm of her father in a black gown.

They seemed to be coming down the aisle in slow motion, each step taking half an hour, each glint on the rabbi's glasses reflecting the looks on four hundred faces, one face at a time, each breath exhaling a universe. After millennia, they reached the *chuppah*. Suddenly Naomi was beside me and her father was opposite us, no longer her father, but the rabbi. Balloons were coming out of his mouth. "This day . . . do you . . . Robin Marc David . . . go forth . . . solemnly . . . daughter . . . take this . . . kiss the . . . be your . . . lawfully . . . vested . . . painful . . . mother . . . ocean . . . Scranton . . . Knoxville . . . God . . . the future . . . braid, breed, bride, broad, brood . . . down the road . . . together . . . gloom . . . asunder." Alan was nudging me in the ribs: "The glass, step on the glass." *Mazeltov.* Mendelssohn. Astaire and Rogers. Turn to the audience. One, two, three, tap dance.

"Why, Miss Naomi, you look beautiful. Like Princess Grace, only Jewish of course."

"Thank you, Jimmy."

"This is a great day for this temple. My, my, my."

At the entrance to the reception hall we formed a line. How do you do? Congratulations. Thank you very much four hundred times. Shake, shake. How do you do, congratulations, thank you very much. Yes, yes, no, no, thank you very much. No, he's my uncle. Shake, shake, congratulations, how do you do, thank you very much. The vase, how lovely, thank you very much, how do you do. Thank you, thank you, thank you, thank you. Shake, shake four hundred times. Yes, she is. Yes, she does. Doesn't she, though. How do you do. Soon, soon. I don't know. Maybe. I don't know. No, as a matter of fact, he's my uncle.

*   *   *

That night, Naomi's parents gave the last party—for the out-of-towners. Her mother excused herself before the filet mignon and went to bed. "I'm just so tired, honey. They'll understand." Rabbi Jo sat stoically through it.

After dinner, my uncle asked for silence. "Excuse me, I am an old man. My English is not good. But the rabbi has been kind enough to allow me to address a few words here in front of family and friends. I think perhaps for five minutes it is alright if we take a pause, if we do not eat and drink and make noise.

"My dear Robin, my dear Naomi, this is an important occasion. It is also a happy occasion. But it is not only happy. I am here, I speak now, not only for myself, but for my brother, who is not here. He is my older brother and I respect him. He is, for his reasons, not here today. His presence, when he is somewhere, is big. But I should like to say that his absence, when he is not somewhere, is sometimes bigger still. It is with sadness and a mixture of feelings that, in his absence, I presume to speak tonight.

"My dear Robin, my dear Naomi, the world is full not only of sunshine but of pain. Some things are hard to bear. And it is not enough, in this life, to take only the good, the easy, the happy. Much more important is it to take also the bad, the difficult, the unhappy. When we have it good, anyone can take it. When we have our washing machine and our big American car—a Buick, isn't it, *ja?*—when all these blessings fall, then to be together, to be in love, that is no art. But when it is hard, when there is war, when a people, like our people, is for no reason persecuted, when there is evil, when things come between us, when a loved one dies—or worse—when you have no one to turn to but each other, no food, no family, no washing machine, then it is an art, then is what counts.

"And so, my dear Robin, my dear Naomi, I say to you, it is not always happy, but it is not always happy which counts. Unhappy counts, too. Unhappy counts more. I wish for you of course happiness. But I am an old man. I have seen too much. I know it isn't all so easy. So I wish for you also strength and courage and endurance, to face together when it is unhappy. When a father does not appear, when a loved one dies, when, God forbid, there is a war, like the war, Robin, in which you were born, in which your grandmothers both died, then you must be together, then you must be strong, then it is when love counts.

"Robin, your Aunt Bertel, whom I loved, and whom I think you loved too, was sometimes a crazy woman. Yes, really—sometimes she would go to Paris for the collections and she would forget to tell me—but it was she who made the money—truly—and we had our troubles, but through them all, after the war, when we both came back, after her stroke, for six years, she would say: '*Orgi, wir sind beide Lümmels.*' *Ach so*—'We are both scoundrels.' I wish for you, my dear Robin and my dear Naomi, that when things are hard, when the rain falls, you can still turn to each other and say: '*Wir sind doch beide Lümmels.*'

"Now, I am also a Jew, and, you will forgive me, I lived for years in Palestine, I am used to a little Hebrew. I know here one worships without hats and without Hebrew. But I would like, my dear Robin, my nephew—I do not have a child, so you are almost my son—to put on my old yarmulke and if the rabbi will permit me, to say in Hebrew a few words: *Yivorechechu adonai v'yishmorechu* . . . My dear Robin, my dear Naomi, in the company of all assembled, and in the absence of loved ones, I repeat the old Jewish blessing: May the Lord bless you and keep you, may He cause His face to shine upon you and be gracious unto you, and may He give you, and your children, and your children's children, above all else, peace."

I went into the center of the room, embraced my uncle, and holding onto him, I wept.

Three months later, after a summer of being rained on in West Virginia, Virginia, Washington, Maryland, Delaware, Pennsylvania, New Jersey, and upstate New York, we returned to the city.

On our first day back, without a place to live, without a job, I am walking down 57th Street when a voice hails me. It is Yuri Krasnapolsky, Michael and Fara's son.

"Robin, I thought that was you. How are you? I hear you and Naomi got married—is that true? Congratulations."

"Thank you. What are you doing in New York?"

"Well, I'm just making a few final concert arrangements. Everything is done in New York—recordings, guest artists, and so on."

"And then back to Omaha?"

"Hub of the universe. Listen, my parents are leaving for San Francisco tomorrow to see my sister. But I know they would love to see you. They have an amazing story to tell you."

That night we went over to Michael and Fara's.

"Congratulations," said Michael. "We take you out for Chinese dinner."

"Oh, Michael, Chinese—he's so provincial."

"I'm sorry, my dear. I have made arrangements. Yuri is coming too with his wife."

"With his ex-wife. Oh, Michael, you are so tiresome."

"She is still his wife. They are not yet officially divorced."

"All this nonsense. Much more interesting is—Robin, I have amazing story to tell you."

"Fara, you think you should tell?"

"Oh, Michael—is he not impossible? Of course I tell."

"Alright, my dear, you tell."

"Robin, Naomi, we are in Europe this summer, on tour of five Eastern European countries. We are in Czechoslovakia, we are in Poland, we are in Hungary—all terrible—and we are in Yugoslavia. We stay in Dubrovnik in this little hotel, all these steps to climb—it is very hilly, Dubrovnik. And one day we are climbing up these steps—very wide—and there is somebody coming down, and I say to Michael: 'Michael, this man I know, this man I know. Hey, you.' And he keeps going. And I say, 'Not so fast. Not so fast.' And he looks round and he sees me and he keeps going. And I call him by name—ah, I see you guess already. And I say, 'Mr. Hirsch. Mr. Hirsch.' And he stops, and he looks at Michael and me, very cool, very brusque, and he says, 'Yes?' And I say, 'You know us. The Krasnapolskys. We are friends of your son, Robin.' And he was going down to his big fancy hotel and we were climbing up to our little *pension*. And I said, 'Where is your wife?' And he said, 'She is not here.' And I said, 'Robin, how is Robin? We have not seen Robin for a long time in New York.' And he looks at his watch and he says, 'At this precise moment, Robin is getting married in Charleston, West Virginia.' 'Aha,' I said, 'so that is where your wife is. So they are getting married. So why are you not there?' 'Too expensive,' he says. 'Good day,' he says, very cool, very brusque. And he turns and he goes on down the steps. What do you say to that?"

That night we had Chinese dinner with Michael and Fara and Yuri and Yuri's wife or ex-wife. Michael broke his rule about not drinking and ordered a terrible bottle of something Californian.

"We are going tomorrow to San Francisco to see our daughter and our grandchildren. Yuri is leaving for Omaha. You have just come back to New York. Everybody is moving. Nobody stays still."

"Oh, Michael, let's drink."

"Alright, we can drink."

"To San Francisco," said Yuri, "and this is a great occasion because my father is having wine." We drank to San Francisco.

"To Omaha, Yuri," said Michael, "and to your future as a great conductor." We drank to Omaha.

"To New York," said Fara. "To Robin and Naomi—this is their time now." We drank to New York.

"And one more toast," I said—and who could resist it?

"Yes, Robin?"

"To Dubrovnik."

And in a crowded Chinese restaurant in the middle of New York, with our elderly Russian hosts and their son and their Italian daughter-in-law or ex-daughter-in-law, I and my American wife raised our glasses of California Chablis and drank to Yugoslavia.

Rosh Hashanah

i. 1975

In New York Fritz Schoenheimer, my father's oldest friend, is approaching his eightieth birthday. The Schoenheimers are as close to family as I have in New York—Fritz and Ellen and their son Pierre. If there is a Schoenheimer family occasion I am invited. I remember the joint celebration almost five years ago, when Fritz turned seventy-five and Ellen sixty-five. Up in their elegant apartment on East 69th Street, on the nineteenth floor, with a terrace that looks out on the glittering forest of Manhattan, a sit-down dinner for fifty people, and witty, elegant, and moving speeches in German, French, and English. Various distinguished German Jews spoke. Pierre spoke. Even I proposed a toast. Just before dessert the phone rang and it was my father calling from London. He spoke to Fritz, he spoke to Ellen, and then Ellen called me into the kitchen and insisted that he speak to me. I sat on a stool and had the usual transatlantic shouting match.

"Hullo, who is zis?"

"Robin."

"Who?"

"Robin."

"*Who?*"

"Your son, Robin."

"Ach, *ja*, RRRawbeen. And why don't you write?"

When we finished, I got up and discovered that I had been sitting in the exquisite Dumas gâteau that was about to be divided into fifty pieces, and that as a result the trousers to my only suit were saturated in whipped cream and chocolate shavings. Ellen looked at me, I looked at her aghast, and slowly she burst into a long intoxicating laughter.

Now, almost five years later, Fritz Schoenheimer, my father's oldest friend, is approaching his eightieth birthday and he is dying. He is suffering from a disease of the motor system. He deteriorates slowly, but he deteriorates. Every so often Naomi and I go up to the apartment and tiptoe somberly into the bedroom. Fritz lies in bed, each time a little less mobile, his great head propped on pillows, still noble, but the skin sagging, the nose more prominent, saliva collecting at the corner of his mouth. His right hand, with the thumb missing, clutches the bedclothes, his eyes stare forthrightly out, and his voice tries and fails to create my name. Ellen wipes his mouth, strokes his arm, and caresses him tenderly with her voice. And later in the living room over tea in the Dresden china she tells us, "He will die in this bed, in this apartment. We do not want him in a hospital or, *Gott behüte*, in a nursing home."

In London my father now decides, his son having been in the New World for lo, these eight years, to come to New York, not to see me, let alone Naomi, with whom he is barely speaking, but to attend the deathbed of his old friend from the rowing days. Always one to hunt around for the best possible deal, he takes three months getting a flight, with the result that the night before he is finally due to set off, Fritz dies. Pierre calls me with the news. I call my father. But this is now, *endlich*, a bargain, so he cannot get a refund.

I see him going to the airport now, alone, leaving my mother because either it's too expensive or she would only get in the way, bulling his way through passport control, carrying his own suitcase, furious as usual at a world that somehow, and continually, mocks him. Two wars and enormous upheavals have taken place and here he is at Heathrow boarding a jet plane, having finally found the perfect flight, and Fritz Schoenheimer is already dead. And I think of the more than sixty years of their friendship—from a time before jet planes, before so many things, when they were young, younger than I am now.

And I think of them as youthful Zionists together in Berlin, of the Jewish rowing club on the Spree, of the First World War in which they both fought, my father winning the Iron Cross (Second Class), Fritz, two years older, winning the Iron Cross (First Class) and losing the thumb on his right hand.

And I think of them coming back from the war, wounded, decorated, hardened, still young, Fritz twenty-two, my father barely twenty. Veterans.

And Fritz in the twenties traveling round the world for the family business, by boat to China, to Australia, to Malaya, to Japan. And my father staying home, nursing his ailing father's firm through the ravaging inflation, and watching his father die.

And a lunatic strutting in Bavaria.

And Fritz marrying and deciding early on to leave, moving to Paris with Ellen and her mother; and establishing himself in the French recording industry; and having a son in Paris and naming him Pierre; and Fritz and Ellen and Pierre and Ellen's mother moving into the fabled apartment on the Bois de Boulogne.

And my father visiting occasionally, en route to Rotterdam or Lille or Manchester to sell bakelite.

And in Berlin the Olympics. And the Reichstag fire.

And my parents hanging on till the last moment, my father till '38 and my mother, to whom he is not yet married, till '39, both their fathers, my grandfathers, now mercifully dead, both their mothers, my grandmothers, yet to die in the unimaginable horrors yet to come.

And Kristallnacht.

And my father escaping at the last moment, by train to the Dutch border, and my mother, well connected, shipping out furniture and her own wrought-iron work and leaving her mother who will never leave and her sister who will end up in Argentina, to join my father in London; and my parents marrying and moving into the small flat in Grove End Gardens.

And the Anschluss. And Czechoslovakia. And the division of Poland.

And Fritz in Paris and my father in London and the second great war of all their lives breaking out, Fritz and my father now a quarter of a century older and living in the capital cities of the countries they fought as young men.

And Denmark and Norway falling. And Belgium and Holland falling. And then, inconceivably, France.

And in France the Occupation, and Fritz, one step ahead of the Germans, fleeing Paris, alone, and hiding out in the mountains near Spain.

And in London, the bombing, and the Germans poised to invade England and my father interned as an enemy alien on the Isle of Man.

And Ellen and Pierre and Ellen's mother fleeing Paris. And Pierre, eight years old, shot in the neck and nursed back to health in a convent near Chartres, Ellen tending to the sick and to her mother.

And my father released, a naturalized citizen now, up on the roof with a tin hat searching for the planes of his erstwhile countrymen.

And Ellen and Pierre and Ellen's mother finding Fritz in Marseilles, and the four of them escaping on a boat to New York.

And my parents living out the war in London and having two children during the Blitz—me and my sister.

And Fritz, with his charm, his acumen, his integrity, and his connections, establishing himself almost immediately for the third time now, in a third country—America, the promised land.

And my father in London banging fruitlessly on the doors of men with whom he had done considerable business before the war.

And after the war, Fritz Schoenheimer growing rich, respected, loved even, maneuvering his Lincoln through the hard, clean, diamond-bright, and unscathed city of New York.

And in London my father, close to fifty, riding his bicycle through the rubble-strewn streets to Westbourne Grove, to the workshop of Michael Beasley, bookbinder, where together they cut and press and glue and tool fine leathers and old prints.

And every so often in the early morning in the small flat in Grove End Gardens before my father sets off, I remember, the bell rings and it is the postman and in his hand is a package and on the package in big letters it says FAMILY HERBERT HIRSCH and inside the package at night when we at last unwrap it are tinned food and books and clothing for the children and on the label under "Sender," which my father shows me, it says, "SCHOENHEIMER, NEW YORK."

And my father, much more slowly and less dramatically, reestablishes himself. And twenty years or more later, a Fulbright scholar, I sail for New York on the Queen Elizabeth and on board in Southampton is a letter for me from Fritz and Ellen with a hundred dollar bill inside it and in the middle of the Atlantic there is a phone call for me from Fritz and Ellen on the beach in Montauk and when I arrive in the gleaming city I am collected by Pierre's wife Janet in Ellen's Mustang and I stay with Pierre and Janet and their three children in the enormous house in Fieldston.

And five years after I arrive, when I am about to marry Naomi and my father has his apoplectic fit, who else on this planet exists to dress my father down but Fritz Schoenheimer? And where does he do this? *Aber selbstverständlich*, on the beach in Tenerife, where the four of them, my mother, my father, Fritz, and Ellen, meet in the rich late afternoon of their rich long lives to expose their aging bodies to the winter sun and recline on the expensive sand. And Fritz tells my father whatever he tells him. And my father, *dafka*, still refuses to come to the wedding.

But now, three years after Tenerife, three years late for my marriage to Naomi, eight years after my arrival in this country, more than sixty years after rowing to victory with Fritz Schoenheimer on the Spree, my father is flying over the Atlantic and Fritz is already dead. And while he is forty thousand feet above the ocean, in a private ceremony, in a cemetery in the pastoral northern fringes of the Bronx, in the presence only of his widow Ellen, born in Brussels, his son Pierre, born in Paris, his three beloved grandchildren, born in New York City, Fritz Schoenheimer is consigned to the same hard earth where his younger brother, Rudi, born like him in Berlin, lies buried, Rudi, who had preceded them all to New York, who had guaranteed their passage from Marseilles, who had stood ready to receive the Nobel Prize in Physiology, and who thirty years before almost to the day, in the garden of their first house in America, had put a gun to his head and brought his brilliant and tormented life to a premature end.

So when my father gets off the plane at Kennedy at four o'clock in the morning Fritz is not only dead but buried. And since the purpose of his visit has now been mocked again, and since he has little to say to me and even less to my wife, and since after a few perfunctory hours in our apartment he insists on moving into the cheap hotel on East 53rd Street which comes with the package, there is little for him to do. He visits Ellen whom he upbraids for having buried Fritz before he even landed— "*Aber warum* you have to do this so rush-rush is beyond me." He visits one or two other elderly *Bundesbrüder*. He even on Sunday comes down to the Lower East Side to our apartment—"Vot is zis 'branch'?"—to which we have invited Ellen and Pierre and Janet and the children and several other New Yorkers who know or would like to know my father. And in front of them all he glowers at the array of smoked fish from Russ and Daughters and Russian bread from Moishe's and with his cigarette holder clamped between his teeth, he hisses, "Und *vot*, may I ask, comes from *zis* house?"

And one afternoon, after I have walked with him through the fish market and underneath the Brooklyn Bridge and up and down Wall Street and in and out of discount houses on Church Street—"*Ach, ja,* I used to like this sort of thing, but now no more"—I sit with him on a rotting pier by the East River and we eat a sandwich, and the accumulated awkwardness, distrust, violence, and stifled love of more than thirty years of our hard-bitten, failed relationship surfaces and sits between us like a stone. Why could we not have eaten in some restaurant? Why had he not taken Naomi and me *once* during his time here? Why had he been unable to accept her in the first place? What is the fury that burns in him and that will not ever burn out? And no doubt he has his own thoughts— about me, about Fritz, about dying—but I cannot think them.

And when the silence becomes unbearable I ask him what else he wants to do in New York, whether he has plans for tonight, and would he like to come for dinner.

No, it is not necessary, he will not bother us, and anyhow, yes, he has plans.

Oh, what plans?

He shrugs as much as to say, "None of your business, doesn't matter."

I persist but the best I can elicit is a grunt and another shrug and a dismissive gesture in the general direction of uptown. So I assume that somewhere on the upper reaches of Broadway is an old flame. And the light on the pier begins to die and we gather the wrappings of our sandwiches and I walk him to a bus.

The next day I see him and I ask, "Well, did you have a good time last night?" Same grunt. But I am determined and eventually I wheedle out of him something about a cousin. "You mean you have a cousin in New York?" A grunt and a nod. I am dumbfounded. I have been in America eight years and I have family in New York and he hasn't told me. "You mean, I have been in America for eight years and you have a cousin in New York and you never told me?"

"Well," he says, "you never asked."

The cousin, it turns out, is a second cousin—my generation, but twenty years or so older—why would I be interested?

What is her name?

Her name is Herta.

And when did she leave?

In '39.

And where, to New York?

No, to Shanghai.

Shanghai?

She was ten years in Shanghai.

And then?

And then in New York.

And does she live alone?

No, she is married. To a Hungarian Jew. Also from Shanghai. No, not originally, *Herr Gott noch Mal*, originally he was from Hungary. There is also a daughter. Linda. She must be now twenty or maybe twenty-one.

It is hard work. I ask him about other scattered family whom I know. About his cousin Martin in Haifa who owns a delicatessen—delicatessen, *keine Rede davon*, it's a sweetshop. About his cousin Rudi in Tel Aviv who is a director of El Al—*ach ja*, Rudi . . . and he gives a little grunt.

I ask him about his brother, my uncle, Georg, in Amsterdam, who was betrayed and shipped to Auschwitz. "Mummy says that when you heard he had survived, it was the only time she saw you cry."

"She does?" And again the little grunt.

Finally I ask him about his father.

"My father? I had nothing but the utmost respect and admiration for my father."

The next day his two weeks come to an end. I take him to the airport. I carry his suitcase to the gate. Tersely, we say good-bye.

"She is not so bad," he says and turns on his heel.

I watch him, still broad, still strong at seventy-seven, framed in the metal detector, picking up his case—"No, no porter," he brushes one aside. I watch him striding down the long corridor, and I wonder, not for the first time, "Will this be the last time?" And I go home.

In the course of the next year, Naomi and I painfully separate. Up in the empty apartment on East 69th Street Ellen no longer has Fritz to nurse, her memory begins to evaporate, and when I visit she is less and less certain who I am. Pierre arranges for twenty-four-hour home care and contemplates the inevitable—like her mother, with whom Fritz and Ellen and Pierre had escaped to America, her body will remain strong while her mind disintegrates and one day even round-the-clock care will not be enough and she will have to move, *Gott behüte*, into a nursing home. An elderly Polish nurse moves into the study. I visit less and less frequently. My own world becomes more and more circumscribed. I have my own unhappiness to wrestle with. I see almost nothing of Pierre. I am in danger of losing touch with almost everyone.

One day, living now in a sublet apartment, a fifth-floor walk-up on East 22nd Street with, incongruously, a grand piano in the tiny and dilapidated livingroom, I realize as I pound away that the phone has been ringing for some time. I pick it up.

"Hullo, is this Robin Hirsch?" Ah, the old familiar accent. "This is Herta Shriner. Do you know who I am?"

It takes me a moment. "Oh, yes, of course I know who you are. We are related."

"Yes, your father and my mother were cousins. That makes us second cousins. I am much older than you, but don't worry, we have a daughter. It is Rosh Hashanah next week. Can you come for dinner?"

Over the next few years I climb on my bicycle at Pesach, at Purim, at Chanukah, on the first or second night of Rosh Hashanah, after the fast on Yom Kippur, and pedal up to 98th Street and Broadway. I have family in New York and they have been here all the years I have lived in America and for whatever complicated or simple reason my father has kept their existence a secret.

ii. 1939/1993

"Ach, those were different times. Now my grandson, Elliot, he's four years old, I say to him: 'Is Molly your girlfriend?' and he says to me, 'Omi, Molly's not my girlfriend. She's like a brother, only with a vagina.' We, we were so sophisticated. But you think we knew what a vagina was? We would sit, Edith and I and my other friend, Ilse, who ended up in Rio, on the top deck. In Berlin, like London, the buses had a top deck, but in Berlin they were open. And there you could smoke cigarettes. And we would smoke and buy the *Times* of London which we couldn't read of course. But we'd open it up and smoke and talk very loud. We were sixteen, seventeen. Very sophisticated. But vagina? Edith comes to me one day and says, 'Herta, I think I'm pregnant.' 'Pregnant?' I say, and she says, 'Yes, sure, he touched me down there, you know—you can get pregnant from touching? I think I'm pregnant. See?' And she made a big *Getü und Geta* about her tummy. And I said of course not. Impossible. But, you know, I wasn't completely sure. You want some coffee?

"The same with Hitler. I mean, he was there, but we were on the top deck of the bus, reading the English papers. And, sure, some people left. Dr. Glass, for example, Werner's father. In '33 already. For Shanghai. But my father was a wholesaler. Business was still good. He thought Dr. Glass was a complete idiot, an alarmist. To leave Germany with all his possessions. For China! *Meshugge!*

"But of course Dr. Glass got everything out in '33. And we had to turn in our jewelry and silver. At the *Sammelamt,* the collection office. But you could still send packages out of the country. Of course if you filled out the card there was a record and that was a very dangerous business. But there was a porter at the *Hauptbahnhof,* everybody knew, you gave him some money and he put packages on the train with no card, no sender. And then you sent the information in a letter to London or Zürich and somebody picked it up and kept it for you.

"Of course, after Kristallnacht even my father realized it was time to go. He purchased visas for Peru. I *natürlich* had become engaged. *Tüpisch.* Not because I was madly in love, but because he was a nice guy and he asked me and I called my friend Edith and said, 'Look, Heinz wants to become engaged. What do you think?' And she of course said yes. And I told my parents and they of course checked out his family. You know how that mattered in those days. And he came from a very good family. His grandfather already had been a judge. So they agreed. And I of course—so sophisticated, so stupid—was very excited—the first in my circle. And my father even purchased a visa for Heinz. And my mother of course said,

'If you're going on the ship with a man . . .' That's all she said but it was obvious. We had to get married. So we got married and when we got to Hamburg the visas turned out to be forgeries. All that money that my father spent was gone for good. How much? I don't know. You know how it was in Berlin, the men went into another room when it came to money. Children and women had no idea. Another cookie?

"Well, one could still go to one place. We were stateless refugees by this time, all Jews. But one place you could still go—even stateless refugees— and that was Shanghai. Where Dr. Glass had gone, my father's cousin—on the other side, not your side, my father. My father must still have had some money left, because somehow in Hamburg he bought tickets for Shanghai and suddenly we were on a boat for three months. Me, my parents, and my new husband. How old I was? Nineteen.

"Well, I pretty soon discovered Heinz was a nice guy, but he was pretty much of a nothing. When we got to Shanghai, he started to work as a cook. He had studied cooking at a hotel school, that's when we met. I guess I must have a thing for cooks. Lacy, later, you know. But the Chinese are very clever at copying. In two weeks they could do everything he did. And so he grew bored and he stopped working and became a big *macher* with the Committee, the Jewish Committee. And he went his way and I went mine. And he had a Russian girlfriend. And I had an Italian boy-friend. And of course everybody knew. But it was Shanghai and it was the war and nobody cared. And that's how we lived.

"And after the war the Americans came in and the Jewish boys worked on their trucks and drove them and became mechanics. Jewish mechan-ics, imagine. And we all worked for the Americans. And we all wanted to get to America, of course.

"And one day at the American consul, they ask my father if he knows in America a Paul Levine. And my father says no, he's dead, long dead. Paul was his brother, my uncle, and he left for America when I was a little girl. It had nothing to do with Hitler. He was an apprentice in a big firm and you know how they treated them, like gofers. So they used to send him down with money to bet on the horses. And he does this for a certain amount of time and he sees how stupid, the horse never wins. So one day he doesn't put the money down, he puts it in his pocket. And he does this several times. And then of course one day the horse wins. And he doesn't have the money and he goes to his father, my grandfather, and my grand-father says, 'Alright, you made a mistake. Once you can make a mistake.' And he gives him the money. But then it happens another time. And my grandfather gives him the money again and a ticket to America and tells him, 'I'm not made of money. Now you go to America and make your own money.' And so my Uncle Paul went to America and nobody heard from him again. And my grandmother said when it came Rosh Hasha-nah, 'That he doesn't write to his own mother for Rosh Hashanah, it's not possible, he must be dead.' And so everybody thought he was dead. But he wasn't dead. He was living in Madison, Wisconsin, and he had put out a search for my father through the Red Cross.

"So there we were in the American consul with everybody else apply-ing for a visa, and suddenly we had a sponsor. But of course there were quotas. The German quota wasn't filled, the Austrian quota wasn't filled either—which is how Lacy came here, he had an Austrian passport. But the Polish quota was filled. And my father, always honest, even when it's stupid, he was born in this tiny town called Seefeld and I remember the consul looking at the map and saying Seefeld, never heard of it, oh, is this it and he points to a town in Germany and my father, how can one be so *meshugge* honest, says no, no, it's this Seefeld and he points to a town and it's on the wrong side of the German Polish border—you know how the border kept changing—so now he and my mother are classified as part of the Polish quota and the Polish quota is filled. So they are sent to Europe and they live in a DP camp for more than a year until they can apply again. But Heinz and I we are born in Berlin, so we are part of the German quota. We have in our pockets a Chinese divorce, but—so what?—we are part of the German quota, so we get a visa together and in a few weeks we are on a boat to San Francisco.

"But before we go to San Francisco I want in addition to the Chinese divorce a Jewish divorce. So we go to the rabbi who was a *gonif* and instead of saying, like a rabbi should, can't you work it out, aren't you still in love, even a little, he says you want a divorce you have to come today because the scribe is leaving tomorrow for San Francisco. Such a divorce I didn't want in such a hurry. So we get on the boat with only our Chinese divorce.

"But in San Francisco I want a Jewish divorce because Heinz is staying and I'm going to Madison, Wisconsin. And there he is again, the same rabbi. Forty dollars, he says. And Heinz says if it's so important to you, I have no objection, but you pay. So somehow I found forty dollars and I put it in an envelope and we went to see the rabbi and he sits there for the whole interview, I never forget, feeling the envelope with his fingers. He can't open it of course but he wants to be a hundred percent certain the money's there.

"So I get my Jewish divorce and I go to Madison, Wisconsin, and Heinz stays in San Francisco. But in Madison my Uncle Paul has in the mean-time died, so I stay with his wife—widow. Very nice woman, not a Jew. And I work as a waitress in a soda fountain. Amazing, America. Ice cream sundaes in the middle of winter. Never heard of such a thing. But I work hard and they even promote me for a day. Behind the bar. But I don't know how to turn off the machine that makes the whipped cream so I'm spraying the whole counter with whipped cream, all the people are covered in whipped cream, and I say thank you for the honor, but I think I go back to being a waitress. And they let me do what I wanted because, I guess, I was a bit of a celebrity. There were not too many German Jews from China in Madison, Wisconsin.

"But after a year, when my parents could apply again, they got in. So I went to New York to meet them. And I had a little room high up on the corner of 96th Street. And when I looked down what did I see? Barton's, the sweetshop chain. I didn't know that I would work for them—at Times Square, remember?—for more than twenty years.

"And then one day at a Bar Mitzvah I met Lacy. A girlfriend of mine said you must meet this man, he's a cook, also from Shanghai. *Schon wieder ein* cook, just what I needed. I was once burned, that was enough. But he was so shy. He asked me out for tea and he could hardly talk. But I talked enough for the two of us. And sure enough he was in Shanghai, he even knew Heinz from the Jewish Committee, he knew Dr. Glass, but he never knew me. He lived in a barracks, a dormitory, for thirty men. He loved it. After all what he went through, after all what he lost. You want some more coffee?

"You know, they were on the border back and forth, Lacy and his family, between Hungary, Austria, and Romania, hiding out for more than a year. And finally they escape to Yugoslavia but there most of them are caught and put in prison. Then they are made to dig their own graves, and shot. Lacy, his sister, and his brother all escape. His sister and her husband, they get on a boat but they are caught and turned back and taken ashore and also killed. His brother, Linda's Uncle Ernst, you know, who ended up in Santo Domingo and now lives in New Jersey, escaped too, to Austria where somehow he managed to alert the relatives. 'You have to leave, now, immediately, over the mountains to Switzerland,' he told them. They didn't believe him. He went on foot alone over the Alps with a rucksack and survived. They stayed and were killed.

"And Lacy. Somehow Lacy got on the last boat out of Trieste. It was sailing for Shanghai. So there we were for ten years in Shanghai. And we never met. For ten years we walked the same streets, we bought from the same shops, we had dinner in the same restaurants, we went to the same synagogue—the little refugee synagogue—we went to the same German operettas which the refugees put on—you know how the *Jäckes* are, *Kultur, Kultur,* even in China—we went to the same doctor—Doctor Glass—and we saw the same dead children lying in the gutter—Chinese children wrapped in bamboo. Lacy even knew Heinz, like I told you, from working together in the Jewish Committee.

"So there we were for ten years in Shanghai and we never met. And there we were in a tea shop in New York and we decided to get married. Forty years ago. 1953. I still remember going down to City Hall with my Chinese divorce. And they look at it and look at it. And they pass it around. And they say no, it doesn't look good. And then suddenly it's lunchtime and suddenly it looks fine to them. And so we got married. And then we had Linda. And now, suddenly, Linda is thirty-eight. And she and David have two children, Elliot with the vagina and Kayla. And Lacy, it's hard to believe, has been gone for almost two years now. And every day I miss him. And suddenly in this house I am alone."

iii. 1979

Tonight is the first night of Rosh Hashanah and I am invited to the Shriners. It is raining and so, instead of my bicycle, I take the subway. In a brown paper bag I carry a bottle of kosher slivovitz, an offering for the New Year.

I have come to look forward to these occasions. There is always food. There is always talk. And there are always people. Friends from their temple on 100th Street, friends from Shanghai, friends of Linda's, the daughter, from college, strangers, lost souls who have somehow wandered into their lives and whom they have invited into their living room. And presiding over this informal and unpretentious salon—refectory, perhaps, or Jewish café—are Herta, the daughter of my father's first cousin, and her husband, Lacy.

Herta works in a sweetshop—Barton's—in Times Square, a gemütliche, portly, German Jewish hausfrau, friendly, welcoming, any suffering hidden now behind aspirations to a normal New York Jewish lifestyle. A matron, but younger perhaps than that implies. Lacy has retired as a cook in an exclusive men's club on Park Avenue—"Jewish members? Not a bit of it. Once, I think, they had a Jew, but it was a mistake." He is one of those figures that Jews seem so often to throw up—a simple man with no pretensions who is yet learned in the Law, an observer, a Talmudist even. A small man, where Herta is large. Quiet, thoughtful, a chronicler.

Needless to say, the food is abundant—soup and chicken liver, and gefilte fish with *Remouladen Sosse* and horseradish, and cold carp in aspic, and boiled beef with carrots and pineapple, and roasted chicken, and broccoli and brussels sprouts and mashed potatoes and gravy, and then desserts—stewed fruit and four different kinds of cake. Everything of course made on the premises. And before the meal, blessings over the wine—dreadful, sweet Jewish wine—and over the bread—wonderful, sweet Jewish challah—and raw apple and honey, a traditional sweetness for the New Year. The setting is simple—the formica dining table, the plastic-covered seats, the hideous light fixture, much too bright, in the ceiling, and the window which looks out on a dirty brick wall, permanently gated and covered in a nubby orange plaid. But the table is set lovingly with embroidered linen and gold-rimmed glasses and china from Europe and, standing majestically over the meal, two magnificent silver candlesticks.

But more than the care which goes into the preparation, what makes these occasions special is the company. There is always a great raucous joyful mix that manages to bridge the generations without effort, to be funny, sly, bawdy, solemn, concerned, sometimes all at once, with half a dozen conversations careering across the dinner table at the same time, and on the more serious festivals—Pesach, for example—continuously interrupted with Hebrew prayers and chanting. An uninhibited Babel. All carried on in a mixture of German and variously accented English with snatches of Hebrew and Yiddish thrown in, depending on who's present.

Tonight is a small gathering. Herta, Lacy, Linda, their daughter, who's doing graduate work in Boston.

Now, a curious thing about "zis Linda" as my father called her. At Rosh Hashanah three years ago when we first met, we discovered that we had our own small story, she and I, and in one respect it resembles the story of her parents in Shanghai, one generation later and half a world away.

More than four years ago, in the summer of 1975, the summer before Fritz died and my father came to visit, I was in Lancaster, Pennsylvania, directing a couple of plays. One night, when I had no rehearsal, I was invited to a production at the local college—a fairly grueling production as I remember of *The House of Bernarda Alba*, two dozen American coeds in black shrouds tromping about the stage as Lorca's tragic villagers. The performance finished, my rehearsals finished shortly thereafter, I returned to New York. Fritz died, my father arrived, I learned of the existence of the Shriners. And at the following Rosh Hashanah, three years ago, I met them for the first time. Linda, it turned out, was finishing her studies at Franklin and Marshall College, majoring in theater. "That's funny," I said, "I was there last summer. You don't by any chance remember a production of *The House of Bernarda Alba?*"

"Remember it?" she said, "I was in it."

So in a small Amish town in the middle of Pennsylvania I had seen onstage in a black shroud a cousin about whose existence I hadn't the slightest inkling, whose mother like my father had left Berlin almost forty years before, whose family's journey to New York had taken them via

Shanghai, Hawaii, San Francisco, and Madison, Wisconsin, and whose arrival onstage at that moment in a small college theater in Lancaster, Pennsylvania, had been every bit as unlikely as my arrival in the audience.

And here we are now, Herta, Lacy, Linda and I, from Berlin, from Shanghai, from Pennsylvania, from London, at festivals like Rosh Hashanah, sitting around the same table as though it's the most natural thing in the world. And in many ways it is.

Family.

The others here tonight I mostly know too: Werner Glass, fifty-two, son of the doctor, also from Germany, also in Shanghai during the war; possessed of a remarkably facile wit and a nice line in self-deprecating humor, which comes in handy since he works for Exxon, scarcely a popular thing to do these days, and if you're Jewish and it's the Arabs who're causing all this trouble and you're a speechwriter for one of the oil companies—well, he was a boy when the war broke out and his English is excellent, honed in Shanghai on the *Times* crossword puzzle, published, a day late, of course, every day in the *North China News*.

Next to Werner is his wife, Irma, an American Jewess, a schoolteacher, who still after twenty-seven years of marriage hasn't learned a word of German— "Oh, I know a few things— '*Ich hab' ein Loch im Kopf*' (I have a hole in my head) —things like that, but I knew them before I met him." She seems simple, sometimes almost simple-minded, until you realize it's not really simplicity but a kind of absolute openness, an unguardedness, which allows her to confess to the most embarrassing ignorance or reveal a foible that's so unexpected you burst out laughing.

Another regular also here tonight is Chavah, a woman no longer young though one somehow wishes she were, delicate, with stooped shoulders, glasses, and, most unexpected, a dazzling and impish smile. She arrived in Palestine also from Germany, when she was one year old. She and her father now work as metalsmiths in America, making Jewish artifacts, religious and secular. Her hair is graying, she says little, but there is something irrepressibly girlish about her, laughter that bubbles out at the bawdiest moments, an occasional bon mot slipped into the whirlpool like a stiletto.

Finally—or, finally, as I think of it—there is the star of the show, Herta's childhood friend from Berlin, Edith, known to everyone as Tante Edith. Now Tante Edith is a lean, hard, tough old cookie, whom you'd expect to elbow you out of the way in the subway, with the heaviest accent you can imagine and a mouth that can match any sailor in any port you care to name. Married to her second husband now, a non-Jew, lives upstate on a farm, owns fifty-seven apartments, all old people, the price of heating oil is going to do her in, they want their apartments always at seventy-eight degrees. Also does insulation, can never remember the word, much too long, I call it blow job, we blow the stuff in, I ask them how many blow jobs they do today, what's so funny? Talks a streak, with a voice that cuts like a knife, devastating, outrageous, thoroughly aware of how outrageous and thoroughly relishing it. Escapes from her pastoral goyish surroundings several times a year to be with Herta and Lacy, travels with them, tours Europe with them, has a ball.

One Tante Edith story tonight brings us closer than we've ever been, she and I. In Innsbruck—or perhaps Copenhagen—with Herta and Lacy this summer, strolling in the evening looking for a café, they pass an automat: "How many boxes would you say? Twenty-five? Thirty? Alright, thirty, doesn't matter, anyway a lot. All different. Condoms. *Ja*, condoms. All kinds. All different colors. Oh, thirty different kinds of condoms."

Uproar from everybody except Irma, the one native American, who doesn't know what condoms are. More uproar.

"You don't know what condoms are. Vell, honey, I can tell you. I used to pack them. Yes, sure. In London, during the war. With my first husband, Bergman. He sold them, I packed them. Sure. Three to a package. For ten months. God, what a job. I had a wooden penis. Yes, penis, honey. What you think, I use a live model? A wooden penis. They arrive like balloons. You roll them on, like this. Then you roll them off, like this. Three to a package. Flat, in a paper bag. Three for two-and-six. My husband he would sell them to fire stations, police stations. God, what a job. So boring. Some I'd prick. Yes, with a pin. Oh, I know, awful, *ja*. But it was so boring. No, my husband, he never knew. Awful, yes, but the English, they needed people, *nein*?" Then, suddenly, to me: "Ven you born? 1942? Maybe you one of my babies, ha! Your father was in the Home Guard? My husband he sold to the Home Guard too. He was up on the roof with a helmet? *Ja*, me too. Yes, sure, my husband sold to the Home Guard too."

Tante Edith is the star of the show, but there is one last person here tonight, a newcomer for me, although a long-standing friend of the family, a prim, sweet-eyed lady in her fifties, well-spoken, careful, the most proper person at the table, a spinster. She lives in the same apartment building and rarely ventures out. "It is so dangerous," she tells me in the living room before dinner. "I am afraid for my life. Truly. It used to be different. But there is a different element now. And drugs. And guns. Even in the day."

"Oh, Katherine, you mustn't let that stop you," says Herta, "I go to work every day. Doesn't bother me. I give them a piece of my mind."

"I admire you, Herta. But I couldn't. I am too frightened."

"She is right, Herta," says Lacy, "things have changed. What one sees sometimes is terrible. And what one hears is worse. But one cannot live one's life in a jail."

"You should move to the country. Cows, manure," says Tante Edith, "No, really, how you can live in the city is beyond me."

"Is there anywhere else to live?" says Linda.

"Ah, you young people," says Katherine, "when you are young, everything seems possible."

Katherine does not open up until long after Tante Edith's condom story. She too spent the war in England. She and Tante Edith know the same parts of London—Belsize Park, Swiss Cottage, Finchley Road, the refugee section. Katherine's mother had opened a German Jewish restaurant in 1943, the Blue Danube, on Finchley Road. It became quite famous. A well-known actor-comedian from Berlin, Peter Adler, would entertain there, supported by all the German Jewish actors in London. My parents, I'm sure, knew it. The restaurant closed in 1954, just before that stretch of Finchley Road became my home territory, but I have a dim memory of it too.

She speaks an almost accent-free English.

"Well," says Herta, "she was educated at Cambridge, what do you expect?"

"Not at the university," Katherine says modestly, "at a girls' school in Cambridge. And then at the London School of Economics. But that's a long story."

"Tell it. Tell it," says Lacy.

"In this company you want her to tell a long story?" says Herta.

Her full name is Katherine Lee. But this is of course not her real name. She too was born in Germany and her original name was Liselotte Kohn. She changed it as a young woman in England at the end of the war. The Lee came easily because there was a street named Lee in Aylesbury where she was working and nobody could pronounce Liselotte and called her Lee anyhow. Katherine came from her best friend, a Dutch girl, with whom she hitchhiked round Europe after the war.

"You hitchhiked round Europe," Chava asks incredulously.

"Yes, for a year. After the war."

"But wasn't it, you know, dangerous?" asks Linda.

"Perhaps it was," Katherine half smiles, "but, you know, when you are young, you don't think about it."

After the war she was hired, with sixty others, as an interpreter by the American army and spent a year in Germany. It was after that year that the two Katherines began to travel. Her first trip in particular was difficult—

two young women hitching through a ravaged Germany, cadging rides on all kinds of military vehicles, trying to reach some remote hamlet in the Harz Mountains where her old nanny lived, telling one story to one authority, another to another, finally getting within six miles, to the nearest village, then leaving their escort on some pretext and trekking through the countryside, arriving late at night for a tender reunion after the war.

This nanny had been an important figure to her. Apparently as a small child, when the time came for her to be taken away from the nanny, or the nanny to leave, Liselotte had been heartbroken and went into a decline. Eventually the doctor had recommended that they be reunited and the nanny became to all intents and purposes her real mother.

"And what did she do during the war?"

"Oh, Werner, don't ask such questions. She was an old woman, she loved me. I loved her. She lived in a remote village. If you had seen how they all lived in '45, '46 . . ."

Somehow the mention of her nanny, of her childhood, unlocks her heart and she begins to describe her arrival in England, how she left Berlin in 1939 as a young girl of sixteen. "You know, my father was born in Prague, so I had a Czech passport. It was very difficult to get out, there were so many regulations, not just in Germany, but abroad also. But because of my passport I could still travel. So my father sent me to England. There were friends of the family—the Blumenthals, he was a big banker, or he had been—and they had sent cartons of silver and jewelry, and furniture even, to London. This was still possible, though it was illegal. The Blumenthals could not get visas. This was quite serious because in London there was a thirty-day time limit. If nobody claimed the cartons within thirty days they would be returned to the sender. Then of course they would be opened by the German authorities and then the Blumenthals . . . well, one knew what would happen. I was the only one who could leave, so I was sent to England with the claim ticket."

"And did it work?" Irma asks.

"Well, the plane was three hours late. I had no authorization to enter England. I didn't speak any English, not a word. But I was a young girl. Nobody really checked me at Tempelhof. And there was a child on the plane who fell sick—you know, those were terrible flights before the war—a little boy and I looked after him, and one of the stewards—BOAC only had stewards in those days—was grateful, and he of course spoke also German and so he helped me at Passport Control when we landed in Croydon. But I was still three hours late and I was clutching the claim ticket and looking for a Dr. Levy who was supposed to meet me and take me to Victoria. And he was furious that I was late, because he had some medical convention. He took the ticket and we rode on the train all the way to Victoria in absolute silence. You know the approach to Victoria? England looked so dark and grim. Anyhow, he attended to the baggage and then he gave me a shilling and the address of a hotel in Russell Square and disappeared. So now I had another piece of paper in my hand, with the name and address of the hotel. And I got on a bus and I gave the driver my shilling and he gave me seven big coins in return. It was night and it was raining and the bus emptied out until I was the only passenger. I got up at a stop and tried to leave, but every time I did the driver pushed me back. Honestly, I thought I'd had it. I thought the bus would stop in a dark street somewhere and the driver would rape me, and that would be the end. But eventually we arrived in Russell Square and he let me off and pointed the way to the hotel. When I entered there was a big English landlady and she asked me immediately for money. 'Five and six,' she said. You know, the old English money system. I gave her my seven large coins and she laughed at me. 'Dr. Levy,' I said. He was supposed to have made arrangements."

"And he hadn't?" Irma interrupts.

"Well, no, but he came back after his convention and paid for the room for a few days. He was staying there too." She paused. "I wanted so much to go home. But Dr. Levy said I had to wait for instructions. So I walked around London. And you know, it's a beautiful city."

"And the Blumenthals?" asks Lacy.

"I never heard of them again."

"Did they . . . ?"

"I don't know. I'm sure they did."

"And your parents, and you . . . ?"

"Well, my father of course . . . died. But my mother and my sister got out. My mother even sent me instructions—by the regular post—to stay in England. Dr. Levy sent me to Woburn House and I met there a German-speaking lady and she befriended me. She even told me about a school that Freud's daughter Anna was starting outside London, but I was too old. Oh, I wanted to go so badly. I begged and begged her to use her influence, and she did and I was even accepted. But I couldn't go because I had no money and I had to find work."

"What kind of work? Domestic?" Tante Edith asks.

"Yes, they needed domestics and my friend at Woburn House got me a job with an English lady—a real English lady, Lady Evesham, who lived in Aylesbury. For a week it was unbelievable. She took me round London, she introduced me to her friends, I felt like a princess. And when the week was up, we drove to this huge estate in Aylesbury. But there everything changed. I was the kitchen maid. The hierarchy was so strict among the servants that nobody spoke to me. I worked six days a week scrubbing the floors. Imagine, the daughter of a department store owner scrubbing the floors. And on my day off I was completely alone."

"And how long did that last?"

"Not too long, a few months. But long enough. My mother and my sister, I told you, got out and they went into domestic service in Cambridge. And of course they wrote me letters. And this was a completely different situation. Two spinster sisters and their brother. Helpful, friendly, with only my mother's well-being and interests at heart."

"Were they Quakers?" Tante Edith wants to know.

Katherine nods.

"*Ja*, the Quakers behaved fine to us during the war. Not like the others," Tante Edith spits. "The others treated us like dirt."

"Well, when I heard from my mother how fine things were in Cambridge, I asked permission to visit them on my day off. It went all the way up to Lady Evesham but she refused. But I decided to go, anyhow. I packed my little suitcase, I crept out of the house, I got on a bus to Cambridge, and I never came back."

Irma applauds. "Good for you," she says.

"So, you see," Katherine says, turning to me, "that's where I went to school. In Cambridge. And then eventually we moved to London. And my mother opened the restaurant, where your parents I'm sure had dinner."

"Domestics. Yes. I, too," says Tante Edith. "But that's another story."

"Ach, you all had it so hard," says Herta. "We, we had a nice cruise. Ten years in an exotic country. See the world, courtesy of Adolf Hitler."

"Don't joke, Herta. You had it pretty hard, too."

"We all had it hard. So, who wants coffee?"

Everybody wants coffee. Lacy pours. Everybody wants cake. Herta cuts.

"You were in domestic service, too?" says Katherine.

"Yes," says Tante Edith. But that's not how she came to England. She returned to Berlin from finishing school in Florence in the spring of 1939 — "What's so funny, you don't think I was at finishing school?" Because she had been out of the country and because things were moving so fast nobody had stamped her passport with the obligatory red *J* for Jew or changed her first name to Sarah. So she was relatively free to travel. She decided to go to London and was given a visa for a month.

In London as the end of the month approached, things became desperate. She had ten shillings to her name. She applied for an extension to her visa. She was refused. But at the same time because she had no *J* in her visa she was denied refugee status. The refugee family with whom she was staying in Greencroft Gardens asked her to leave. She begged them to let her stay. She would do anything—clean the house from top to bottom, cook, act as maid for their little boarding house, anything. They relented, but after three days the woman said, "No, we need the room. It is our livelihood. You have to go." She had nowhere to go. She packed and left and stood outside the front door, frozen in place.

"Suddenly, across the road, coming down the street, I can hardly believe my eyes, I see a woman and her daughter whom I know from Berlin. Frau Rosendorf. The Rosendorfs, oh, they were beneath us in Berlin. We ignored them. Terrible, no? But we did. A fat woman. And her daughter, Ruth, fat, too. I ran over the street and embraced them. So nice I was never to them in my life. I begged them to help me. And they did. Terrible, no?"

They had an attic with a mattress, where she would be safe. For four months, until the war broke out and she could claim asylum, she lived in hiding.

"Then of course the war broke out. I married Bergman. We had a daughter. Then the bombing started." She turns to me. "Were you evacuated?" she asks.

"Yes, my sister and I were in a village called Thundridge, in the house of a bookbinder, with whom my father worked in the city."

"My daughter, too. I sent her to a school in the country. I worked as a barmaid in the Hotel Picadilly. The Americans, they tipped well. They wanted other things, too, oh, sure, what do you think? But they tipped good anyhow. All the tips went in my shoe. We were not supposed to take tips but all the girls did, so—I'm not stupid, I took tips too. Then, two, three in the morning, I walked home. I tell you, it was painful."

"From Picadilly?" I marvel.

"To Belsize Park, yes. We slept in the Underground station."

"Because of the bombing."

"Yes, because of the bombing."

"We went into the basement."

"Yes, you had a basement. We lived in a boarding house. So we slept in the Underground. Every night. On a step."

"On a step?"

"Yes, sure. A step. If you had kids you were on the platform. But my daughter was in a fancy school in Kent. So we got a step. I tell you it was hard. But the money in my shoe paid for my daughter's school. And every Sunday after I finished at the hotel I would take the train to Kent—the milk train, it took all night. And there would be Lady So-wie-So, or your Lady from Aylesbury, in their fancy cars. And nobody knew that I had come on the train. And this went on until the end of the war. Then I became a pig farmer."

"Come on, Tante Edith."

"Yes, sure, a pig farmer. You didn't know? In Ireland. Bergman stayed in England. I went with my daughter to Ireland and we raised pigs. I read about it in the library. I got me a book and I raised pigs. You want to know hard. That was hard. We rode down to town on a bicycle, rain or shine, my daughter and me, once a week for the rations. They lasted three days—four days if we were lucky. Herta, give me another piece of that terrible *Nusstorte.*"

"*Schlagsahne*, Edith?"

"Of course. What do you think, I have to watch my weight? Hm, it's not so bad. They could use a little of this in Ireland, to go with their potatoes."

"You were a pig farmer in Ireland?"

"Yes, sure. I was a pig farmer also in America. Later. I even won prizes. Long time ago."

"Before you did blow jobs."

"Yes. Very good. Before I did blow jobs." She laughs. We all laugh.

"But all this is nothing," Tante Edith continues. "What is something is my cousin Hans. One day, in London, before I am completely underground, I meet my cousin Hans. He is in London for a week, staying on a German boat—*ja*, he was on some government scheme as a reward for hard work—*Freude durch Arbeit.*"

"Joy through work?"

"Yes, something terrible like that. Anyhow, he begs me to help him stay. I go to Woburn House, like you, but by the time they get a lawyer to follow up on the case the boat has left and he on it. So, that's that. I will never see him again. I am underground, I'm a domestic, I marry Bergman, I pack condoms, and I begin to hear these strange rumors. Hans was a traitor, he had joined the Nazis—can you believe it? People had seen him in uniform. *Unglaublich.*

"Well, one day, in 1943, it's four years, five years later, I'm riding on the top of a No. 2 bus, where you can smoke, on the corner of Baker Street and Marlborough Street, and out of the window I see three British soldiers. And I cannot believe my eyes, one of them is Hans. I jump off and he tells me the whole story.

"The boat went back to Germany. In Hamburg he and two other Jews are taken off by the SS, and they are tortured for three days. Then they discover—typical German efficiency—that he doesn't belong in Hamburg, he belongs in Berlin. So they send him under guard by train to Berlin. He sits in a compartment, handcuffed to a guard, and he realizes, this is it, it's all over. They let him go to the lavatory—*ja*, they release him—and as he is about to go in, the train slows down and, he doesn't even think about it, he opens the door and jumps. But the train picks up speed again immediately and is gone. So he lies there for two hours in the undergrowth and then he starts walking back along the track, fifteen kilometers to the last station, and then to the station before that. From there he calls his sister in Berlin. No reply. His father. His father, my Uncle Erich, answers. 'You have to help me. I have to get across the border,' Hans says. There is nothing Onkel Erich can do. Hans hangs up. The next day they pick my uncle up, put him on a train, we never hear from him again. The phone was tapped.

"Hans makes his way to France. Then the Germans invade France, so he goes south, to Marseilles, and ends up in Casablanca where he joins the Foreign Legion. Then the British arrive, you know, looking for Rommel, and Hans becomes a spy for the British. He is given an SS uniform and he becomes a Nazi—imagine a Jew in an SS uniform. So they were right, all these people: he became a Nazi. Anyhow, he infiltrates the German ranks. And he is so successful that he is allowed to join the British army. When I met him it was his third day in London. Incredible, no?"

"*Ja, ja,*" says Herta, "We all have stories."

"So, Robin, slivovitz?" Lacy asks me. It has become a ritual, he and I, when the evening winds down, a shot each of slivovitz. "*L'chaim,*" he says.

"*L'chaim,*" I say.

"Ach, how you can do that is beyond me," says Tante Edith.

And, to applause, in one gulp, down it goes.

More dessert is served, more coffee. And then brandy. I am so full, not just from food, I want to leave. Instead I go into the kitchen. Lacy is washing the dishes. No, no, nothing to help. In the dining room the women are entertaining each other. Werner and Irma have left. Linda's boyfriend, David, is coming the next day. He is going to spend the night. "Oh, he'll sleep with me on the sofa," says Tante Edith. "I'll show him a thing or two." Everybody laughs.

I learn one other thing tonight. Herta is clearing the table. The candles are guttering out.

"What about the candlesticks?" I say.

"No, no. They stay here. We have guests again tomorrow night."

"They are really magnificent," I say.

"Yes," she says, "Those candlesticks belonged to my mother, also the linen and the china. And you know who saved them, who got them from the station in Victoria and kept them during the war? Your father. He kept them in London in the basement and we were afraid to have them in Shanghai, but when we were all reunited in New York he packed them up with quite a bit of money and sent them to me. I think of him every time I light the candles."

Outside it is still raining. I walk Chavah to her car. It is one in the morning. A gang of street kids is hanging out by the car. We lock the doors from the inside. She drives me to the subway. We wish each other *leshanah tavah.* And she speeds off through the rain in the direction of the Queensborough Bridge. The next day she has another celebration to go to in the afternoon. I have theater tickets. And Herta and Lacy and Linda and Tante Edith are having Rosh Hashanah guests again.

Yom Kippur

It took me weeks to pluck up the courage. Finally, one spring afternoon, with considerable trepidation, I walked down West 13th Street, stopped in front of an ivy-covered four-story building, took a breath, and opened the door. Inside, at a desk, a monk in an orange-colored robe picked up a telephone: "Integral Yoga Institute. May I serve you?"

I don't know why these things scare me. Perhaps it's the aura of holiness, the whole idea of Indian gurus in white robes and bare feet, lighter than air almost, their eyes liquid, faces aflame, flesh melting into nothingness, some primordial groan rumbling up from the stomach, or from the ground, whole body a drum, whole being a top, moaning, spinning, streaming, swirling, a hum curling up toward the lip of Heaven.

When I was fifteen, in Switzerland, stranded at a ski lodge half way up the Piz Palu, the last of the afternoon sun dying away, a snowstorm threatening, the rest of my party from school already gone, cold beginning to set in, waiting for a guide to help me down, suddenly from above, with unearthly speed and quiet—whoosh, whoosh—a lone skier flashed into view, coming down the mountain as though on wings, cutting the ice like a dancer, this way and that, a man in his thirties with long dark hair and a beard, an incongruous sight in the Alps, a hippie before there were hippies. In an instant, in a plume of snow, he stood before me. His pale blue eyes looked at me for a moment, held me transfixed, and then as suddenly as he had come he was gone, dancing down the mountain towards the lights of the Engadine. I thought he was Jesus. It scared me to death.

The monk behind the desk looked up at me: "How may I serve you?"

"Um, I'm here for the class."

"Hatha?"

"I guess so."

"It is in the Gold Room. You have a towel?"

"A towel?"

"Yes."

"Er, no."

"Do not worry. You may borrow a towel."

"Thank you."

Behind the aura of calm, beneath the orange robe, I was dimly aware that the monk was a young American, younger perhaps than I. There was no mark on his forehead, his head was not shaven, there was nothing beyond the robe and the sense of self-possession to distinguish him from the throng of New Yorkers shuffling by outside.

"Please sign your name here."

I signed.

"The contribution is $1.50."

I pulled out $1.50.

"And 25¢ for the towel."

"Oh, of course."

"Please take off your shoes and leave them on the rack outside the door. The men's changing room is to your right. Once you are inside, please remember to keep silent. You may change and then, when the doors open, you may go in."

I nodded imperceptibly, took the proffered towel, and tiptoed stealthily over to the shoe rack. I took off my shoes and opened the door to the men's changing room.

Inside, in a half light, various men were in various stages of dress and undress. On racks were suits from Wall Street, jeans from the Lower East Side, the clothes of old men, young men, respectable burghers and revolutionaries. Some stood ready in white cotton, in running shorts, in sweatsuits, some crouched cross-legged on the floor with their eyes closed. I hung my jeans and sweater on a hanger and stood with the rest in the running shorts and T-shirt I had put on underneath. A sign read, "Not everyone is a Yogi. Please take your valuables with you." I fumbled in my jacket for my wallet. A sign by the sliding doors read, "Do not enter while chanting is in progress." From behind the doors came a dull responsive moaning. A third sign read, "Please observe silence." Some of the men, old comrades obviously, were whispering greetings to each other, a low undercurrent of muttering to the distant moan from beyond. It was not unlike an Orthodox shul where the men and women are separated and down on the main floor—the orchestra—the men keep up a hubbub of greetings and congratulations and inquiries after business, health, and family, while on the dais the rabbi and the *chazan* drone imperturbably on. Presently there was a furtive scratching at the doors and they slid open. A handful of somnambulists, leaden-footed, heavy-lidded, dribbled out, towels in hand. The crouchers near the door sprang up and leapt in and the rest of us followed, some more purposeful than others, I less purposeful than all.

The Gold Room was perhaps fifty feet long with a skylight running its entire length. From an identical sliding door to our left the women entered. To our right was a low white table with flowers, a candle, and incense. Above it were portraits of Swami Satchidananda, whose beautiful serene face with its long hair and beard I recognized from Woodstock, and of his guru, a severer bald-headed man, Swami Sivananda. There was also a huge, intricate, colorful mandala, in which the symbols of all the great religions were intertwined. I watched as men and women scattered quietly across the golden carpet, spread their towels in neat rows, and lay down on top of them, feet facing the walls, head towards the center of the room. I spread my towel and lay down too.

The room was very peaceful; early evening light flooded in from the long skylight, suffusing the room in a warm glow. The floor felt firm and solid beneath my back. Presently the doors to both the dressing rooms were slid shut and fastened and a pair of feet padded softly towards the altar. A match was struck, a candle evidently lit, and then the sweet and acrid smell of incense crept through the air. A moment of silence, some whispered incantation, and then the feet padding the entire length of the room between the two rows of prone bodies. Another moment of silence and then from the other end of the room a woman's voice: "Please come to a comfortable cross-legged position facing the center of the room."

I was completely taken aback. The voice spoke with a pronounced German accent. It belonged to an elderly gray-haired woman in a white cotton meditation suit.

"Please check that your posture is correct, straight but not rigid, chest out, shoulders relaxed, head centered, eyes closed."

It was a voice that could have belonged to any one of my mother's bridge partners.

"Now we will chant together three times the syllable *Om*. *Om* is the sacred sound of the universe. It will help us to come together, to put aside all thoughts of what happened before we came into this room and all thoughts of what will happen when we leave. Now, breathing in fully and deeply for *Om*."

I breathed in fully and deeply. "*Om*." A long low rumble beginning in the stomach and rising to a hum in the head. "*O-om*." A long low rumble like the sound of the shofar on Rosh Hashanah. And a third time, "*Om*," the body vibrating, the head beginning to swirl.

"We will now chant responsively."

It was the first time, I thought, with the possible exception of Jochem, who had died a year earlier, that a voice with a German accent had ever sounded soothing.

"*Om namashivaya guravay,*" the voice sang out softly and we responded, some more expertly than others, all more expertly than I.

"*Satchidananda murtayay,*" she sang and we followed.

"*Nishprapanjaya shantayay/Nira lambaya tayjasay.*"

The class proceeded: eye movements; sun worship; backward-bending poses—the cobra, the locust, the bow; forward-bending poses—the head-to-knee pose, the half-spinal twist, the shoulder stand, the fish pose; the seal of yoga; deep relaxation.

"Please lie with your head toward the center of the room. The corpse pose. We will now tense and release each muscle independently. And then we will check the body with our mind. Stretch out the right leg along the floor. Tighten it. Raise it off the ground a few inches. Tighter, tighter, and release."

Two dozen right legs dropped to the floor. Left legs followed. Then the arms, the buttocks, the stomach, the chest, the shoulders, the face, the back of the neck, the scalp.

"Think of the body floating in a soft sea. The water bathes and relaxes the toes; the feet; the calves; the knees; the backs of the knees; the thighs; the pelvis; the whole genital area; the buttocks; the stomach; the small of the back; the upper back; the chest; the fingers; the hands; the wrists; the forearms; the elbows; the upper arms; the shoulders; the neck; the throat; the jaw; the chin; the inside of the mouth; the tongue; the teeth; the lips; the nose; the cheeks; the eyes; the eyebrows; the forehead; the back of the neck; the ears; the scalp; the crown of the head; the hair."

This voice, the voice, I was sure, of a German Jewish refugee, a voice associated for me with all kinds of terrors, the terrors of childhood, of my father's ranting, of Hitler, of bombing, of propaganda, of Auschwitz, of Germany after the war, was leading me, lulling me, into a kind of sleep. I thought of *Demian* and I felt as though a mystical guide had arrived to take me through a secret door.

"Slowly become aware of your breathing. It is very shallow. You are floating on the breath. Now become aware of your thoughts. If a thought arises, see it. Look at it. Let it go. This is yogic sleep. It is seven times more restful than normal sleep."

I was so tired, so tired. It was so restful. Suddenly a hand touched me. I started.

"You fell asleep."

"Mm?"

"You must try to remain conscious."

I tried. I fell asleep again. I awoke again. She was speaking to us all.

"Return your awareness to the breath. Allow the breath to become deeper and deeper. Gradually stretch the toes and fingers, the arms and legs. When you feel ready, come slowly to a comfortable cross-legged position facing the center of the room, for the final chants."

In slow motion I sat up and turned to face the center of the room.

"Now the breathing. Eyes closed, posture erect but not rigid."

Three-part breathing, bellows breathing, alternate nostril breathing. In, out. In, out. In, out.

"Now we will chant responsively, and then a moment of silent meditation. For those of you who have a mantra, you may use it. Otherwise you may use *om shanti*, for example, which means peace, or concentrate on a beautiful object—a candle flame or a flower. Now, responsively, please," and she began a lilting chant: "*Rama, rama, rama, rama, rama, rama, rama, ram,*" and we followed, and she picked up again and we followed, and faster and faster, and then slower and slower, and softer and softer, until it died away altogether and all that was left was silence and a sound or a picture reverberating in the head. And then after the silence, again "*Om,*" and we responded, three times in all, and then the closing chants— "May the entire Universe be filled with peace and joy"—and then finally spoken, "*Jai sri satguru maharaja ki*" and all those more familiar than I answered, "*Jai.*" "Victory to the guru who is within us all," she said. "Thank you. My name is Ma Nishalananda. I thank you for a wonderful class." And slowly, in the now gathering dark we collected our towels and somnambulated towards the changing rooms.

"Naomi," I said when I got home, "you won't believe what this was like."

"Oh, you, you're such a romantic," she said when I had told her. "*Demian!* It's just a little *Jäcke* who's doing something with her life apart from playing bridge."

"Oh, Naomi."

"Oh, Robin."

"You don't understand. It was very moving."

"It's not that I don't understand, darling. It's just that sometimes you go a little bit overboard."

"O.K. O.K."

"You little Jewish romantic."

Naomi at this time was beginning to sing in public and perhaps the habit of getting up in a nightclub in a silver lamé gown and performing for a generally inebriated clientele was not entirely compatible with the notion of a mystical experience. She was actually getting to be rather good, and whenever I could I would go to Reno Sweeney's or the Ballroom to cheer her on.

One night she was singing in a small place on 45th Street. Her father's cousin Madeleine was coming and Naomi asked me to keep her company. Madeleine was the one member of her family for whom we felt a genuine affinity—she was a painter who had resolutely stuck to her guns in New York and who maintained an amused and healthy detachment from her cousin, Naomi's father the rabbi, and the contrived gentility of their life in West Virginia. I arrived late and Madeleine was sitting at a table close to the stage and I didn't want to push through. Naomi's sister, Julie, and her husband, Tony, were at a table closer to the entrance and I joined them. Naomi was singing "Someone to Watch over Me."

"Doesn't she look great," said Julie.

"Yeah, but she sounds terrible," said Tony. I kicked him, our usual greeting.

"Madeleine's here with a friend of hers she wants you to meet. She's a translator. She's just done a play by that Polish playwright friend of yours, you know."

"Mrozek?"

"Yeah, him."

Mrozek, by a peculiar combination of circumstances, I had met the previous year in, of all places, Pennsylvania, when I returned for a week to revise my dissertation and he turned out be playwright in residence. My God, how things had changed—in my day, when I arrived, they wouldn't have known how to spell his name. Now here he was in person, the gloomiest of exiles. For a week we made quite a pair. While I expounded on the ritual nature and origin of the drama and how those primitive religious forces could be discerned beneath the surface not only of Aeschylus and Shakespeare, but of Miller and Beckett and Ibsen and, yes, even of Mrozek himself, Mrozek concerned himself entirely with living conditions. They had given him a hideous apartment with cinder block walls and even more hideous furniture. But . . . he had figured out a solution. In the living room was nothing but a card table with a typewriter and an open tin of cat food. I never saw a cat. I never saw the furniture either until I looked in the bathroom. The entire bathroom including the tub was piled to the ceiling with American motel furniture.

"Slawomir, how do you wash?"

He shrugged. "Cleanliness is next to Godliness. Neither of them is so important."

"She knows Mrozek?" I asked.

"I don't know, you'll have to ask."

Naomi finished and we gathered some tables together and joined Madeleine up front.

"Hello, Robin, my dear. I want you to meet my friend Lola. She's from Berlin like your mother. She also knows that Polish playwright you're always on about, with the unpronounceable name."

"Mrozek."

"Yeah, that's him. Lola, this is Robin. Robin, Lola. Wasn't she great by the way—Naomi, I mean."

"Yes, she was."

"Can't sing, though"—this from Tony.

"You were wonderful"—this from Julie.

"Yes, wonderful, wonderful"—this from Lola. There was something vaguely familiar about her but I couldn't quite place it. "So, you know Mrozek?"

"Well, we spent a miserable week together in the middle of Pennsylvania, I don't know how much that counts. How do you know him?"

"I have been translating some of his plays—from the German, I don't read Polish. Would you like an English cigarette?"

"Thank you, but I've just given up."

"Oh, good for you. I try and try, but I don't succeed."

I laughed. Why did a cigarette seem so incongruous somehow? "This may seem like a very strange question, but you don't, by any chance, teach yoga, do you?"

"Oh, my God, I've been found out. Smoking. In a nightclub. They'll drum me out."

"My God, I don't believe it. Naomi, Naomi, this is the woman I told you about." I suddenly became very shy.

"How do you know? You go to the Institute?"

"Yes. In fact, the very first class I took, you taught."

"How was it—awful?"

"No, it was wonderful. It made a very big impression on me."

"You're pulling my leg."

"No, he's not," said Naomi. "He couldn't stop talking about it. I even started to tease him."

"Well, Madeleine, you see, I even have students. She doesn't believe in all this yoga nonsense. She thinks I invent it."

"Robin, is this true?"

"Certainly, it's true."

"Well, that's wonderful. Let's have another round. Waiter! Unless of course it's against your religion."

Lola, it turned out, had become involved in yoga through a friend, initially for the physical exercise. "But there was something so peaceful about it. I went more often. I did a retreat. It's lovely. No talking for a weekend or a week or ten days. Peaceful. And then I asked if I could take the Teacher Training. Some of the *asanas* I couldn't do but they let me anyway. And so I teach. You know, it does a lot for me. Even my voice. You are not the first one to say it. I have normally a terrible voice. This German accent, it's horrible. And God forbid, I should sing. Naomi, you would run away. But in the class, when I do those chants, for some reason, I cannot explain it, it is alright. I can feel it. I don't even need to be told. Though it is nice. And I thank you."

"I thank *you*."

The reason I hadn't seen her again was that she now taught almost entirely at the uptown center, where she had developed a class for older people. "Madeleine, you should try it."

"Sure, sure. Their father should try it, *he*'s an older person. His congregation could send him up from Charleston. Do him a world of good. Judy too, I can just see her." We laughed.

"Lola, don't you have to do all kinds of things—not smoke, not drink, not eat meat?"

"Well, I'm supposed to. But I'm old, what can I do? What can *they* do? I do what I can. You gave up smoking—good for you. I like it too much." She lit up. "Listen, when you've been through the war, and all that that involves, a cigarette here, a cigarette there, it doesn't make so big a difference. I have a fondness for these English ones. It's from when I lived in England." She, like my parents, had escaped to England just before the war. "I still have friends there. Next time, when you go, you must look up Helen Greene. Will you? She's Graham Greene's sister. Have lunch with her. Tell her how you know me."

Lola's spiritual peace—or perhaps more accurately, truce—was hard-won. It amazed me. But then these things always amazed me. I was such an extremist. I assumed that if you embarked on some spiritual path, that was it, *finito*—no more sex, no more booze, no more earthly pleasures, no more cigarettes. Somewhere it was all laid down hard and fast, chiseled in stone. The notion that you might wrest from the negotiation some tiny personal plot on which to plant your flag, that indeed that might be the struggle without which no victory was possible, that the struggle and the journey were one, that notion flew by me. Oh, I understood it intellectually. I understood that letting go was what it was all about, that letting go was necessarily a process, that it was a question of slowly discarding. But deep down in my bones I knew that wasn't true. It was a precipice towards which you were dragged blind and screaming, at the edge of which you were left teetering, until some kick, some poke in the ribs, some breath on the back of the neck sent you hurtling into the unknown. If I didn't watch out I'd wake up one morning in an orange robe with my head shaved, except for one bizarre lock flapping in a chilly breeze, and other people in orange robes with shaven heads and similar locks would be mouthing some unpronounceable Indian name at me and it would be mine. And there I would be walking the streets of New York, barefoot, banging a drum. It might be alright in New York. But how could I ever go home again?

"Hullo?"

"Hello, Daddy."

"Hullo?"

"Hello, Daddy, it's Robin."

"Who?"

"Robin."

"Who?"

"Your son, Robin."

"Ach, RRRawbeen."

"Well, as a matter of fact, that's why I called. It's now Swami Pravadananda and when I get off the plane tomorrow I want you to be prepared for a shock."

And so, perhaps understandably, I was continually astounded when I bumped into people who were on that path, who nevertheless walked the planet like normal people with normal problems, that the two things could cohabit, that one could be a rabbi and a woman and have sex, that one could be a rabbi and a mystic and play the guitar and be divorced and have affairs, that one could be a priest and an alcoholic, that one could be a minister and a pianist and a political activist and a homosexual—that one could be a German-Jewish refugee who practiced yoga and smoked English cigarettes.

In the course of the next year or so, in the private and peculiar and imperceptible way in which those things happen, quietly, like the movement of tectonic plates, Naomi and I began to drift apart. At first we didn't notice.

In the summer we went to Europe for six weeks. They sped by in a series of snapshots: my uncle picking us up in Amsterdam; my uncle driving us to the country house in Ruurlo; Naomi with Lex and Marjanne in Enschede; the four of us in their car driving to Paris; Paris in sunshine; Lex and Marjanne waving good-bye at the Gare de Lyons; Naomi and I on the train to the south of France; Naomi and I on the Riviera; Florence, Siena, Pisa, Rome; exhaustion; the night train back from Venice to Paris;

Mrozek in Paris; this time, *bien sûr*, raining; the boat to Dover; Marlborough Mansions; family wounds which refused to heal; and on our last day
lunch at the Albany with Helen Greene.

"And how do you know Lola?"

"Well, we actually met through yoga."

"Yoga? She's studying yoga?"

"As a matter of fact, she's teaching it."

"Good Heavens! And why did she send you to see me?"

"Well, amongst other things, she thought perhaps you might be interested in publishing my dissertation."

And in that marvelous flat in the Albany, in the shadow of Oscar Wilde
and Algernon Moncrieff, not to mention several British prime ministers
living and dead, I started to elaborate to Graham Greene's sister and two
gently intoxicated aristocratic young Englishmen on the common bond
we all shared way back in the rituals of sex and sacrifice and tribal execution.

Back in America, on the Lower East Side, amid the junkies and the
delicatessens and the Jewish monument-makers and the bodegas and the
burnt-out buildings, our marriage slowly fell apart. And in the increasingly frantic, lonely, unstructured, Naomiless life that emerged, I involved myself in a series of promiscuous flirtations: I was Rolfed; I whirled
like a dervish; I sang with the sufis; I meditated chaotically in the manner
prescribed by a guru in Poona—I screamed, I panted, I danced; I sat for
hours with Buddhists, more varieties of Buddhist, I am sure, than ever
existed in Tibet; I wept, I shouted; I even dined with monks in orange
robes and shaven heads with solitary locks who chanted during dinner; I
tried to reexperience the moment of my birth.

And every so often, under the assault, a door would open: in a moment of excruciating pain, the Rolfer kneading the inside of my mouth,
trying to dissolve the accumulated tension in the root of my tongue, I
would realize how many screams and shouts and cries I had held back as
a child; in a silent encounter, sitting cross-legged on the floor, face to face
with an enormous fat woman, gazing into her eyes, I would suddenly see
past the unwholesome blubber into the soul beyond; in a moment of
levity, dancing, singing, in the company of strangers whose hipness and
cool and general savoir faire had reduced me only moments before to
stuttering paralysis, all barriers would suddenly fall away, a deep rolling
tide of joy would take hold and sweep me into communion—every so
often a door would open, but only a crack, and then it would close again.

And every so often my steps would take me, towel in hand, over to 13th

Street and I would pad over the golden carpet underneath the skylight and incline my head ever so slightly as I passed the altar and chant and breathe and stretch and relax—and, not infrequently, fall asleep.

One day I saw a notice. It was fall. I was vaguely conscious of the High Holy Days approaching. I rarely did anything religious on the High Holy Days. On one of the evenings of Rosh Hashanah I might go to my cousins on upper Broadway. On Yom Kippur I might fast. But it was a hollow gesture. Most of the Yom Kippur observances I had been to had seemed empty—the huge ceremonies in London at the Odeon Swiss Cottage, which the Belsize Square New Liberal Jewish Congregation rented for all those who became Jews again (and paid their dues) one day a year; the glib, denatured, passionless services of Naomi's father's congregation in Charleston; the immense parade of wealth at a temple Naomi's cousin Eddie took us to in Philadelphia. When we lived on the Lower East Side I often wondered about the little shuls and what the old pious Jews did on Yom Kippur, but it was frightening, I didn't have even the rudiments of Hebrew, and stepping across their threshold would have taken far more courage than I possessed, far more courage than it had taken to enter the Institute on 13th Street almost four years before.

Naomi and I had been separated now for two years. I was cut off from my family. I had no community, except the self-invented horizontal community of friends who perhaps had nothing more in common than the fact that they knew me. A sense of solitariness stole up on me. So when I saw the notice, I resolved that this time I would not allow my fears to get the better of me. It said: "Yom Kippur for Yogis. All welcome. Rabbi Samuel Seligman, a close friend of our beloved Swamiji, will hold an ecumenical Yom Kippur Service at the Institute on . . ." I made a note of the time and date. It was the Sunday morning after Yom Kippur.

I paid my money. I removed my shoes, although this time I did not change. I stepped into the familiar room. A table had been placed underneath the skylight. A few figures sat on the floor facing the table. I sat. To my right was a young woman. One or two people were talking softly to each other. "Excuse me," I said to the young woman. She didn't respond. I touched her hesitantly on the arm. She turned around. "Excuse me," I said again. "Is it alright if I sit here?"

She smiled and nodded. "Yes." She looked at me with great concentration. "What is your name?"

"Robin."

"Sarah."

She held out her hand. I shook it. "Do you know what's going to happen?" I asked.

She shook her head.

"Do you come to yoga classes here?"

"No. I have a friend who teaches here. Scott. He told me about it."

"Is he here?"

"No. He's a doctor. He's on call. Maybe he'll come later." She continued to look at me. I looked down.

"I'm sorry to look at you like that."

"Oh, that's alright."

"I can't hear you when you look down like that."

"I'm sorry." I turned to look at her again.

"I'm deaf. Not completely deaf. But it helps to see your lips. And this helps." She pulled the hair back from her ear to reveal a hearing aid.

"I'm sorry." I moved closer.

"No, don't be sorry. Just accept it."

"Do you know the rabbi?" I asked.

"You don't have to mouth the words like that—I'm quite skilled. No, I don't. Do you?"

"No." I shook my head.

She touched my arm. "It's O.K."

I nodded, "O.K."

"What brought *you* here?"

"Well, I come to yoga classes here. I guess I'm sort of a dislocated Jew. I don't go to synagogue."

"So you're looking."

"I guess so."

"Who isn't?" She gestured around the room. It was filling up, a mixture of yogis and disenfranchised Jews, orange robes, white robes, yarmulkes, no yarmulkes, men and women, bearded and clean-shaven, neat and unkempt, old and young. Jews and yogis and a whole host of gradations in between—here a meditation suit, there meditation pants and a yarmulke, here a cross, there beads and a tiny mala of the guru, here and there a tallis.

"What a mixture," I said.

She smiled and nodded.

There was a commotion behind us and a phalanx of monks came in with a corpulent figure in a blue suit and a white yarmulke. There was much whispering and flapping of robes and a parting as it were of the Red Sea to enable the Israelites to get through. Some of them were lost on the journey, sitting down on the floor in odd remaining spaces, but the body of them reached the table and settled down beneath the sky-light, spreading their robes on the floor, except for two who sat on chairs and the incongruous figure in blue who was whispering into the ear of one of them.

"My God," I said to Sarah, "do you believe it?"

She laughed.

"Look at his cuffs." On the cuffs of his shirt was embroidered the Hebrew letter *shin* in a blue as brilliant as the blue of his suit. "And look at his watch." He had taken from the pocket of his vest a large gold watch which was attached to the rest of his considerable bulk by a large gold chain. "This is everything I've always hated. I don't believe it. I don't believe it."

Sarah touched me on the arm. "He's going to begin."

"Well, it's almost time. Everything at the Institute begins exactly on time. Everything in Judaism begins late. So we'll split the difference." He waited for a few late arrivals to settle down. "Ma Prem has been kind enough to invite me into her house so I will ask her to extend the kindness by beginning." He turned to the monk in one of the chairs.

"It is not my house, as Rabbi Seligman knows well. It is a house of the spirit. It is Swamiji's house. And in the name of our beloved guru I bid you welcome. Let us begin as we always begin by closing our eyes. Exhale. Breathe in deeply for *Om.*"

And obediently, in front of a fat rabbi in a blue suit, all of us, this crazy mixture of God's people, lost, found, and seeking, closed our eyes, in-haled, and let out a long, low, rumbling *Om.* And then a second time. And then a third. I looked at Sarah. She was looking at me.

"Feel it in the top of your head."

"I did," she said.

"Good girl."

"And now responsively."

I faced Sarah.

"*Om namashivaya guravay/ Satchidananda murtayay . . .*"

"I bet you weren't expecting this," I whispered.

"You're right," she said, "Were you?"

"Nope."

Ma Prem was speaking. "Rabbi Seligman is a close friend of Swamiji's. They have conducted many services together. It is a pleasure to welcome him into our house."

The rabbi was half sitting on the edge of the table, one foot balancing him against the carpet, the other dangling. They were both sockless.

"My friends," he began, "it is not Yom Kippur and this is not a temple, but I have never seen so observant a congregation. Why, you ask. It is enjoined that on Yom Kippur one does not wear shoes. Even the orthodox generally compromise. They do not wear leather. They wear canvas. But here, I look round the room and not one of you is wearing shoes. What a *frumme* congregation. How observant." There was scattered laughter. "Do you know why? Anybody?"

A voice from the back: "Because it is wrong to wear the skin of an animal on a Holy Day?"

"Well, that's one reason. But wherever you have two Jews you have three reasons. Rabbi Menahem Mendel said it is because all the worlds are elevated on Yom Kippur, the earth on which we live is elevated too, and is called holy ground, and it is written—you know this from Exodus: 'Put off thy shoes from off thy feet, for the place whereupon thou standest is holy ground.' But Rabbi Moses Hagiz says that the only reason we wear shoes is so our flesh may not touch the earth, for the earth is cursed because of the sin of Adam, but in holy places, where the ground is holy, we must go barefoot. This is a holy place and you are all good Jews, better than you know.

"I want to thank Ma Prem. I want to thank her for her hospitality, for her invocation, for offering us this holy ground. I want to say how conscious I am, how conscious we all are, of the absence of my friend, my brother, our beloved Swamiji. But I look at the altar, at the picture of his beautiful face, and I realize that he is with us in spirit.

"And I look at the great mandala with all its symbols and I see among them the Maagen David and I think it is alright if today it radiates with a special light. And I see the candles burning and I think it is like the candles we are enjoined to light, the candles which burn for twenty-four hours on Yom Kippur. And I look at some of you in your white robes and dresses and your white meditation suits and I think of the white we are commanded to wear on Yom Kippur, for it is a Holy Day not of awe only but of joy, for 'the Divine Presence does not rest . . . in the midst of sadness . . . but in the midst of joy at the keeping of a commandment.' And I look at some of you with your beards and long hair and I think of the Nazarites, for whom one room in the inner court of the Temple was reserved, the Temple of Hero which took eighty years to build and was destroyed by Titus and which we still mourn, I think of the Nazarites, who were under oath not to cut their hair—and not to touch wine.

"And I think above all of the principle of yoga, the yoke, the principle of balance, and I think of the complex duality of the Jewish God, the eternal complexity, the God of compassion and the God of justice, the God to Whom we pray, '*Avinu Malkeinu*, Our Father, our King, let Your compassion overwhelm Your wrath,' the God who Himself prays, according to legend, 'May it be My will that My love of compassion overwhelm My demand for justice,' the God in Whose presence we are commanded by the Psalmist 'to rejoice with trembling,' the God Who creates a world where, in the words of Rabbi Simcha Bunam of Prysucha, 'Every man—and woman—should carry in his pockets two scraps of paper, so he can reach in and pull out which one he needs; on one should be written "For my sake the world was created," and on the other, "I am dust and ashes."' You know, maybe that is the quintessential Jewish joke. St. Augustine said, 'One of the thieves was hanged: do not presume. One of the thieves was saved: do not despair.' Perhaps Augustine was a Jew. Certainly there were three Jews up there. Just like Yom Kippur. On Yom Kippur there are three men on the *bimah*. Three men constitute a rabbinical court. It's why I have asked Ma Prem and Swami Mugdananda to sit on chairs up here with me. Together we constitute a Beth Din, in whose presence we can begin."

And he began: "'By authority of the Court on High and by authority of the Court below, with divine consent and with consent of this *frumme* congregation, we hereby declare it permissible to pray with those who have transgressed.'

"On Erev Yom Kippur, the eve of Yom Kippur, this is repeated three times. We hereby invite all Jews, even the most recalcitrant, to return to the fold on this sacred day, *the* day, the Sabbath of Sabbaths, and we hereby absolve our brothers and sisters of the normal duty, which is to keep the transgressor at bay. There is a legend that this custom originated in Spain at the time of the Inquisition, when Jews were forced to convert, to become *conversos, Marranos*, 'pigs,' and that on this one day, this day of days, they came back secretly to join their brothers—their brothers and their sisters—and to pray for divine forgiveness."

Rabbi Seligman had left his precarious perch on the edge of the table and was walking up and down in front of us. Now he took off the jacket of his blue suit and went behind the table and hung it on the back of the chair.

"We gather on Yom Kippur to atone for our sins, to ask forgiveness. For the sins against our fellows, our brothers and our sisters, we must ask their forgiveness, we must seek them out, for God will not pardon us unless they first have pardoned us. And for the sins against God, for our transgressions, we confess together, for we are all one people, one congregation, we are all responsible for one another—if someone has sinned, I confess to it, for if someone has sinned, it is as though I have sinned."

He paused. "Now this is all very heavy, and we here at the Institute are not one people, we are not one congregation. So I think I should stop for a moment and I should ask you if there is anything on your mind, anything at all, anything you want to confess, to talk about, to question." He looked around the room. "Yes?"

He looked directly at me, but a woman behind me started to speak. Very softly she said, "Rabbi, I sit here in a room full of strangers. I know no one. Maybe, if I knew anyone, I would not speak. But no one knows me and I feel I can speak. Something troubles me. I am vain. I look at myself. I admire myself. I think of other people admiring me. I think always of the impression I make. I put myself always in a certain light. I cannot simply be. Even now, when I talk to you. When I confess."

"Oh, my dear," said the rabbi, "Vanity, do I know from vanity." He laughed. Sarah and I exchanged glances. "This suit." He picked up the jacket from the chair and laid it on the table. "This blue suit is an expensive suit. It has an expensive lining." He opened the jacket and revealed a blue satin lining. "I ask myself, why do I need such a suit? This shirt, this shirt with the embroidery." He held out the cuff of his right sleeve. "This *shin* embroidered in blue to match the suit. Why do I need it. Is it not vanity? Of course it is vanity. It troubles me terribly. But if I were not to wear it? It would sit in my closet like a guilty secret. And if I had not bought it? It would be the same thing.

"You know, in the afternoon of the day before Yom Kippur it was customary for each member of the congregation to receive thirty-nine lashes. There are all kinds of reasons for the number thirty-nine, but it is curious that in the Torah it is written, 'Forty lashes he may give him.' Now a story is told of a certain Hassid who went to see his rabbi and on the way he thought, 'Perhaps it would be worth it to receive the forty lashes, so my rabbi will find no fault in me,' and while he is still thinking that, the rabbi comes out to greet him, and says, 'Why do you think the sages took one lash away from the forty, making thirty-nine, when the Torah expressly says forty? Because when a man commits a transgression and receives the full forty lashes, he may think he has wiped away the iniquity, but if he receives only thirty-nine, he will know he has not yet received his full punishment, and he has still to better his ways.'

"For me, my suit is that missing lash. For you, too. Our vanity, your vanity and mine, tells us we are not perfect, it tells us we have yet to wipe away our imperfections, it tells us we are still human."

Quietly, behind me, the young woman started to weep.

"Yes?"

The rabbi turned to another questioner, a man who asked bitterly: "Why all this breast-beating, all this mea culpa? We fast, we mortify the flesh, we say over and over again how terrible we are. All this guilt, it's too much."

"You are wrong. There is a beautiful passage in the Haftorah portion for Yom Kippur about fasting. It is from Isaiah. I will read it to you." The rabbi thumbed through the book lying on the table, found his place, and began to read: "'"Why have we fasted," they say, "if you see it not? Why have we afflicted ourselves if you know it not?" Behold, on the day of your fast, you pursue business as usual, and oppress your workers. Behold, you fast only to quarrel and fight, to deal wicked blows. Such fasting will not make your voice audible on high. Is this the fast I have chosen? Is this affliction of the soul? Is it to droop your head like a bullrush, to grovel in sackcloth and ashes? Is that what you call fasting, a fast that the Lord would accept? *This* is my chosen fast: to loosen all the bonds that bind men unfairly, to let the oppressed go free, to break every yoke. Share your bread with the hungry, take the homeless into your home. Clothe the naked when you see him, do not turn away from people in need. Then cleansing light shall break forth like the dawn, and your wounds shall soon be healed. Your triumph shall go before you and the Lord's glory shall be your rearguard. Then you shall call and the Lord will answer, you shall cry out and He will say, "Here I am."' "

The rabbi looked up. "It is not to mortify you, it is to set you free; it is not to inculcate guilt, it is to resolve it; it is not to weigh you down, it is to lift you up."

"But, rabbi, I am not light."

"Ah, that is because you do not dance. Later, we dance."

"Rabbi," another voice came from the floor, the voice of an older woman, weary, calm. "Rabbi, you talk of light, of joy, of dancing. Do you deny suffering? What *about* the naked, the homeless, the oppressed. And what about the Jews? Why always the Jews? Why harp on that? My father was a banker. In Frankfurt. He never went to temple. His mother wasn't even Jewish. But they took him anyhow. They put him on a train. I am not a Jew. I am a devotee of Swamiji's. And yet, if it happens, they will take me too. Why? I do not have children. I will not bring children into such a world. But, if I had children, were it to happen, they would seek them out, they would take them too, they would put them on a train. Little children. God in Heaven. Why? Why? Forgive me, I didn't mean to speak."

The rabbi looked at her for a long time. "For some questions, there are no answers. Or maybe there are answers, but I don't have them. In the Mussaf Service on Yom Kippur, the Additional Service, there is a section—the *Eileh Eskerah*—where we commemorate the martyrs. You are right. It is like touching bottom. Rabbi Ishmael, Rabbi Shimon, Rabbi Akiba, Rabbi Judah, Rabbi Hanina, all slain, all martyred, all going to their death—their terrible individual deaths—for faith. All going *bravely* to their death because they were Jewish. All going bravely to their death because they chose to. All dying secure in their faith.

"But what about the six million? What about your father? What about your father who had no faith. Who did not choose to die. Who died anyway. To those questions I have no answers. As Swamiji might say, it has always been, it is, it will continue to be. It is the very depth. It is the moment at which even the Psalmist can see no light: 'Confusion confronts us constantly, our face is covered with shame. All this has come upon us, yet we have not forgotten You, we have not been false to Your Covenant. For Your sake are we murdered constantly, treated as sheep for slaughter. Why do You hide Your presence? Why do You forget our affliction, our oppression? Our spirit is down in the dust, our body cleaves to the ground.'

"It is the bottom from which there is no way out. It is the moment where we can no longer pray. It is the moment where we pray to be able to pray. It is the depth from which we must rise but cannot. It is the depth beyond which there is no further depth. It is the very bottom. It is the depth beyond which we cannot fall. It is the depth from which we cannot rise. It is the depth from which we can only rise. We pray to be able to pray. We pray."

The rabbi broke off. There was a silence. Then faintly a melody. The rabbi was singing: "Lai, la la lai lai lai, la la lai, lai lai." And then again: "Lai, la la lai lai lai, la la lai, lai lai. Come, we pray." And he began to chant:

> *Ashamnu bagadnu gazalnu dibarnu dofi.*
> *He'evinu vehirshanu zadnu chamasnu*
> *tafalnu shaker. Ya'atznu ra, kizavnu latznu*
> *maradnu ni'atznu sararnu avinu*
> *pashanu tzararnu kishinu oref. Rashanu*
> *shichatnu ti'avnu ta'inu titanu.*

"Lai, la la lai lai lai, la la lai, lai lai. What shall we say before Thee, O Thou Who dwellest on high, and what shall we recount unto Thee, Thou Who abidest in the heavens? Dost Thou not know all things, both the hidden and the revealed? Thou knowest the secrets of eternity and the most hidden mysteries of all living. Thou searchest the innermost recesses and triest the reins and the heart. Nought is concealed from Thee or hidden from Thine eyes. May it then be Thy will, O Lord our God, and God of our fathers, to forgive us for all our sins, to pardon us for all our iniquities, and to grant us remission for all our transgressions.

"For the sin which we have committed before Thee under compulsion, or of our own will. Come, cast it away. Lai, la la lai lai lai, la la lai, lai lai. And for the sin which we have committed before Thee in hardening of the heart. Lai, la la la lai lai lai, la la lai, lai lai. For the sin which we have committed before Thee with utterance of the lips. For the sin which we have committed before Thee by unchastity. For the sin which we have committed before Thee by wronging our neighbor. Come, cast it away, like *taschlikh*, upon the waters. Lai, la la lai lai lai, la la lai, lai lai."

Slowly, as the great recitation unfolded, and as the little melody bore it away, the mood began to lift. I felt something inside giving way.

"And for the sin which we have committed before Thee by the sinful meditating of the heart. For the sin which we have committed before Thee by despising parents and teachers. For the sin which we have committed before Thee in presumption or in error. Lai, la la lai lai lai, la la lai, lai lai."

I did not look at Sarah and she, I was sure, did not need to look at me.

"And for the sin which we have committed before Thee by profanation of the Divine Name. Lai, la la lai lai lai, la la lai, lai lai."

Sarah was singing loud and clear.

"And for the sin which we have committed before Thee wittingly or unwittingly. For all these, O God of forgiveness, forgive us, pardon us, grant us remission."

How we finished, whether we confessed all our sins, whether the rabbi accomplished the closing of the gates, I do not know. But I know he blew the ram's horn a long, long blast— *Tekiah*—I know he said the only joyful kaddish I had ever heard, I know he poured honey on bread to signify the end of fasting. And I know he blessed us.

And I know that before the monks arrived with huge platters of fruit and bread and vegetables, we were all on our feet dancing, a mass of robes and yarmulkes and flying hair, and people laughing and crying, and tears streaming down our faces, singing and clapping, and the monks going, "Rama, rama, rama, rama, rama, rama, rama, ram," and Seligman going, "Lai, la la lai lai lai, la la lai, lai lai," and everybody picking it up, picking it up, sending it round, sending it round, embracing, hugging, kissing, crying, singing, shouting, laughing, jumping, and the door opening just one hair's breadth further than it had ever opened and holding it one instant longer than it had ever held it, before it closed again.

Border Crossing

Airports and train stations. There's always something quickening about both of them for me, a combination of exhaustion, anticipation, worry, crowds, loneliness, newspapers, chocolate, and fleeting encounters. And timetables. And barriers. And all one's belongings. And a certain inescapable sense of life in the balance.

I'm flying to Europe again, so many times now it's routine, I've lost count. Fourteen years in the States. My uncle has invited me to spend a week in the Dutch countryside, at his little house in Ruurlo. He will pay for the flight. But we never do anything the normal way in my family, when there is a way of making it cheaper and more complicated. So I'm flying with Romanian Airlines to Amsterdam.

We gather, several hundred of us, by a hand-lettered sign at a desk borrowed from an orthodox carrier in an obscure wing of an obscure terminal at Kennedy. Short squat men with loud voices in ill-fitting clothes carrying suitcases seemingly bigger than themselves, cigarettes glued to their lips, shout at short squat women who seem to have no other form of expression but the cough—phlegm-filled, full-bodied, rasping, symphonic. Everyone smokes, everyone elbows everyone else out of the way. Everything bulges. Shirts hang out of trousers, necks burst from collars, bosoms from overcoats, overstuffed suitcases tied with string leak their contents—undergarments, sweaters, canned goods, electronic gadgets, toilet paper.

On the plane, the shouting, the smoking, the coughing continue. The flowers of Romania's National Air Hostess Training School elbow their way down the aisle. A certain longing for the efficiency and plastic smiles of American airlines takes hold of me. Fourteen years in the States, is it too long? What is happening to me? Shouldn't this kind of surliness seem refreshing?

I am distracted from my reveries by Germans—I am entirely surrounded by Germans. Behind me a blond Nazi lout drinks beer and shouts with the best of the Romanians. From time to time he pauses to harrass my neighbor, a young woman. She is an art student from Hamburg. The two Germanys. Trains and planes and the shadow of history.

Nanna, my neighbor, the art student, has been hitchhiking round America for two months. In her travels, she says, she found only one person—an eighty-seven-year-old woman in Maine—who had any political perspective, who could understand, for example, why Germans might be upset at having America's nuclear weapons stored on their land. A certain nostalgia for the European worldview sweeps over me, as so often in transit. It's not simply politics, but the nature of the national dialogue: in Europe the answers are no clearer, but the questions are still framed—aren't they?—by artists, by philosophers, by politicians; in America by TV. I carry with me as a kind of race memory, a kind of bedrock ontological comic routine, a late-night discussion between Johnny Carson and Don Rickles on the subject of the Middle East, both earnest, both ignorant, the news as game show, complete with contestants, clues, live audience, music, laughter, applause, and commercials. And then, from behind, just to keep me on my toes, the thump-thump-thump of the Nazi jackboot as our beer-swilling companion bangs out a charming ditty on the back of Nanna's seat: *"Einz, zwei, drei, vier/Hab'n wir noch ein Tröpfchen Bier . . ."*

In Amsterdam I have a couple of hours before the train. It is early morning. At the Centraal Station, where I have arrived, departed, changed trams, changed trains, so many times before, I bump into Nanna and a couple of American boys.

I take them for a cup of coffee off the Rokin. The boys have never been to Europe. They are starting in Amsterdam. They want to see the prostitutes, and, of course, the van Gogh Museum. Nanna is spending the day before catching the night train to Hamburg.

The boys have eggs, Nanna has honey cake, I have tartare.

I am trying to decide whether it's too early to call Mama Pauka. Is she still alive, will she remember me, why haven't those fuckers written to me?

I decide to call. The proprietor unlocks the booth and I dial. Presently someone answers: *"Met Pauka."*

"Mama Pauka?"

"Robin? Oh, Robin, it is you. Oh, how wonderful. Where are you?"

"Ich bin in Amsterdam, aber nur für eine couple of hours." We speak in a mixture of German and English. It is like old times. Nothing has changed.

"Lex and Marjanne, they know you are coming?"

"No. I'm staying with my uncle in Ruurlo. Those fuckers never write."

"They don't write. That's terrible."

"No, no. They write in their hearts."

"But, Robin, you will see them."

"Of course I will see them. You think I come to Holland, even for a day, and not see them . . . ?"

"Then I will see you. I am going to Enschede this afternoon for the weekend. It is David's birthday."

"Perfect. Perfect. I can't wait."

"Oh, Robin, they will be so happy."

"Mama Pauka, I love you."

"*Und ich dich*—oh, terrible language."

I come out of the booth laughing, almost dancing.

"You look happy."

"David Robin Alexander Pauka is going to be six years old tomorrow."

"Who?"

"Forgive me, it's a long story."

I tell them the story. Köln, Münster, Bochum; my first morning; the landlady bursting into my room, quiet, crazed, spitting: "*Scheiss Engländer! Scheiss Jude!* And how come you speak such good German?" And I, naked, trembling, racing out; and her mops and pails and imprecations tumbling after me; and my flight that first weekend across the border into Holland; and my magical encounter with Lex and Marjanne; and our instantaneous and enduring friendship; and the birth six years ago tomorrow, long after I had moved to America, of their first child, one of whose many names is mine. David Robin Alexander Pauka.

"Come on." We walk down a side street to a department store where in the back they used to serve *Geldersche Wurst* hot.

"Where are you taking us?"

"Listen, you only have me for an hour. Take advantage. This is incredible sausage."

"Sausage at this time of the morning?"

"Eat. Eat. It's good for you. Now take a canal trip. Go to the Anne Frank House if you want somewhere to stay. And come back here at night if you want to see the prostitutes. Nanna, good luck with your painting— take them to the van Gogh. Have fun."

I returned to the station. Behind me, I am sure, they are stuffing into a neat Dutch receptacle the remains of their *Geldersche Wurst*. I don't care. I'm dancing.

The train is crowded. It pulls out of the station, through the flat suburbs, into the flat countryside. The green, the cleanliness, the clarity. The cold, clear dappled Dutch light. And the faces, from Dutch masters.

I change at Amersfoort. Beside me, across the aisle, on the next train a glorious Dutch-American couple, he Dutch, she American, eating each other up. A reunion? Something wonderful about this type of European man. Something enviable. Fourteen years in the States, have I become American? Something enviable. Something lost. The fluency of conversation. The immediacy of feeling. The ease of sexuality.

I change again at Apeldoorn. The last train takes me through rich farmland to Ruurlo. I am the only passenger to get off.

It is Saturday afternoon. There is no one around. Even at the station things are wonderfully green and quiet. Outside in the station yard there is a phone. I call Georg. I cannot get through. I call the operator. We cannot make ourselves understood. I try again. I cannot get through. I call the operator again. I cannot get through.

I walk into town. It is Saturday afternoon. Everything is closed. I walk back to the station. It is eight kilometers to Georg's house. A car pulls up on the gravel, parks. A man gets out. I approach him. "Telephone," I say. "Not working."

He looks at me, shrugs, goes into the station.

Suddenly it hits me. The travel. Coming back. I sit on my case in the station yard. I am very tired. I am almost crying.

Presently another car pulls up, a gray Lancia. It is Georg.

"*Süsser, du bist doch hier*. Why didn't you ring?"

"I tried but I couldn't get through."

"And from Amsterdam?"

"I'm sorry."

"*Macht nichts*. You're here. That's good." He kisses me. "*Komm*."

I put my bags in the back seat and climb in. "How is Mart?"

"She is fine, working in the garden. She figured out this train. I of course—*Idiot*—came to meet every one."

"Oh, Georg, I'm sorry."

"You remember Ruurlo?"

"No, not really. It's been a long time. I remember the house."

"*Ist doch schön, nein*, a little Dutch village?"

"Yes."

"And the countryside, you like?"

"Yes, Georg, it's beautiful."

We are onto the dirt road now, Georg driving in his reckless fashion. Suddenly, abruptly, almost without slowing down, he turns the car left over a tiny moat between two poplar trees and we pull up beside the house.

"You remember?"

The last time I was here was with Naomi seven years ago. Georg whisked us down in the car from Amsterdam, straight from the plane, and in the sudden stillness of the Dutch countryside we sat before the television set, my Dutch uncle, my American wife and I, and we watched the World Cup final between Holland and Germany. Germany won.

And eight years before that—fifteen years ago—living in Germany, at the home of wealthy Germans in Dortmund, entirely surrounded by Germans, I had watched the World Cup final between England and Germany. England had won. I thought they would lynch me, a Jew and an Englishman. But no, I had been carried through the streets on German shoulders.

"You remember?"

Yes, I remember. I remember the house. Bertel still living. The wheelchair. The blanket. Georg leaning over her. Sister Marie.

"Things have changed," Georg says.

Mart comes across the lawn to greet us. The golden light illuminates the grass, the banks and banks of flowers, the old pigsty that is now garage and workroom, and the gray-haired figure in rubber boots coming towards us.

"Robin, you are welcome."

"Hello, Mart." I kiss her.

"You see, I said he would be on this train. Come." She takes me inside, across the stone floor, to the room beyond the kitchen. "Put your things down. Wash and when you are ready we have coffee outside, alright? I leave some clogs for you at the front door."

It is Sister Marie's old room, still spartan. It has a sink, a bed, a table, a closet. I put down my bag, wash perfunctorily, put on a clean shirt and go outside, slipping my feet into the clumsy wooden shoes on the way out. Funny how they slow you down.

We sit at a small folding table with coffee and six small pieces of honey cake, two each.

"And now for to jog, *ja?*"

"No, no, Georg, now for to sleep."

And I stretch out in a garden chair, in that gold light, with the trees swaying and the birds singing, and sleep a dreamless sleep. The rush, the frenzy, the clatter of New York fall away and when I awake I lie for a few moments in the late afternoon light, trying to adjust my rhythm to the slow tread of the Dutch countryside, to fix myself forever in that moment, in that garden, in that light.

"I have run a bath for you. The water is not so often hot." Mart is standing a few feet away.

"Thank you, Mart."

I rise like a somnambulist, pick up my clogs and trail my bare feet through the grass towards the house. As I leave the border and step over the shoe grate to the lintel I see they are completely green. I bathe quickly, luxuriantly, and pick my way through the kitchen to my room. Mart is at the sink, peeling potatoes.

There is something so quiet, so soft-spoken, about the house, it encourages me to meet it. I sit on the floor and slowly, with control, go through my yoga *asanas*. When I am done, however, I do not meditate: it is cocktail time; I join Georg and Mart in the living room for a drink.

"Mart has a sherry. But we, we have a whiskey, right?"

"Right."

Georg pours me a measure of whiskey into a glass. "It is cold. From *Kühlschrank*. But you are American, you need ice."

"No, no, Georg, it's fine."

"Ah, whiskey, the best drink in the world."

And we sit there, the three of us, in silence, looking out through the picture window at the last light as it brushes the delphiniums and the sunflowers and slowly, slowly turns itself out. How many times had I sat here and watched Bertel in her wheelchair gaze out through this same window at this same sight.

"*Ach, Gottchen*," says Georg.

"Now, I must make dinner. And Robin must call his friends. And Georg of course must watch the news."

"*Ja, ja.*"

Mart goes into the kitchen. Georg goes into the other room and switches on the television. I pick up the phone.

"*Met* Lex Pauka."

"You motherfucker, why don't you write?"

"You son of a bitch, where the fuck are you?"

"I'm closer than you think."

"London?"

"No."

"Amsterdam?"

"No."

"Ruurlo?"

"Maybe."

"Marjanne, Marjanne, pick up the phone, Robin is in Ruurlo."

"Hey, you, motherfucker, you don't write us before you come?"

"You don't write me, I don't write you."

"Hey, man, it's perfect. David's birthday is tomorrow. There'll be a thousand screaming children. You'll fit right in."

"Oh, great."

"You take the bus at noon. We'll pick you up."

"*Geweldig.*"

"*Tegenliggers.*"

My old Dutch practice words. I never could pronounce them. We crack up.

"Hey, Robin, Lex and I are so happy. David will be six tomorrow. Can you believe it? Everybody has a baby. Jelly has a baby. Bert and Quinte have a baby. But it's still the same. Still crazy after all these years. You too, right?"

"Me, too."

"Robin, give our love to Onkel Georg. See you tomorrow."

"*Tot siens.*"

"Your mother has a belly like a percolating coffee pot."

"Fuck off."

"Fuck off."

"Fuck off."

"*Nu,* how are they?"

"They're fine. They send you their love."

"*Ach. Danke.* You will see them?"

"Yes, tomorrow, after Daddy calls, I'll take the bus. They have two children now. The oldest one is named after me. It's his birthday tomorrow."

"He is named Robin?"

"No, his second name is Robin. His first name is David."

"David? *Ein ganz jüdischer Name. Wie kommt's?*"

"I don't know. Is it Jewish here? Lex is half Jewish. His mother. From Vienna."

"*Ach so. Vielleicht darum.*"

My father is due to call the next morning. Some of the restitution money my parents receive from Germany is held in a bank in Düsseldorf. Georg's too. It is an hour and a half or so beyond the German border. Once a year Georg drives over. "I pick up my interest. I wanted a bank, a reputable bank, near the border. I did not want to stay the night in Germany, you understand."

It is that time of the year now, and Georg thinks to take advantage of my presence and take me with him. It is time, he thinks, and I think also, to introduce me to the arcane mysteries of banking.

Money has always been the thorniest of subjects between my father and me. Where it comes from is a mystery, where it resides is also a mystery, how much there is is the biggest mystery of all. From the look of his desk when I was a child I can only assume there are scraps of paper scattered across Europe. What significance they might have, if any, I have never been able to discover. My father attributes this to my utter lack of interest, if not stupidity; I to my father's determination to keep it all a secret.

"Yes, your father. It is not easy. Those endless details. The endless questions. He does not understand why you are not a stockbroker. That he should write like that to you, terrible. That he should do so many of the things he did, terrible. Or did not do, also terrible. But his whole life is devoted to providing for his family."

"Yes, but . . ."

"But. He is impossible. He is difficult. Sometimes he makes me furious. But there are three people who meant something to me in this world—Bertel, Mart, and your father. And your father first of all, he is my brother. Now we will go through some of these things together so you have some idea because in some of these matters, frankly spoken, you are an idiot."

I laugh.

"Don't laugh. It is true."

"I know it is. But somehow it doesn't hurt coming from you."

We spread out the most recent statements on the dining table. Figures wrapped in German banking terminology swim before my eyes—*Auszug, Blatt, Buchungstag, Beleg-Nr., Buchungstext, Postenanzahl, Wert, alter Saldo, neuer Saldo, Währung, Wertpapierbezeichnung, Fälligkeitstag.*

"Alright, enough. We make ready for dinner."

Soup. Then a small piece of meat with potatoes and gravy.

"Many things I owe to Mart. Many things I have learned. But the thing I have learned for which I am the most grateful is moderation."

"Oh, he thinks I am modest. It is really he who is *mean*—like your father."

Georg laughs. "Maybe it's true. But still tonight it is an honor. We have my nephew all the way from America. All this way to spend with two old foggies—is that right?"

"Fogies."

"Oh, fogies, of course, thank you, fogies. So we must have wine."

Mart looks at me and winks. "Miracle of miracles."

Georg produces a bottle of Lambrusco. "It is alright?"

"Of course it's alright, Georg. Thank you."

He pours a little into each glass. "*L'chaim.*"

"*L'chaim.*"

"You see, for a good Dutch Protestant, her Hebrew is perfect."

We drink and Mart is right: it is a miracle; in this slow, sedate, measured household, the three of us—me, my seventy-eight-year-old uncle, and his chaste sixty-four-year-old companion—between the three of us we polish it off.

"We are privileged persons," Georg says, and indeed something touches a longing in me here—the control, the peace, the moderation. Everything at its appointed time—a slow, leisurely, appreciative, savoring routine. The light, the garden, the quiet, the dusk, drinks, dinner, news, conversation, reading, and after dishes, bed. In the morning to rise early for a little yoga and meditation—only to get drunk and debauched later at Enschede. But Enschede's my youth.

The next morning my father calls. How was the flight? Fine. No, he has no objection to my going to Düsseldorf. He has no instructions either. My mother gets on the phone. What, I would only be in London so short? Soon, soon. Georg and my father speak rapidly in German. When he hangs up, he shakes his head. "*Nein, nein, nein.*"

"What is it?"

"It's nothing, it's nothing. Sometimes he talks to me like a child too. Come, I drive you to the bus."

Outside the post office at Ruurlo, he waits till the bus comes and then he kisses me good-bye as though I am going on an ocean voyage. And in a way I am. I will be back the next day, but I know how Georg looks on that day away: it is a kind of betrayal—him I see out of duty, but Lex and Marjanne I see out of love.

On the bus through these small Dutch villages the familiar sense of being in transit settles in, a sense of loneliness, of privacy, of having my world completely with me, even as I pass through, a small figure in a landscape. Blond children and farmers and old women get on and off. Rivulets of rain slide down the window. I sit looking out as the countryside rolls by and listen to the polite Dutch chatter of alighting passengers.

Some things change. And nothing changes. Marjanne has put on weight. She now wears glasses. Lex still looks like a boy, though a slightly older one. They have two children, they have moved, their business is prospering, they work very hard.

But nothing has really changed. Their house is still the same crazy mix of people coming and going, children, animals, neighbors, strays, activists, homosexuals, yachtsmen, bartenders; Lex still sails through it all with an uncapsizable bonhomie, drinking, talking, laughing, filling his pipe, weaving people together, clearing the debris, changing the baby, never breaking stride; Marjanne still rolls her cigarettes in the twinkling of an eye, flirts, laughs, dances, sings, cooks, swears, throws down her glove and challenges the world to pick it up half as fast as she.

"Oh, Robin, you look so good, you like it in America?"

"Mama Pauka, you haven't changed. Not one bit."

And she hasn't, not since the day I first met her sixteen years ago, rolling out strudel dough on the kitchen table in her tiny apartment in Amsterdam.

Nothing has changed. Music, food, drink, laughter, cigarettes, and above all talk. When the kids are asleep, when everyone else has been bundled off into the night, out come the beer and the genever and there we sit talking, talking, into the morning. Late, late, we tumble into bed.

We're up at seven. Lex sets off on his *bromfits*, that marvelous Dutch improvement on the bicycle, for Hengelo. It's the only time he has alone. As he put-puts along, he speaks into a little tape recorder slung around his neck. It's the way he organizes his thoughts for the day. By the time he gets to the office the day is pretty much mapped out. The design and advertising business is growing. Soon they will move into their own building. It's a big step. It is still fun, but there are more and more details to keep track of.

Marjanne and I follow in the car, after David has been taken to school and Lukas, the baby, deposited with Bert and Quinte. She has a shoot for the next three days in the south. She and Lex will leave the office at the end of the morning and take me back to Ruurlo. "No, no, we do it, of course. Lunch at Avenarius."

Lunch at Avenarius, the big hotel on the edge of Ruurlo, like long ago, like yesterday. Carpets on the tables, newspapers on the racks, an elderly waiter somnambulating between the tables with a tray of genever and beer, coffee and evaporated milk, half a dozen genteel customers, the gray light glancing in through the windows, the three of us talking, talking, in our outrageous mixture of languages, laughing, remembering, touching, shrieking, and every so often a genteel gray head turning slowly in our direction and then slowly back again, with sometimes, just sometimes, the faintest beginnings of a smile upon it.

At 1:30 I call Georg. "Georg, it's Robin."

"*Nu, wo bist du?*"

"I'm at Avenarius. I tried to reach you at 11:30 from Hengelo but there was no reply."

"*Natürlich*, I was mowing. Mart was in the garden. There is much to do."

"I'm with Lex and Marjanne."

"*Immer noch.* You are spending the whole day with them?"

"No, they are bringing me back."

"Not now. Now is not good. I expected you sooner."

"I'm sorry. When is good?"

"After we sleep."

"Three?"

"Is better."

I pad slowly back. "Listen, we have an hour to kill. I think Georg is upset with me. He's jealous, you know."

"Of course. He's your uncle. You rush off with us."

"But this is a bit *übertrieben*."

"So?" Lex laughs, "What else is new?"

We drive a couple of miles out of Ruurlo in the direction of my uncle's house and park the car. Marjanne, exhausted, sleeps in the back seat. Lex and I go for a long walk in the woods. More talk—John Cheever, maturity, marriage, small business, sex, heartaches, plans for the future, children, dreams.

"So, Robin, are you happy in America?"

"Happy . . . Lex, you know me. It doesn't change so much inside, how much difference does it make outside?"

"David calls you my brother in America."

He looks at me and puts his arm through mine.

Mart has made tea. We are five. Lex bounces in, Marjanne is remarkably deferential. She remembers Georg from Oestgeest fifteen years ago with his gray Lancia, his gray hat, his gray gloves—my mother there from London, her old friend Betty Joseph from Los Angeles, my cousin Ellinor from Israel, and my uncle driving down from Amsterdam in his gray gloves. He is a different man here in the country, almost a farmer.

He remembers her as the most striking beauty—now she wears glasses, she is almost a matron.

Bringing them together after all these years, I suddenly see them all with different eyes.

The phone rings. It is Antwerp calling for Lex. He winks at me on the way to the phone and says, "You feel like a child here? *I* feel like a child here," and he laughs.

I look at Mart and Georg on the sofa—a nun and the Ancient Mariner. And yet hovering overhead is always Auschwitz.

In the evening, after Lex and Marjanne have gone, after we have spent some energetic hours mowing, we sit down with drinks and Georg confesses how taken he is with both of them. He asks about Lex's Maagen David. I tell the story of my first day in Germany, the Nazi landlady, the trip across the border, my first encounter with Lex and Marjanne and Lex's brother Guus, the safe harbor they provided all my time in Germany—Germany, Germany, the constant trauma.

"Yes, I know. Imagine your mother, sick, seventy-eight, and you forced to put her on the train."

He pauses.

"It is the whiskey that makes me talk. Something came up last night for me, we go to Düsseldorf tomorrow, maybe that's why. It is the whiskey. I have never talked about this, even to your father. Even Herbert doesn't know. That they could take me, that I understand—a Jew, an enemy of the German people—but that they could force a man to put his own mother, sick, on a stretcher, on a train to Auschwitz, no, that I cannot forgive."

"Georg."

His hand is clenched around the glass, white, trembling. "There are Jews who can forgive. There are even German Jews who can forgive. But not the Jews from occupied lands. The Jews from Israel, they are the first to return . . ."

"Yes, I knew some of them in Hamburg . . ."

"The first to return, the first to drive German cars—Audi, VW, not Mercedes, that far they do not go, that was Hitler's car," and as he says the name his hand rises automatically in salute.

"Georg." I fill his glass.

"*Ach. Gott.*" He looks at his hand and brings it down. Then he picks up the glass and takes a sip. "My father, your grandfather, he was a lovely, charming man, a sweet man, almost a goy. A gymnast. Every Wednesday night he would drink beer with Herr Ludwig, a bigger goy—and a real one. My mother kept almost kosher—two sets of dishes. My father kept something always underneath the table, not kosher *natürlich*, for the dog—and for himself: he slipped himself something, too. His father, my grandfather, was a tailor—I visited him once in an old-age home. He manufactured corset sticks—is that right?"

"Stays."

"Stays, *ja*. But my father saw it wouldn't last, so he changed to buttons.

In 1926 I was in Palestine—I lived there for three years. If I had stayed maybe I would drive a German car—no, no, not Mercedes—but I was called back home because my father was sick. Herbert had a big job at Oerstein und Koppel, but he left and we took over the firm—Max Hirsch und Co. Herbert looked after abroad, I after domestic. Two years later my father died. He was sixty-three."

He breaks off.

"I am older than my father."

He shakes his head.

"A sweet man. I still have poems he wrote to my mother from Wiesbaden where he took the cure for rheumatism—eventually it got his heart. '*Mein Maitröpfchen, meine süsse Blume.*' In some ways it is a blessing he did not live longer."

He takes another sip.

"We lived at home, your father and I, till 1935. Hard to imagine, no? Two grown men. Your father was almost forty. But we had our mother. And servants. It was a different time, a different world. And then of course, orders—no more Jews in the same house with Aryan women. And then more orders. And restrictions. And fear. And destruction. And the decision, not so easy, to leave. But where to? Amsterdam? I always liked it. Decent people. I sent Bertel and my mother to Amsterdam. I went to Palestine to see what could be arranged. But for an old woman, too difficult. I came back. A nice flat, a good neighborhood. And then, *tzak*, the occupation. Jackboots. Gunfire. Tanks in the street. Everything broken. Hiding. And I, *Idiot*, to go back for such a *Kleinigkeit*—a bracelet. They saw me. My neighbors. *Tzak, tzak* on the door. The Gestapo. They took me and beat me."

"Georg."

"One is not so strong, you know. One breaks. Imagine. Your wife. Your mother. In hiding. And they beat you."

He stops.

"They took us to Westerbork. The three of us."

He stops again.

"And then, and then, imagine, you cannot imagine, the trains . . ."

He shakes his head.

"Georg."

"*Ja*, it never leaves."

He sits for a moment and then he turns to me. "Your glass is empty. You can survive without a drink?"

"It's alright, Georg."

"You are sure?"

I nod.

"*Komm*," he says, "enough. We play piano." And he leads the way to the piano. "*Komm*, we play together."

"No, you play. I enjoy it when you play."

"But it is so old-fashioned."

"I like it."

"*Ach*, this piano. It gives me so much pleasure. You see, your father has a good heart."

And indeed, this piano, which gives my uncle so much joy, arrived one day from my father, a gift for his brother's seventieth birthday. And on it for hours my uncle bangs out the waltzes, the operetta tunes, the mazurkas from their youth in Germany, tunes I have heard in London at my Bar Mitzvah, in West Virginia at my wedding, and since the arrival of the piano, every time I come to Holland.

"*Komm*, you play with me."

And I sit down next to him and on my father's piano his brother and his son, an old man and his nephew, the concentration camp survivor and the expatriate, in the peace and stillness of the Dutch countryside, play cocktail music together.

"It is so nice to see the two of you together," Mart says after dinner as we do the dishes. "Such things come up for him. Such dreams, such nightmares. It happens when he has to go to Germany. All this money. It is so complicated. My father was a banker. It was never so complicated. We lived very simple. Of course I never lacked for anything. We were not poor. We were even rich. But it is the Dutch temperament. A house, a garden, food on the table, a car even, but what more does one need. There is a little money. It looks after itself. I no longer need to work. With Georg it is more complicated. I don't say anything. It is not my business. And with your father, it is much more complicated. With your father it is not so good, hein? I had it with my mother. You know, when I was twenty, she became paranoiac. It was terrible. One cannot live with that. Quite literally, people were after her, I was after her. She had to be, how do you say, restrained. Violent, very violent. She lived a long time. One copes. My sister—did you meet her, she does yoga too, she lives in South Africa, she comes back from time to time—she is glad now she never had children. It is a not so good inheritance. I never married. Because of that? I don't know. Now you dry and I put these away." She gives me a towel. "We bought this house together, the three of us, your uncle, your aunt and I. Bertel I met when she arrived in Amsterdam in '38. Georg I met only later when he arrived from Palestine. Later they were moved to the Jewish quarter. One day I went to see them. 1944. They had been taken. The neighbors, good Dutch neighbors, the Dutch you like so much, were stealing everything. I have never seen anything like it. Terrible."

The next morning in the Lancia we drove rapidly through eastern Holland to the border, crossing into Germany at Emmerich.

"*Weiter.*"

Border control waves us through. We never leave our seats. How easy for terrorists in Europe. And what a contrast. Fifteen years ago I crossed all the time. The Dutch never gave me trouble. But the Germans would hold me up, sometimes for an hour, while they examined my passport with its East German visa and its many destinations.

And more than forty years ago, at this same border crossing, my father sits in a German train, alone at night, at the very brink of freedom, while two SS men with guns take away his passport. That morning in Berlin the final ordinance has been passed: no more Jewish males to leave the country. My mother has heard it on the radio. They are not yet married. She tells my father to take the train immediately to the remotest border crossing— perhaps orders from Berlin will not have reached there yet. My father's passport has a *J* for *Jude* and visas permitting business travel for Max Hirsch and Co. to Holland, France, and England. He takes the train to Emmerich. "It was the only time Daddy ever listened to me." He sits and waits. After an hour the SS men return. They unlock the compartment. They look at my father in his overcoat and hat and gray silk scarf. He looks at them in their jackboots and riding breeches and leather pistol harness. On the platform soldiers in greatcoats with dogs and machine guns. In the compartment two SS men with pistols and his passport. Slowly he reaches into his overcoat and pulls out a silver cigarette case. He opens it, extracts a cigarette, snaps it shut, replaces it. Methodically, he tamps the cigarette on the back of his hand. He produces a lighter, snaps a flame, puts the cigarette to his lips, lights it and inhales. He looks up at the SS men. They look down at him. Then they give him back his passport.

"*Weiter.*"

The train moves slowly into Holland.

We speed on towards Düsseldorf.

We park beneath the bank in a private car park. In the bank itself, middle-aged functionaries, all male, in somber suits, sit at large isolated empty desks, not a scrap of paper on them, with nothing to do but motion you on through the carpeted halls to the next. We arrive at the final desk.

"*Herr Hirsch*," Georg says. "*Verabredung mit Herrn Henken.*"

"*Moment, bitte.*"

The official speaks into a telephone.

Presently a portly man in a similar suit appears from behind glass doors. The man at the desk announces, "*Herr Hirsch. Herr Henken.*"

My uncle announces, "*Mein Neffe aus New York,* Dr. Robin Hirsch."

A discreet inclination of the head, an almost imperceptible click of the heels.

Georg plays the farmer. "I'm here, you know, to pick up my interest. I must say I'm leery about walking around with a couple of thousand Deutschmark in my pocket."

"For us, that's nothing. Why, yesterday, a client came in, withdrew 350,000 in cash, put it in his attaché case and walked out, just like that. Now then I might worry . . ."

Georg's interest is authorized and made available to him at the *Kasse.*

"You have an appointment also with Herr Dr. Niens, *nicht wahr?*"

"*Jawohl.*"

"I will ring for him."

Dr. Niens is a courteous, quiet, gray-haired *Leiter* who speak excellent English. "Herr Hirsch. Dr. Hirsch. Come with me." He leads us into an elegant private room. Two of the walls are glass, one with a glass door through which we have just entered, giving onto the reception area, the other with a glass door giving onto banks of files. "Won't you sit down?"

The entire furnishing consists of a sofa, two armchairs, and a glass table. On the table are a telephone and three envelopes.

Dr. Neins asks me about my doctorate and chats knowledgeably for a few minutes about American literature. Then he picks up an envelope. "This account . . ." and he sketches out the details of the account.

So, the family is not poor. My father has done a good job.

Dr. Niens picks up the second envelope. "This account is a joint account which you share with your uncle . . ."

Did he enjoy it? Is he happy? Why did he need to keep us in the dark? Did he need respect so much he had to beat it into us?

"And this account is with our sister bank in Luxembourg. A moment please." He picks up the telephone. "*Luxemburg, bitte.*"

Düsseldorf, Luxembourg, Zürich—scraps of paper scattered across Europe.

"*Danke.*"

Some further details, a handshake, an even discreeter inclination of the head, *auf Wiedersehen.*

*   *   *

Mart has packed us sandwiches. I half believe, knowing Georg, that, having traveled to a foreign country, we would sit in the car in the concrete car park underneath the bank and eat them. But no, after the bank, we walk through the *Altstadt*, we have *Reibkuchen* at a stall in the open-air market, we stop at a brewery, drink beer and eat *Bockwurst*. We even have coffee and chocolate in a *Kaffeestube*. Two cups, I almost faint.

Everywhere, people are polite, unbelievably polite.

At the *Brauerei* a pensioner at the next table engages me in conversation. He is of that age. Georg averts his eyes.

He is from not far away.

Oh?

From Bochum.

But of course he knows the university.

And how come I speak such good German?

The following afternoon, after a hard day's mowing, I take Georg's bike and pedal the eight kilometers into Ruurlo. At the bank I buy a ticket for the Hook of Holland. I run a few errands and then in the golden rays of the afternoon sun I sit on the terrace at Avenarius and have a genever.

I am in Georg's boots, covered in grass, a farmer from the feet down. I look out over the flat landscape, warmed by the sun, a little tipsy. In two days I will be on the train again—Zutphen, Arnhem, Utrecht, Winterswijk, Rotterdam, the Hook, and then the ferry.

Trains and planes—there's always something quickening about both of them for me. Cigarettes. And passports. And memories. And the shadow of history. And all one's belongings. And a certain inescapable sense of life in the balance.

The Imperial War Museum

Birthdays were always a big deal in my family. Even in the early days when there was very little money and England was still coming out of the war and we were still on rationing, somehow on birthdays there was always an abundance of food and a veritable mountain of presents. In the early years the big thing was that the birthday child, for breakfast, got a whole soft-boiled egg. I never figured out how my mother accomplished this—whether she did some bartering on the black market or some judicious haggling with the grocer or whether, which seemed the most likely, in the week previous to the birthday she had gone without. In any case, sitting there in anticipation with a whole egg in front of you instead of the customary half, made you feel more special than anything: like the Sun King with all of Versailles stretching into the distance.

Birthdays always brought out the best in my parents. My mother would bake her extraordinary rich chocolate birthday cake with Smarties around the perimeter and the appropriate number of candles and the age of the birthday child also written out in Smarties at the center. And endless whipped cream, the cream patiently collected over weeks by skimming it off the top of the gold label milk bottles which the Express Dairy left every morning outside the front door, and whipped up the night before with lots of sugar and a little vanilla. One slice would be eaten at breakfast and the rest served in the afternoon when friends of my parents came round with more presents or friends of ours came for a party. And there would also be endless sandwiches and a nut cake or a cheesecake or a *Streuselkuchen* so the guests had something else to eat besides the birthday cake and so a few slices of the birthday cake could be secreted away and consumed in a kind of glowing aftermath the next day.

Birthdays also allowed my father to display his generosity. His customary tightfistedness and ill humor melted away on birthdays and they became a big production number and a model of organization.

One birthday I remember going into the living room in my dressing gown—it was the one day in the year when getting up early was no problem. The living room was off limits until everyone was ready. So going into the living room—or, rather, being asked to come into the living room—was always the beginning of the ritual. There on this occasion was the usual pile of small presents around the birthday cake. I unwrapped them—a pen, a book, a toy, a diary, a sweater, a scarf, a woollen hat, a pair of gloves—all very nice, but nothing significant. When I had finished unwrapping, and reading the cards, I felt somehow let down. I knew it wasn't right to expect something big but somehow something seemed to be missing.

"What's the matter? *Ist etwas los?*"

"No, no, no."

"Why do you look so unhappy?"

"No, no—I'm very happy."

"You don't like your presents?"

"I do, yes, I do. The pen is lovely, and the socks, um, . . ."

"*Gut, also, Käthe, Frühstuck. Ach,* it's so dark. Robin, *mach die* curtains *auf.*"

I almost didn't. I almost said, "It's my birthday. Barbie should open the curtains." But some guardian angel made me think better of it. I opened the curtains. There in the bay window stood a beautiful big black bicycle. I screamed with joy. My first full-size—or almost full-size—bicycle. "I don't believe it. I don't believe it. It's beautiful. Can I take it downstairs?"

"In your pyjamas?"

That bike became a significant companion of my childhood. I could rush off on it and ride around the neighborhood. I could ride up and down Loudoun Road with the other kids and do tricks on it—standing on the crossbar, sitting on the luggage rack and coasting down towards Boundary Road with my feet on the handlebars, lying face down with my stomach on the saddle and my legs stretched out behind, my arms in front steering, flying downhill like a toboggan. It became my friend, my companion, my means of escape. It almost eclipsed the pain of first learning to ride under my father's tutelage, my father barking out orders in German at the top of Loudoun Road like an SS officer. "*Weiter, weiter,* pedal *Herr Gott nochmal. Ach, kannst du nichts tun?*" and then as I fell, "*Idiot, Idiot,*" his cigarette holder clamped between his teeth, some private frustration, some private fury, driving him to make me ride. "Come back here." Over and over again, up and down outside Arnold House, my father violent, trembling with anger and disappointment, I cowering, terrified that someone from school might see me.

"Hirsch is a Nazi. His parents are Nazis. I know. I've seen them."

Birthdays, at least our birthdays—my sister's and mine—were a warm respite from all that, an oasis, an occasion when we felt loved and cared for. They didn't work so well the other way round. I never felt as though we could provide the same warmth. My mother of course would accept any gift—a snowflake—as though it were a wonder. I could make the most clumsy contraption—a bowl, a desk calendar—and my mother would be genuinely awestruck that I could have labored over it so many days—"So, it isn't finished, it's still beautiful." But there was always tension in the air between my parents. As for my father, I never gave him a present which wasn't criticized, or even rejected—a waste of money, where did you get it, I could have got better, I'm perfectly happy with the one I have. Once I gave my father a diary. He kept it for a day. Then he gave it back. "Give it to your uncle. He likes that sort of thing." My uncle was in Amsterdam. Like a dutiful son I got on a plane and went to Holland.

Birthdays were a different thing for my parents. Perhaps it had to do with the passing of time. Perhaps they were less sanguine than we about kissing good-bye to another year. Perhaps that explained the tension, the lack of excitement, a certain sense of rue in the air.

And as time passed, the significant birthdays were marked with increasingly formidable celebrations. For my mother's seventy-fifth birthday, my father took the family to a country house in Weybridge for the weekend—my uncle, who came over from Amsterdam, my sister, her husband, the kids. I arrived late from New York and greeted them on their return.

For my father's eightieth I received an invitation for dinner at the Hotel Westmoreland. This time I made it.

I arrived in London not quite knowing what to expect. My father had arranged everything, down to the tributes. "Sixty people. Sit-down dinner. Georg will speak. You will speak. Mr. Battsek who is ninety will speak. Mr. Nelken will speak. Dr. Falk will speak. I will respond."

"My God, how formal is this?"

"Dinner jacket."

"My dinner jacket is in New York."

"*Warum?*"

"You didn't say anything about dinner jacket."

"You should have known.

"How should I have known?"

"It's my eightieth birthday. Of course it's dinner jacket."

"I have a sports jacket."

"*Ausgeschlossen.*"

"I could buy a suit."

"*Nein.*"

I borrowed a dinner jacket from a friend of my sister's.

"Ladies and gentlemen, it is both moving and intimidating for me to see so many of you gathered here tonight to honor my father on his eightieth birthday. It has fallen to me to act as master of ceremonies. Since all of you know my father well, you can probably surmise how much choice I had in this assignment.

"My father is a meticulous planner and to all those of you about to speak I should warn you that my father has a stopwatch by his plate and no matter how lavish the praise, you better not go over your allotted time.

"I look around this room at this impressive gathering and I realize that my sister Barbie, my nieces, Nicky and Tanya, and I—the perennial kids' table at these events—are the only ones here in this room at the Westmoreland who can pronounce the name of this hotel. We are the only ones who were born here. I must say, as I look at all of you, and as I think of similar gatherings over the years, at Zion House, at the Theodore Herzl Society, at the Belsize Square New Liberal Jewish Congregation, I am struck with admiration—that you survived at all, that you made it to a foreign country, that you withstood the hardships and indignities of starting again from scratch, that you prospered, that you built institutions, that you gave your children the best possible education—and that you still can't speak the language.

"I should like in particular to welcome my Uncle Georg, whom many of you know, and who is here from Amsterdam. He is my father's younger brother, and as a result a kind of Honorary Life Member of the Children's Table. Georg, I think you have been present at all the important moments in my life. You spoke at my Bar Mitzvah here in London more than twenty years ago; you spoke at my wedding in America. I feel somehow the occasion is not important if you are not there to make it important. Ladies and Gentlemen, it is with great love and affection that I call upon my Uncle Georg to say a few words."

Georg spoke. Mr. Battsek who was ninety spoke. Mr. Nelken spoke. Dr. Falk spoke. My father wittily and with aplomb responded.

Much later as we drove back to Marlborough Mansions in the car, my father said: "But that you didn't bring a dinner jacket, it's beyond me."

More than four years later, as my mother's eightieth birthday approached, I made the familiar trip to Kennedy Airport, climbed aboard the huge jumbo jet with hundreds of other passengers and sped again across the Atlantic. How many times had I made this trip in the last fifteen years, how routine it had become, how many more times would I still make it? Time was passing, gathering momentum. My parents, who had always seemed so indestructible, were passing milestones where in the conventional world there were fewer and fewer survivors.

My father still, at the age of eighty-four, crawled under the car on Cannon Hill to drain the radiator, he still read the papers late into the night, he still smoked his endless half cigarettes, cut precisely down the middle and screwed resolutely into his holder, but his trips to the fruit and vegetable markets on Church Street or the Portobello Road had become less frequent, his daytime dozes, slumped in the armchair in his smoke-filled study, lasted longer and longer, and since the dog had died he no longer took his nightly walk, and when he walked it was more slowly and with less conviction.

My mother still went down to the shops on West End Lane to buy groceries or do the laundry, she still cooked three meals a day, she still kept the books of the Henrietta Irwell Group, her chapter of the Women's International Zionist Organization, but John Barnes, the huge department store on Finchley Road, which, with its delicatessen in the basement, had served as a meeting place for a generation of German-Jewish women, had closed down, her trips were now confined to the immediate neighborhood, her step was more diffident, her breath shorter, she had to stop sometimes on the street, she had even fallen a couple of times, and the doctor had diagnosed angina.

And at night now when my mother wheeled the tea trolley into the living room with an assortment of cakes and biscuits and a pot of tea, she and my father would sit for longer and longer stretches in front of the television. And the volume would get louder and louder. And they would talk to each other less and less.

"God, Robin, I don't know what this will be like," Barbie clutched my arm. "Daddy's so generous in some ways and so mean in others. We're going to the Royal George in Tunbridge Wells. Georg and Mart are coming. You have a room. They have a room. Mummy and Daddy have a room. I have a room with the kids. Three days in an English hotel with every bloody meal in the hotel because it's cheaper that way. Georg and Mart won't eat enough and Daddy'll be furious because he's paid for it and they're not giving him his money's worth. Mummy will stuff herself, which she shouldn't do, not because she likes it, but just to please Daddy. The kids can't stand all that arguing and all that German and there'll be nothing for them to do and they'll be miserable and they'll get on everybody's nerves and I'll get it in the neck because they're not being grateful. So the only one I can see having a good time is you. So, you better enjoy it."

"Gosh, it sounds wonderful. I can hardly wait."

*   *   *

Barbie and Nicky and Tanya and I drove down together, through town, across the Thames, through the endless dreary suburbs of South London, onto the motorway, cutting through the lush green countryside of Kent, to the eighteenth-century city of Royal Tunbridge Wells.

The hotel was something of a surprise, a large elegant Georgian estate on the outskirts of town with landscaped formal gardens stretching off into the distance where they were swallowed up by wilder woodland. In the drive were Rovers and MGs and large family estate cars and the occasional Rolls and Bentley. We parked and took our luggage out and stepped inside to the reception desk.

"Ah, the Hirsch party."

"We're the advance guard. The grown-ups are coming later."

"Mrs. Goodman, this is your key. And you're the young Mr. Hirsch—this is your key. Rupert will take you upstairs."

It was extraordinary, after so many years in America, to encounter again that strange mixture of solicitude and distance. Rupert took us upstairs—a strange, circuitous journey, up stairs, along corridors, down stairs, up stairs, round corners, along more corridors, across landings, down and up and around, the patchwork refurbishment of a great English country house into a genteel English hotel, the quality of the carpeting and the furnishings slowly diminishing the further we got from the impressive public rooms.

"'Ere we are," Rupert opened a door. "Madam is around the corner, and across the landing."

I slipped him what I hoped was an extravagant American-size tip for the voyage—"much obliged, sir"—and stepped inside. A rather dowdy room with two twin beds, a dresser, a night table, and a sink. I had forgotten the paucity of baths in even the finest English hotels. But a lovely view of the gardens and on a low table an electric kettle with tea bags and packets of creamer and instant coffee.

I unpacked. Presently there was a pounding at the door.

"Uncle Robin, we're going to explore. You want to join us?"

"I think that's a brilliant idea, but later, O.K.? I want to settle in a bit. You go ahead and let me know what you find."

Barbie appeared. "Off. Go. Go. You're not going to get much opportunity. *Raus*," she screamed at the top of her lungs.

The kids laughed.

"Alright. Alright. We get the message," said Nicky.

"KNW," said Tanya.

"What's that?" I said.

"Kids Not Wanted."

"O.K., enough of your charm—vamoose, scram, out."

"Alright, Mum, alright, we're going."

"Race you down to the desk."

"And don't terrorize the natives."

They were gone.

"Nice room."

"Yes, it's not bad."

"It's as big as ours. What are you going to do with the extra bed?"

"I don't know. You think Daddy'll want to rent it out?"

"Come on, Robin."

"I don't know. In some ways I'm amazed. I expected this to be a lot, I don't know, shabbier."

"Weybridge wasn't shabby."

"I wasn't in Weybridge."

"Oh, right."

"I don't know, I thought we'd all be in one room, huddled like refugees, one happy family—'Robin, tonight it is your turn to go downstairs and eat—you vill take ze doggy bag . . .' This is actually quite impressive."

"They have money now. There's no reason not to spend it. They travel a lot. They're mellowing."

"Oh, come on, mellowing. They still drive you crazy."

"Robin, you know, it's easy for you. You live all the way over there in America. You come back once a year, maybe twice, for a week. You bring presents. Your nieces love you. Mummy can talk of nothing else. Even Daddy, beneath his impossible behavior, he's glad to see you—you're the only person in this family he respects. But I have to deal with them day-to-day, all that fussing, that interference, those fucking questions. Yes, I have a temper, I'm like Daddy that way. They drive me bonkers. But it's still not like it used to be. Christ, I need a cigarette. Do you mind?"

"If you have to."

She pulled out a packet of cigarettes, shook one loose, put it to her lips and lit it.

"My God, you look like you're trying to inhale the universe."

She laughed. "Yeah, I know, Nicky does a great imitation of me smoking."

"I've seen it. That's the difference. We could never make fun of our parents."

"You could."

"Rarely. Mostly things were too grim. And anyhow, that was Mummy's worst weapon."

"You mean, 'Have a sense of humor'?"

"Yes."

"Yes, I have more resentment about that than you. Always coming between us. Whenever Daddy did something, making us apologize. I hate her for that."

"Barbie."

"I do."

"What could she do, she was caught in the middle."

"Rubbish. She should have stood up for us."

"Maybe you're right."

"Of course I'm right. A kid gets humiliated, beaten, and then you make him apologize for having provoked Daddy, for having made him lose his temper? It's terrible. It's a betrayal."

"You never lose your temper with your kids?"

"Of course I do, you've seen me, that's unfair. But after it's over, *I* apologize. I don't say, 'Look what you made your mother do.'"

"So there's hope."

"I don't know if there's hope. I'm divorced. You're divorced. Neither of us could hold a marriage together. Nicky and Tanya have it a little better than us. But I don't know how much. I'm a thirty-eight-year-old woman. I'm a little more mature now than when I was a kid. But some of those things are still fresh. They still hurt. I still react like a fucking infant. But I have my own kids to worry about. And they're smart. Kids are smart. They pick up on things. They see Daddy and Mummy for what they are—the violence, the tension, the anger, the manipulation. Tanya's a charmer, a flirt, she can wind Daddy round her little finger, but she always keeps a little distance. And I keep a distance too. Kids want love so much, they give it so freely, but they don't want it on terms, and they don't want to be force-fed it, and they can smell conditions a mile away."

"God, Barbie, you're a wisewoman."

"Bullshit. I'm just a mother. You were always the bright one. Oxford. Fulbright."

"That doesn't mean anything."

"Yes, it does, don't put it down. But I didn't have any of that. Nobody ever thought of me as smart. And maybe in some ways it was a blessing. Anyhow, I see things pretty straight. I love my children. I'm mean to them sometimes, but I won't let anybody else be. We had a rotten childhood, you and I, and I don't want any of that in my children's lives. Or as little of it as possible. So I keep a distance."

"Whew. I could use a drink."

"Well, tough luck. This is England, remember—no drinks in the afternoon, no buses after eleven."

"I have some cognac from the plane, you want some?"

"No, but you go ahead. I'll have a coffee."

She put water in the kettle and plugged it in. I poured a little cognac into a water glass. The kettle boiled almost immediately and she made coffee.

"You want some?"

"No, I'm happy with this."

"Alcoholic."

"Cheers."

"Cheers, *Brüderchen*."

We sat for a moment and drank, brother and sister, the children of refugees, of German Jews, all these years past, almost grown up, almost comfortable in an English hotel.

"It's amazing."

"What?"

"Eighty."

"Mm."

"You think we'll ever be eighty?"

"I don't know, I didn't think we'd ever be this old."

"She's amazing for eighty."

"Yeah."

"They're both amazing. After what they've been through."

"Now don't get all soppy and romantic. A lot of people have been through a lot worse."

"Yes, but still."

"Robin, I'll clean up. You go and round up the kids. They'll need to wash up. Mummy and Daddy'll be here any minute, if they haven't arrived already, and knowing them they'll want dinner right away."

There was a knock on the door.

"Come in."

The door opened.

"Hallee halloh."

"Oh, my God, they're here. Hi, Mummy, I'm just clearing up. Have you seen the kids?"

"Vot, ze children are lost?"

"No, no. Christ!"

"Barbara, don't get so impatient."

"Mummy, it's alright. How was the trip?"

"Hullo." My father had materialized in the doorway.

"Hello, Daddy."

"Hullo, *mein Sohn. Nicht schlecht*, the room. This is your room?"

"Yes."

"It's bigger than Georg's."

"I'll happily swap."

"Barbara, *was machst du bloss?*"

"I'm just washing one cup and one glass and cleaning out the ashtray."

"*Tag*, everybody." Georg had entered with Mart.

"Georg." I went over and kissed him.

"Fine room you have."

"Yes, would you like it?"

"Yes, I like it very much."

"No, *would* you like it?"

"*Ach so, nein, nein*, we have our own room."

"Mart, how are you?"

"Fine, thank you." I kissed her too.

"How was the flight?"

"Fine."

"And the drive down?"

"Well, you know how it is with your father driving."

"You got lost?"

"Only a little bit—shh."

"Barbara, *wo sind die Kinder?*"

"They're exploring. Robin was going to find them. When do you want to eat?"

"Why are you in such a hurry to eat?"

"No, no. I thought you and Mummy . . ."

"*Keine Rede davon.*"

"*Nu*," Georg broke in, "*lass die Kinder sein.* We go to our room. Unpack. *Komm.*"

"Daddy."

"*Ja*, Barbara."

"I just want to say, I think this is incredibly generous of you, and I think the hotel is wonderful, and I hope we all have a fabulous time."

"*Ja*, is not bad."

"And Mummy—you look incredible. We won't tell anyone—they wouldn't believe it anyhow."

"Tell—just you dare!"

"Alright, everyone, it's a wonderful hotel, and Mummy, you look stunning, but it's my room, and I'm going to wash." I bundled everyone out.

"Alright, alright."

"Dinner at 7:30."

"*Ja. Ja.*"

"Dress *dich bloss* up."

"O.K. O.K."

They all disappeared round corners, down corridors, across landings, a last-minute barrage of injunctions and counter-injunctions pattering off the walls in a mixture of English and German.

Dinner was splendid. The eight of us sat at a large circular table in the enormous Georgian dining room and were waited on hand and foot. My father was in an expansive mood and ordered wine. The kids were scrubbed and clean and dressed up. Georg and Mart ate discreetly but not too little. Barbie squeezed my hand underneath the table and whispered, "God, it's going to be alright."

My mother looked radiant in a green shantung gown.

"Mummy, you look radiant," I raised my glass.

"No, no, no more. A long time ago, maybe."

"Yes, you do. Come on, everybody, cheers."

We drank. The dessert cart came round.

"Georg, for God's sake, *nimm.*"

"*Danke, nein.*"

"*Herr Gott.* Robin, take two."

"No, Daddy."

"Waiter, give my son here two."

"Very good, sir."

"No, thank you, really."

"I said two, you take two. Give him some of this and some of this—and also one of those."

"Yes, sir."

"Mummy, is it alright if Tanya and I go to the Game Room and play ping-pong?"

"Yes, Nicky, I think that's a very good idea. Nicky and Tanya ask to be excused."

"Thank you for dinner."

"Thank you for dinner."

They ran out.

I sat with three desserts in front of me. My father took out his cigarette holder, a packet of cigarettes, and a pair of scissors. He removed one cigarette and cut it in half. One half he replaced in the packet, the other he ground into the holder, which he placed between his teeth. The waiter struck a match.

"Oh, thank you."

"Coffee, sir?" the waiter asked me.

"Oh, thank you."

"Cheese?"

I gestured helplessly in front of me.

"Oh, we can take care of that, sir."

Miraculously, the three desserts vanished and cheese appeared in their place. "Double Gloucester."

"Thank you."

"*Was*, you have cheese also. What an appetite."

Georg and Mart retired early. Barbie and I fled to the sanctuary of the Game Room, where my parents eventually followed. The much-vaunted sporting facilities of the Royal George Hotel consisted of either billiards or table tennis. These could not be played at the same time since the two halves of the ping-pong table went on top of the billiard table. The net, a ball, and rackets you had to procure from the front desk. This Nicky and Tanya had done, but there were three young men playing a leisurely game of billiards, pints of beer on the edge of the table, taking their time, chalking their cues, bantering, taking aim. Finally, the last ball was sunk.

"Can we play now?" Nicky asked, a trifle sullenly.

"Yeah, yeah, you go ahead. You need 10p to get the balls though."

"No, we want to play ping-pong."

"Oh, alright. Want a hand then?"

One of the boys gave me a hand with the ping-pong table.

"We live round 'ere, so we just come in for a pint—you're staying at the 'otel, you get priority."

"Thank you."

"Uncle Robin, will you play with us?"

"O.K., but you've only got two rackets, don't you think you should play with Tanya first?"

"Alright, but you play the winner."

"Sure."

"It'll be me. Ready, Tanya?" and she whacked her first serve in.

We rotated. Nicky played me. I played Barbie. Barbie played Tanya. Tanya played my mother. Barbie put her arm around her and said, "Mummy, I think you're incredible. My mother's eighty tomorrow and she's playing table tennis."

"Barbara, shh—ach, Tanya, you're too quick."

"Want to take it again?"

My father meanwhile, at the other end of the room, with the uncanny facility he sometimes displayed, had struck up a conversation with one of the boys. Snatches of it drifted over to me.

"Quite an enterprising young man. How old are you?"

"Seventeen."

"Seventeen? That's my son over there. I wish he were as enterprising as you. He lives in New York."

"New York. Cor, I'd love to go to New York."

Tanya had beaten my mother. "*Oof, sagte Mutter. Nun,* Herbert, it's *doch* time."

We began to pack up.

"Robin, *komm ma' her.* This young man, Harry, *nicht wahr?*"

"Yer, that's right, 'Arry. 'Ow d'you do?"

"How do you do?"

"This young man, Harry, wants to go to New York. I told him you can show him around."

"It would be a pleasure."

"Cor, that's great. Thank you very much. I must say it's been a pleasure meeting you, sir." He shook my father's hand. "And you." He shook mine.

"Look," I pulled out a card, "here's my name and address. If you ever come to New York, let me know."

"I will, I will."

"Enterprising young man," my father said as we walked towards the front desk. "*Gute Nacht.*"

"Good night."

"Sweet dreams," said my mother.

"Same to you."

The next morning at breakfast my father appeared in his undershirt with a cardigan.

"Happy birthday, Mummy."

"Happy birthday."

"Thank you. Thank you."

"You look wonderful."

"*Keine Witze*" (No jokes).

"I don't understand," my uncle turned to me, "my brother appears like a *Bettler.*"

"*Bettler?*"

"Beggar."

"I don't understand either, it's embarrassing."

"All these *anständige Leute.* He can't dress like a normal person?"

"You know him a lot longer than I do."

"*Nein, nein, nein.*"

The breakfast menu was as long as dinner—"What a choice!" said Nicky—kippers and kidneys and eggs and sausages and rashers of rich

English bacon and lamb chops and orange juice and coffee in gleaming silver pots.

"Tanya, you are eating only cereal?"

"I don't want anything else, honestly, Grandpa."

"Barbara, this is not possible."

"Daddy, she doesn't want anything else."

"Barbara, this breakfast costs six pounds fifty. I will not have Tanya only eating cereal."

"Daddy, first of all this breakfast does not cost six fifty for children, secondly it's all part of the package rate, and third I will not have you forcing food on Tanya. She eats very healthily. A lot more healthily than you."

"Barbara, I'm warning you."

"Yes? What are you warning me about?"

"Barbarina, you are making Daddy very upset."

"*I*'m making *him* upset? This is what I can't stand."

"Barbie, it's Mummy's birthday, come on, let's cool it."

"Tanya, *Herr Gott nochmal. Es macht mich rasend.*"

Tanya had left the table and was running through the dining room.

"Tanya," Barbie got up and started after her.

"Mummy," Nicky stood up.

"Nicky," I moved over and sat next to her. "Nicky, everybody else may be having problems, but you and I have appetites and there is tons of food. Let's eat."

"I don't want to. It's not fair."

"Waiter, waiter," my father was shouting.

"Yes, sir."

"I want everything. Fish, eggs, sausage, bacon, meat. Everything, you understand?"

"Yes, sir. How would you like the eggs, sir?"

"What?"

"The eggs, sir, how would you like the eggs?"

"Yes, I would like the eggs. Of course I want the eggs. Eggs and everything."

"Very good, sir. Yes, sir."

"*Idiot.*"

"Herbert."

"*Es macht mich wahnsinnig.*"

"Herbert."

"*Ruhig.*"

Barbie came back to the table. "Tanya has gone to play outside. Nicky, if you want, you may join her. If you want to finish your breakfast, though, you may." The waiter returned. "If it weren't Mummy's birthday, I want you to know, I wouldn't have come back."

"Kippers, sir. Sausages, sir. Lamb chops, sir. Kidneys, sir. Bacon, sir. Eggs, sir. Scrambled."

"Scrambled—I want fried. Like that there."

"Very good, sir." He leaned over the serving cart. "Here we go, sir. Fried."

"*Endlich.*"

We continued our breakfast in silence.

Finally, Mart said, "How is everything in New York, Robin?"

"Fine."

"Are you still living in that, how do you call it, up in the sky?"

"Loft."

"That's right, loft."

"Yes, I am."

"With the skylight."

"Yes."

"Have you seen it, Barbie?"

"Yes, I have, it's quite beautiful."

And somehow we were off and running.

The dining room was now almost completely empty. Tanya appeared at the window and made faces. Outside it had begun to rain. Barbie beckoned her back in.

"Waiter." My father called the waiter over and whispered in his ear. The waiter disappeared and returned with six fluted champagne glasses and a huge silver ice bucket. In the bucket sat a bottle of champagne. My father nodded to the waiter and he picked up the bottle with a napkin and began to unwind the wire clip that held the stopper.

"Oh, how wonderful," my mother said.

The cork popped and the waiter poured champagne into the glasses.

"Hey, what about me?" said Nicky.

"Of course, darling. Waiter, could you bring another glass for my daughter."

"Daugh*ters*," said Tanya.

"Daugh*ters*," said Barbie.

"Certainly, madam."

"This bottle I brought from home. It is quite old."

The waiter returned. "Here we go, madam."

"Thank you, that's very kind of you." Barbie poured some of her champagne into the new glasses. "Here, my darlings."

"This champagne is more than twenty years old. Robin, do you recognize it?"

"No."

"It is from your Bar Mitzvah."

"My God, I hope it's still drinkable."

"Of course, it's drinkable."

"I didn't know we had champagne at my Bar Mitzvah."

"You didn't? You don't know a lot of things. It's French. It's vintage. It is very good."

"Herbert, this is *doch* wonderful." My mother had tears in her eyes. My father lifted his glass.

"Käthe."

In an empty Georgian dining room, the waiter at a discreet distance, a soft English rain gently misting the formal English garden outside the windows, my father in his undershirt, my uncle in his pearl-gray suit, Mart in her glasses and gray hair and prim Dutch dress, my sister, my nieces, and I, the eight of us seated round that table, drank to my mother on her eightieth birthday.

In the car on the way back, Nicky said, "What is it with Grandpa?"

Tanya said, "He's like a baby who never has enough."

"My children," Barbie said, "you are very, very smart."

I spent my last few days at Barbie's. Before I left London I had an errand to run. I had promised to pick up some posters for a production in New York. It was of an English play about the Second World War. On my last night I took a bus south of the river to the Imperial War Museum on Lambeth Road. I had never been there before.

I was completely dumbfounded by its size. I walked up the long approach towards the huge black mounted cannons, past them, up the enormous stairway to the imposing entrance. The great turreted red neo-Gothic castle towered above me. I stepped inside. A guard asked me to check my briefcase. I gave it to an attendant and received a plastic token with a number. I walked down the stone stairs and found myself in the Hall of the Twentieth Century. Before I knew it, I was in a trench. "World War I trench, Battle of Verdun, heaviest artillery bombardment." Sandbags, soldiers, some dead, water, the trench very low, maybe five feet, rifles, bayonets, mud, heavy boots, my father had fought in this battle, tin hats, bandages, stretchers, wounded soldiers, Fritz had lost a thumb in the First World War, the noise, the sheer wall of noise, open your mouth when the cannon goes off or you'll go deaf, my father was deaf in one ear, the sheer screaming terrible noise, bullets, machine gun fire, heavy artillery, shells exploding, hand grenades, the relentless, screaming, shouting, raging, hysterical noise, the noise of a screaming voice, raging, guttural, whiplike, frenzied—*ach, mach, lach, krach*—higher and higher, louder and louder—*ach, mach, lach, krach*—like jackboots, a fever, a fire, a conflagration, Hitler's voice, my father's voice, the voice of my childhood—Second World War, Hitler Arouses the German People, A Slide Show. I sat transfixed.

Less than six months later, Barbie calls me in New York. "Bad news, Robin, Daddy had a heart attack. He's in the hospital. The worst is over. They think he'll make it. I'll ring you if anything happens."

Four days later she calls. I get on a plane the next day.

London. October. Raining. The three of us at Marlborough Mansions. He was alert to the last second. Instructions. Notes. Sell this. Buy this. The three of us around the kitchen table.

"There must be a hundred and fifty bottles of wine."

"My God."

"Some of it's good."

"Cheers."

A new rabbi at the congregation, not Salzberger, not Kokotek, not a German Jew, an Australian.

"Would you like to speak at the funeral?"

"I don't think so."

"Ladies and gentlemen, I didn't know Herbert Hirsch . . ."

Yiskadal v'yiskadash.

All those faces, the German Jews, Mr. Nelken, Dr. Falk. Georg too sick to come over. Friedel Richter, her husband gone. "*Ach, Gott,* Robin."

"*Na ja.*"

"I saw him, you know, in the hospital, after they called. Mummy saw him too. I'm glad I did. It wasn't too bad. You know, the nurses, they really loved him. Funny, no. Eighty-four. I don't know, they really loved him—those last four days."

A year later at the cemetery in Golders Green, Georg has come over.

London. October. Raining.

A black jackdaw cawing way up in the bare branches, Caw. Caw. Caw.

We walk to the gravesite, the seven of us, my mother, my sister, my nieces, my uncle, Mart, and I.

We stand in the rain. Umbrellas.

Georg kneels. He shakes from a phial some earth. *Eretz Yisrael.*

Herbert M. Hirsch. Born Berlin 11 January 1898. Died London 28 October 1982.

He kneels with his brother in a strange country. Earth from the Promised Land. *Na ja. Na ja.*

Epilogue

---◆---

(1991)

Home

I have always had something of a refugee mentality when it comes to settling down. Perhaps it has something to do with my parents who *were* refugees—born in Berlin, fled Hitler, settled (if that's the right word) in London. Perhaps it's something innate in being a Jew—not a believer, you understand, but a Jew nevertheless. I've traveled a lot, I've lived in various countries, I was even married for four years in New York. But I never really felt at home at home. I've always felt more at home in airports, in railway stations, at border crossings. In cafés.

Well . . . fourteen years ago three of us, on a lunatic whim, opened a little one-room café in Greenwich Village. We scraped, sanded, plastered, painted, and did the little dance one does with the authorities who live beyond the Village. Suddenly, after two months, we turned around and, *mirabile dictu*, we had a café. For three more or less starving artists, as we then seemed to ourselves to be, it provided a roof over our heads, a place to eat, and a showcase in which to display our art. In short, you should pardon the expression, a home.

Over the next few years the café grew. It added a room, a kitchen, another room, a bar, a prep kitchen, a performance space. I had begun, without thinking, to put down roots and flourish. I no longer traveled as much. The world seemed to beat a path to my door.

In Year IV of the cafe I met Leona. In Year VI we moved in together. In Year VII we married and then in Year IX, five years ago, we took the plunge. We bought our own crumbling derelict brownstone in the Park Slope section of Brooklyn.

This, for a refugee, is commitment.

We lived in the one habitable room and worked hard—Leona finishing her dissertation, I coordinating the construction. Windows, walls, floors, ceilings, plumbing, electrical. Every day there was more dirt. Then suddenly after four months our contractor turned to us and said, "It feels like a home."

In 1988 our first child was born—Alexander, known to the world as Sasha. We were running up and down stairs. Diapers or a change of clothes always seemed to be two floors away. Two of the fireplaces needed finishing. The front of the building was still crumbling. The front door had been kicked in by local vandals. But Sasha was the first Jewish male born into my family since my arrival forty-five years earlier and so in the living room eight days after his birth, nonbelievers though we were, we had a *bris.*

It took a year, but we fixed the front of the building. Another year and we replaced the front door. The fireplaces are still not done. We have no light fixtures to speak of. But the garden is slowly coming into its own. And five weeks ago, on Valentine's Day, after a difficult pregnancy, our second son was born, Benjamin. Healthy. Mother and son both fine. Another *bris* in the living room. Exponentially more running.

And then on Saturday it was Sasha's birthday. Three years old. The house was full. Children from his nursery school. Parents whom we'd never met. The obligatory presents. Books, a video. A plastic farm. A plastic car wash. Trucks. More trucks. Clutter. Things. And at the end two parents, shell-shocked, war-weary, picking their way through the debris. Home?

The next night, Sunday, I take Sasha into the café. Tonight as on every Sunday night since we opened there is a reading. We've come in because the people reading tonight happen to be friends. Sasha and I have dinner with them, then we go downstairs, where Sasha works on the adding machine in the office, plays piano in the deserted cabaret, dances on the little stage. At the café Sasha is completely at home. Some of the waiters are his buddies. The bartender has made him his assistant. We have established the first International Bartending Preschool.

We are not planning to stay for the reading, our presence is simply a good luck call. However the time to begin is approaching and I am usually the one who does the introductions. And Sasha is now, after all, three.

"You want to introduce them?" I ask.

"Yes, Daddy."

"O.K. We need to rehearse."

We rehearse and then we go into the back dining room and do it for real. Four stools have been set up for actors who are going to read a new film script. I sit on one, Sasha sits on one and I begin: "Ladies and Gentlemen, welcome to . . ." and I pass the mike to Sasha, ". . . Cornelia Street Café," he says, without missing a beat. There is of course applause. We tell the readers, "Break a leg," and dash out. Into our jackets. Into the car. And down Broadway in the direction of the Brooklyn Bridge and home.

At Canal Street we stop at a red light. An elderly man approaches. With Leona in the car I have come to grit my teeth at these occasions and lock the doors. Locking the doors has in New York with children become second nature. But the café and Sasha's performance have relaxed me. The man bears a resemblance to John Huston, an emaciated, anorexic version. He's wearing a big cross. I open the window.

"Happy Palm Sunday," he says.

I reach into my pocket.

"I'm trying to get seven dollars together for a room."

I pull out my change and put it into his outstretched beret.

"Thank you," he says, "I'm sixty-two years old." And then suddenly, "Are you Jewish?"

"Yes," I say.

"Well, then Happy Five Days before Pesach," and he uses the Hebrew word.

"Thank you," I say.

"I have a friend, he's a waiter. Last year he made fifteen hundred dollars. In one day. Tips alone."

"Really?"

"Yes. Pesach."

The light turns green.

"Good-bye," I say, "Good luck."

"Daddy, do you know that man?"

"No, Sasha."

"Why were you talking to him?"

"I gave him a little money."

"Why, Daddy?"

"Because he doesn't have a home."

"What did he say, Daddy?"

"He wished us a happy Pesach. Pesach, darling, is Passover. Seder. When we go to Mimi and Bapa's house."

"Yes, Daddy."

"You know, Sasha, we're Jews, and the Jews have never really had a home. We were kicked out of Egypt, which is what Pesach is about. And we were homeless for forty years. We were kicked out of England. We were kicked out of Spain. My Mummy and Daddy were kicked out of Germany. Bapa was kicked out of Poland. Mimi was kicked out of Russia. Sasha, I don't expect you to understand all this. But one thing is very important. There are people all around who have very little. We have a lot. It's like sharing your toys. It's difficult sometimes. But there are kids who come over who have much less. And when you have a lot you must share. Not only for them. But because it makes you feel good. This man has very little. And there are many people like him in this city. And this is what we must never forget."

We drive over the bridge. We pass our house. There is of course nowhere to park. We go to the lot, a bombed site on the far side of Fifth Avenue, much like the bombed sites in London after the war when I grew up. Only the wars here are very different. They are civil wars.

We climb out of the car, Sasha gets on my shoulders, we lock the gate, and we make our way through the broken bottles, past the winos, the crack dealers, the boarded-up windows. Down the street on Fifth Avenue is Mark's apartment. Mark is an artist who used to work at the café. We have four or five pieces of his work in our house. One of them is in Sasha's room. Another is in Benjy's. Mark no longer works at the café, he no longer lives on Fifth Avenue. He is in St. Vincent's dying of AIDS.

We turn up our street. Lights are on upstairs. Leona and Benjy are up. The house looks beautiful in the lamplight, orange brick and orangestone. I carry my son up the steps and unlock the new front door. Sasha gets off my shoulders. We lock the outside door and open the inside door. "Hello," my three-year-old calls out. And then again, louder, filling the house, "Hello-o."

He is, we are, home.

UNIVERSITY PRESS OF NEW ENGLAND publishes books under its own imprint and is the publisher for Brandeis University Press, Brown University Press, Dartmouth College, Middlebury College Press, University of New Hampshire, University of Rhode Island, Tufts University, University of Vermont, Wesleyan University Press, and Salzburg Seminar.

LIBRARY OF CONGRESS CATALOGING-IN-PUBLICATION DATA
Hirsch, Robin.
    Last dance at the Hotel Kempinski : creating a life in the shadow
of history / by Robin Hirsch.
        p.   cm.
    ISBN 0–87451–713–3
    1. Hirsch, Robin.   2. Jews—England—Biography.   3. Children of
Holocaust survivors—England—Biography.   4. Jews, British—United
States–Biography.   I. Title.
DS135.E6H554   1994
941'.0092402–dc20
[B]   94–48725
⊚